CW01018839

The map library in the new millennium

The map library in the new millennium

Edited by

R B Parry

Senior Research Fellow and Map Curator, University of Reading

and

C R Perkins

Senior Lecturer in Geography and Map Curator, University of Manchester

LIBRARY ASSOCIATION PUBLISHING
LONDON

Published by
Library Association Publishing
7 Ridgmount Street
London WC1E 7AE

Library Association Publishing is wholly owned by The Library Association.

First published 2001

British Library Cataloguing in Publication Data

A catalogue record for this book is available from the British Library.

ISBN 1-85604-397-5

Typeset in 9.5/13pt New Baskerville and Franklin Gothic Condensed by Library Association Publishing.
Printed and made in Great Britain by MPG Books Ltd, Bodmin, Cornwall.

Contents

The contributors

Dr Robert Barr

Senior Lecturer, School of Geography, University of Manchester, UK
E-mail **R.Barr@man.ac.uk**

Dr Christopher Baruth

Map Curator, AGS Map Collection, University of Wisconsin, Milwaukee, WI, USA
E-mail **cmb@uwnm.edu**

Dr David Fairbairn

Lecturer in Geomatics, Department of Geomatics, University of Newcastle, UK
E-mail **Dave.Fairbairn@newcastle.ac.uk**

Dr Pip Forer

Professor of Geography, University of Auckland, New Zealand
E-mail **pipf@clear.net.nz**

Alan Godfrey

Map Publisher, Alan Godfrey Maps, Consett, UK
E-mail **alangodfreymaps@btinternet.com**

Russell Guy

Map Dealer, OMNI Resources, Burlington, NC, USA
E-mail **guy@omnimap.com**

Dr Menno-Jan Kraak

Professor of Cartography, Division of Geoinformatics, Cartography and Visualization, ITC, Enschede, The Netherlands
E-mail **kraak@itc.nl**

Patrick McGlamery

Map Librarian, Homer Babbidge Library, University of Connecticut, CT, USA
E-mail **libmap1@uconnvm.uconn.edu**

Carol Marley

Information Services Librarian and Bibliographer, Hitschfeld Geographic Information Centre, McGill University, Montreal, Canada
E-mail **marley@felix.geog.mcgill.ca**

Nick Millea

Map Curator, Bodleian Library, Oxford, UK
E-mail **nam@bodley.ox.ac.uk**

R B Parry

Senior Research Fellow, Department of Geography, University of Reading, UK
E-mail **r.b.parry@reading.ac.uk**

C R Perkins

Senior Lecturer, School of Geography, University of Manchester, UK
E-mail **c.perkins@man.ac.uk**

Dr Michael P Peterson

Professor of Geography, University of Nebraska, Omaha, NE, USA
E-mail **Michael_Peterson/CAS/UNO/UNEBR@unomail.unomaha.edu**

Jan Smits

Senior Cataloguer and Senior Information Specialist, Koninklijke Bibliotheek, The
Hague, The Netherlands
E-mail **jan.smits@kb.nl**

Jennifer Stone Muilenburg

GIS Librarian, University of Washington Libraries, Seattle, USA
E-mail **jnstone@u.washington.edu**

Preface

Late 20th century developments in information technology have radically changed the nature of map production and the distribution of spatial data to the user. Map libraries in academic institutions, traditionally repositories of paper maps, have come under threat as increasingly maps are stored and manipulated in electronic rather than paper format, and the transmission of digital spatial data has become possible via the Internet. Meanwhile the library as an institution has been forced to respond to social, political and economic changes and pressures and to new educational prerogatives. Issues arising from the nature of digital data, claims on ownership of such data, and concerning their modes of production and use, have also had an impact on the map library.

While some institutions have begun to view the map library as anachronistic and essentially dead, others recognize a continuing but adaptive role for the curators of map collections in providing control of the new data formats and guidance on their use, besides acknowledging a continuing value in the printed map archive.

This book provides a timely exploration of all these issues. We have recruited an international team of authors, drawn not only from map librarians themselves, but also from other cartographic and GIS-related fields. We have asked them to re-examine the role of the map library, and assess its status and relevance in the context of digital/electronic technology, of changing user needs, and of social, political and economic changes at the turn of the millennium. In the event we did not entirely succeed in all our objectives. The content reflects its authorship, which is predominantly English-speaking and from North America and the UK, although we are delighted to include the contributions of two Dutch authors and one from down under.

The book is not intended to be a prescriptive text on map librarianship: the themes discussed are ones that affect all users and distributors of spatial data, and the aim is to raise awareness of the issues among a wider readership. Our remit has been to produce the book quickly, presenting lively views on a range of contemporary issues that affect the future of the academic map library. This has been facilitated by the excellent support of our publisher and the production team at LA Publishing, and by our contributors, most of whom managed to meet (or almost meet!) our very demanding deadlines.

Bob Parry and Chris Perkins

1
Introduction

Bob Parry and Chris Perkins

Although some map collections have a long and venerable history, the development of map libraries servicing academic institutions has essentially been a post-World War 2 phenomenon. Partly this was a response to the explosion in higher education provision which took place in the 1950s and 1960s in Britain, North America and other parts of the developed world. But a lot of the growth of collections at that time was not so much demand- as supply-led. The years of World War 2 had not only stimulated an interest in the importance of maps in a shrinking world, but also resulted in an enormous production of 'war-theatre' mapping, much of which was dispersed to academic libraries in the immediate post-war period. Institutions responded, providing facilities and personnel to curate these nascent collections and, as Ristow observed, the profession of map librarian 'came of age' in the decade after the war (Ristow, 1967).

The growth and appreciation of map libraries continued to be favoured through the 1950s and 1960s by several further factors. Firstly, the supply of new mapping did not diminish. A huge output of topographic and resource mapping began to emerge, undertaken by Western survey organizations in the developing world. In Britain, for example, many collections were recipients of a free distribution of maps produced by the Directorate of Overseas Surveys, covering emerging post-colonial nations in Africa, the West Indies and elsewhere. Similarly, in the USA topographic mapping of many states in Central and South America, undertaken through collaboration with the Inter-American Geodetic Survey, were deposited in US collections by the Army Map Service. Map libraries in the USA in particular benefited from generous depository arrangements which extended to many government publications, including the domestic map series of the United States Geological Survey.

This period was an exciting time of accelerated map production using the latest (but pre-digital) data capture, compilation and printing technologies (Monmonier, 1985), and in Western Europe too, most states embarked on new national mapping programmes. In Eastern Europe and the Soviet Union extensive programmes of topographic mapping to a standardized military specification were undertaken (although during the Cold War these maps did not migrate into academic libraries).

A second factor that undoubtedly favoured map library development over those two decades or so was the perceived close link between maps and geography. Indeed, in the UK it was often the academic Department of Geography rather than a centralized library that harboured and fostered the growing map collection. In the USA, although map collections were almost always administered by the university's central library, they were sometimes deliberately decentralized in location to become part of a departmental (geography) library, in the perhaps mistaken belief that their main users would be found there (Treude, 1972).

While the generous depository arrangements characteristic of the USA, and to a large extent Canada, have continued to the present day, such arrangements were much less common elsewhere. In Britain, the six legal deposit libraries receive home-produced mapping, but the majority of academic collections do not benefit in this way. Nevertheless, the mapping bonanza of those early post-war decades was inevitably reflected in a proliferation and growth of map libraries.

A maturing profession

The 1960s saw the establishment of major professional cartographic societies, and some of these attracted the interests of the small but growing fellowship of map curators. The British Cartographic Society, founded in 1964, developed a strong Map Curators' Group (which later also developed a link with the Library Association). In Canada, the Association of Canadian Map Libraries (now Association of Canadian Map Libraries and Archives) was established in 1967. In the USA, map librarianship had already found its home within the Special Libraries Association, but only much later with the American Library Association, which launched a Map and Geography Round Table in 1980. In other parts of the developed world, other small but active map curator networks developed. In Australia, for example, an Australian Map Curators' Circle was founded in 1973 (and was subsequently enlarged to include the interests of map producers and users as the Australian Map Circle), while in New Zealand, the New Zealand Map Keepers' Circle (now New Zealand Map Society) was founded in 1977. In Europe, map libraries benefited from the establishment in 1980 of a Groupe des Cartothécaires under the aegis of LIBER (Ligue des Bibliothèques Européennes de Recherche). The International Federation of Library Associations (IFLA) also made efforts to support the development of map collections, especially in the developing world, and is responsible for the *World directory of map collections*. These organizations provided useful forums for the exchange of information through conferences, seminars and newsletters, and some of them organized in-service training in a profession in which many participants were largely self-taught (few library schools offered much teaching on the skills needed for running a map library).

In the 1970s, manuals of map librarianship began to appear. In Britain, Harold Nichols' *Map librarianship* passed through two editions (1976 and 1982), and provided a useful collection of information and advice for aspiring map curators. A more hands-on approach was provided by Mary Larsgaard who was able to 'tell it how it was' from her live experience of map librarianship in three editions of a book of the same name (1978, 1987 and 1998). In Canada, Farrell and Desbarats (1981 and 1984) followed with a small but extremely useful *Guide for a small map collection*.

All this networking and guidance was much needed for a small and widely dispersed profession which was feeling its way to developing standards of map collection management.

With the great expansion, the concern for better collection management resulted in the adoption of a variety of cataloguing and classification schemes, some homegrown or based upon the established schemes of Boggs and Lewis or the American Geographical Society, or, in Britain at least, the Ministry of Defence 'Parsons' classification system (Ministry of Defence, 1978) or that of the Royal Geographical Society. In North America, in spite of its imperfections, most libraries eventually settled for the Library of Congress Classification, Schedule G. Most cataloguing standards meanwhile had been brought into conformity with AACR2, using the manual of interpretation prepared for cartographic materials (Stibbe, 1982).

Interest in the automated cataloguing of map collections began in earnest in the 1960s. Several home-grown schemes were introduced by enthusiasts interested in making new technology work for them. In Canada for example, Donkin and Goodchild (1967) developed a system using IBM punched cards. Another relatively early scheme was developed in the UK by Shepherd at Middlesex Polytechnic (now University) (Shepherd and Chilton, 1980). Elsewhere, more partial systems were introduced. For example, in the USA Phil Hoehn and Steve Silberstein developed a system for generating printed listings of USGS topographic quadrangles from sheet data held on IBM cards (Hoehn and Silberstein, 1971). Unfortunately, many of these systems were limited and ultimately doomed by the immaturity of the computer technology available at the time. The prime time of computer catalogues as tools for the user only really came in the 1990s, when the once formidable problem of providing a graphical interface for area searching, and on-screen graphical indexes of map series, was solved. Pioneer work was done by a British Library-funded CARTONET project in the mid-1980s to develop a system that generated customer-defined graphic indexes from a computerized catalogue held in an Oracle database (Bartlett, Irvine and Morris, 1989).

The 1980s also saw the widespread adoption of cooperative online cataloguing using OCLC or RLIN, and the use of variations of the Machine Readable Cataloguing Format (MARC).

More practical aspects of map librarianship, such as the selection of suitable storage facilities for maps, conservation problems, and the problems of selection and acquisition, were covered in the serial publications associated with map librarian organizations, and in occasional special issues of more general journals of librarianship. The problems of map availability and acquisition were also tackled in Winch's *International maps and atlases in print* (1974 and 1976) and Parry and Perkins' *World mapping today* (1987 and 2000).

However, even as map librarianship was developing formal structures for the management and care of maps, the nature and supply of their objects of concern were undergoing radical change. From the mid-1980s, maps were increasingly being replicated or replaced by data in digital form and stored and distributed on media such as magnetic tape, floppy or hard disk, CD-ROM and, ultimately, the Internet.

Decline or rebirth?

If the 1960s and 1970s were a growth time for map libraries, the 1980s and 1990s were in some respects a period of apparent decline. Again, there were complex reasons for this. Globally, much of the post-war boom in mapmaking was over, or much diminished, and the mapmaking industry itself was in decline. The link between geography and maps was no longer as strong as it once had been, and collections that had depended on such a link suffered. In Britain, a number of departmental collections were dismantled, and others were neglected as funds were re-routed to new priorities, such as the provision of computing facilities.

One of the consequences of the great map bonanza of the first decades after World War 2, was an assumption in many institutions that map collections could manage with little, or sometimes even zero, funding. Unfortunately this has never been the case. To maintain a quality collection responsive to users' needs demands considerable outlay. Map curators have always had a hard time promoting the importance of the service they provide, and have had to fight their corner for adequate funding to support those services (Cobb, 1979). It was only by so doing that a high profile for the map collection could be achieved. The importance of funding has grown as the availability of free maps has been reduced, and the pricing of maps and spatial data has become increasingly commercial.

In North America collections maintained their presence numerically, but many were starved of funds and were overly dependent on their depository status for survival. In year 2000, the US depository system was itself under threat due to proposed Government Printing Office funding cuts for FY 2001 (discussed on MAPS-L, see below, in May 2000).

The rise and decline of the map library is illustrated indirectly by Wishard (1997) who has charted the rise and fall of membership of the four principal map library organizations in the USA and Canada. All have been falling since at least 1992, and this has been accompanied by a corresponding decline in the publications of these societies (and the demise of two of them).

This does not necessarily mean that what is left is unhealthy: many of these publications functioned mainly as newsletters rather than as vehicles for refereed papers, and there is now an active exchange of information in electronic form. Indeed it could be argued that the development of e-mail-based listservers and increasing use of the web partly explain the decline in membership of map library organizations. Pre-eminent amongst these electronic bulletin boards, and with a focus upon current mapping and map library practice, is MAPS-L, the Maps and Air Photos Systems forum (available at **maps-l@uga.cc.uga.edu**). MAPS-L has a very active international traffic with about 1500 members, and wide-ranging thematic coverage.

MAPS-Hist, established in 1994 and now with over 600 subscribers, is available from **http://www.maphist.nl/index.html** and offers an equivalent source for historical coverage. Other lists support more local user communities, such as LIS-MAPS in the UK, or Carta in Canada. There is of course also a profusion of more specialist listservers allowing a very focused one-to-many communication, and integrating the isolated map librarian with a wider user community, for example GIS4LIB, aimed at the library GIS-using community.

Meanwhile the web allows wide dissemination of materials from portal sites, and has taken on much of the mantle of formally published literature. Notable amongst resources are the LIBER home pages at **http://www.maps. ethz.ch/gdc-education2. html**, or the IFLA pages at **http://www.ifla.org/VII/s6/sgml.htm**. National map societies in most Western countries also now operate web pages.

It is also clear from the broader cartographic literature that, while an industry (mapmaking), and a service that supports it (the map library), have diminished numerically in staffing, the interest in and utility of spatial information are in the ascendancy. Interestingly, a fifth organization charted by Wishard (1997), the North American Cartographic Association, which is not restricted to the interests of map librarians, showed a strongly growing membership right up to the last year of the survey (1995), and this society continues to maintain a lively and innovative serial publication (*Cartographic perspectives*). This growing interest is directly attributable to the new possibilities for the manipulation of digital data and their graphical representation made effective through computer systems, and it is these possibilities above all that provide map librarians with new challenges.

Evidently, map librarians, and those with a controlling influence on map libraries, need to rethink their role in the changing context of new technology, new media, and of new political and economic perspectives. It is the task of the chapters that follow to map out some future scenarios for the map library at the turn of the millennium.

Map libraries in the new millennium

The authors who were invited to contribute to this book were deliberately chosen from a variety of fields within cartography, in order to give a wider perspective than the narrow spectrum of a book written purely by map curators for map curators. The result has been interesting to say the least! Although we endeavoured to sustain continuity between chapters by providing each author with a suggested remit, an outline of the book as a whole, and an easy means (e-mail) of contacting each other, not only the perspectives but also the approaches adopted vary enormously. Many chapters also reflect rather parochially the developments in the country of residence of the contributor, rather than an international view. This itself is revealing: globalization of data and communication systems notwithstanding, the experiences of data provision and therefore of the changing function of the map library, are as yet not uniform between, say, the USA, the UK or The Netherlands. We have preferred to treat these disparities as a strength of the book rather than a weakness, and so have tampered only minimally with the content of most chapters! We hope they will reveal to the reader some of the divergence in ideas and applications in different countries and continents, as well as the differing perceptions of the providers, managers and users of spatial data. We are nevertheless conscious that the book presents a Western view of map libraries.

In Chapter 2, Carol Marley, a Canadian writing from a North American perspective, illustrates the growing technical knowledge of some (not all) map users and map librarians through two revealing reference interviews. Map librarians now need to be knowledgeable not only about the contents of their own collections but about the web as well; and it is not only knowledge of the resources themselves that is required, but how to access and employ them. After considering some of the literature on user needs in the digital age, Marley concludes that, in research libraries in North America at least, the argument for GIS training and expertise in the map library has already been won. She recognizes the enormous problems faced by map libraries trying to meet the demands of spatial data technology and its users, but does not doubt that there is a future for map librarians in a redefined role.

In contrast, Nick Millea (Chapter 3) offers a mainly European-orientated view of the effects of internal and external political and economic pressures on the map library. He stresses the pressures that might limit organizational responses, detailing the wider context, the role of parent institutions, data suppliers and cartographic agencies, and the varying impacts of technological change. Examples are taken from a global range of map libraries, with comparisons drawn between the variety of responses experienced in different national legal and institutional contexts. Millea concludes by evaluating impacts on map library personnel and users, and argues for more appeciation of local contexts when considering technological change.

In Chapter 4, Patrick McGlamery introduces the multiple uses of automation in the map room. He discusses the development of automated cataloguing systems, and then presents a strong case for GIS as 'the natural successor of the paper map', and therefore the need to rethink and supply revised training for the role of map librarians. The various North American-based initiatives to 'bring on' the map librarian as a GIS specialist are discussed, and the importance of developing communications technologies, from CD-ROM to web delivery of spatial information are also considered.

Jennifer Stone Muilenburg (Chapter 5) also provides a mainly North American view. Her remit was to argue the case for GIS in the map library in greater detail, and this she does with recourse to a new survey into the use of GIS in the map library. Her results, whilst drawing on a relatively small sample of collections, highlight the key role of the map curator or spatial data specialist in the provision of GIS.

In Chapter 6, Bob Parry presents a more detailed review of the role of CD-ROM as a storage device for map data and as a medium for standalone mapping packages in the map library. He argues its value as a user-friendly and map library-friendly medium for disseminating spatial data, and for developing user skills in handling and presenting data cartographically. Although recognizing the growing dominance of the web for the delivery of spatial data, he suggests that, just like paper maps, there is a continuing place for data stored and serviced locally, whether on CD-ROM, DVD or some future medium.

The Internet undoubtedly lies close to the heart of the changes that are taking place in cartography and that are having an effect both on and far beyond the map library. The Internet and the web are recurring themes in most chapters of the book, but two are devoted to it exclusively. In Chapter 7, Michael Peterson traces the Internet and the web back to their origins, and discusses the nature and availability of maps on the web and the problems of accessing them and downloading them. He also suggests that the pervasive mobile phone, using WAP technology, will soon replace the computer as the main tool for accessing data, including maps. Although he concludes that the all-digital, online map library is now possible, he also concedes that use of maps on the Internet may act as a stimulus to the use of mapping in general, including paper maps, something that map libraries are indeed finding. In Chapter 8, Menno-Jan Kraak takes a closer look at the different applications of maps on the web and considers how they might be used in the map library context, for example to provide a showcase for the map collection or as a graphical interface to a map catalogue. He argues for the involvement of map curators in providing metadata and access tools for web mapping, a topic taken up in the following chapter by Jan Smits.

Metadata and standards defining the quality of information that is to be used in retrieval systems are increasingly significant. Jan Smits classifies these according to their complexity into four 'quality' levels. He also introduces some of the ways in which systems have used these different types of metadata, including the development of hybrid systems, before considering how the bewildering variety of standards might come to operate together. Obstacles hindering such a convergence need to be removed if the digital map library is to be used in effective and imaginative ways.

Although the 'new cartography' has mainly focused on the changes affecting contemporary cartography, even academic libraries that cater mainly for interests in modern mapping inevitably have a historical dimension to their holdings. Old maps are of both historical interest – as a reflection of and commentary on past times – and of value in investigating a range of contemporary problems. Chris Baruth (Chapter 10) illustrates the importance of the map archive, its conservation needs, and discusses developments in the transfer of old maps to a digital environment. He also considers the resourcing necessary if we are to preserve our cartographic heritage for the future, and stresses the need for shared responsibility for the digital preservation of our digital archive. To avoid duplication of effort, uniform scanning standards and provision of metadata for scanned maps are required, and the concept of a clearing-house for registering scanned maps is considered.

Chapters 11, 12 and 13 focus upon the changing nature of spatial data and the ways in which map libraries might be able to adapt to these profound shifts in format. Chris Perkins addresses the global issue of varying availability of different kinds of map and spatial data. He charts significant spatial variations in availability and begins to account for these by discussing local organizational, economic and political factors. Whilst there is a global dynamic pushing map librarians away from the acquisition of printed published mapping, and towards facilitating access to a wide diversity of forms of spatially referenced data , the local circumstances of the map library and the context in which data are produced will continue to be significant issues.

Bob Barr picks up these themes and focuses in detail upon the nature of information as a commodity. He too explores the implications that flow from the dematerialization of information and the shift from map to spatial data. He emphasizes the key role of local legal frameworks that underpin the politics of information, and contrasts and explains reasons for a restrictive policy, with the rationales for a more liberal policy stressing the freedom of information.

Pip Forer takes these arguments forward by addressing the tension between the map library as a custodian of publicly available knowledge and the ongoing commercial dynamic generating an entirely new mapping sector. Forer argues that map librarians should aim to provide access to data made available by these new industries, as well as continuing to procure and provide more traditional materials. He recognizes that spatially referenced data from the new mapping sector represent an unparalleled challenge for the map library community, that can only be answered by building proactive relationships with the new mapping institutions.

For Chapters 14 and 15 two British users of maps and spatial data were invited to give their personal impressions of what they expect a 21st century map library to offer and why. Alan Godfrey, a publisher of reprints of early Ordnance Survey maps, calls on his extensive experience as a user of map libraries in the UK to give a personal and refreshingly anecdotal view, and, although no technophobe, argues the case for the continuing importance of access to paper maps. David Fairbairn approaches his task as an academic who uses maps and digital data in teaching, research and recreation, and offers a more studied review of how he sees the map curator meeting the contemporary needs of the map user.

What is the use of a map library without maps? Traditionally among the greatest and yet least written-about problems of map libraries have been those concerned with acquisition: the high price of some mapping, the best sourcing, and (as discussed in Chapter 11) availability. The web has changed all this and, in Chapter 16, Russell Guy discusses these issues from the point of view of a major US-based map dealer.

One of the encouraging things to emerge from these chapters is that many map curators already appear to be ahead of the game. Thus comments by academics such as Kraak and Fairbairn about how curators might extent their role by adding web links to their map library home pages, providing metadata, developing expertise in importing web data into a GIS or creating presentable maps, are counterpointed by Marley, McGlamery, Stone Muilenburg and Smits who reveal the progress being made in these areas.

Cartographers and curators unite! Just as there is a need for curators to keep abreast of what cartographers are doing, so all who are interested in maps need to be more aware of what the map library can do for them. For example, the role of map library as archive is shown by Forer to be even more crucial, now that new kinds of data sets in digital format may find a passing use and then be lost to posterity.

We have chosen to end the book by distilling some of the views and arguments of our contributors into a debate in which we have deliberately adopted opposing views of the future of the map library. Readers will not find it difficult to see through this pretence and realize that as editors we both still have a reasonably strong belief in a future for both map libraries and their curators. However, this must be tempered by a real concern that map librarians must try to stay with, or even ahead of the pack in promoting and disseminating the digital map. Many of the chapters that follow attest that they are already doing so.

References

Bartlett, D, Irvine, J and Morris, B (1989) The map curator in the computer age: the world at your finger tips. In Rhind, D and Taylor, D R F (eds) *Cartography, past present and future*, Elsevier, 97–108.

Cobb, D A (1979) The politics and economics of map librarianship, *Bulletin, Special Libraries Association, Geography and Maps Division*, **117**, 20–7.

Donkin, K and Goodchild, M (1967) A computerized approach to increased map library utility, *The Cartographer*, **4** (1), 39–45.

Farrell, B and Desbarats, A (1981) *Guide for a small map collection*, Association of Canadian Map Libraries.

Farrell, B and Desbarats, A (1984) *Guide for a small map collection*, 2nd edn, Association of Canadian Map Libraries.

Hoehn, P and Silberstein, S (1971) Computerized control file for topographic quadrangles developed for the Bancroft Library, *Bulletin, Special Libraries Association, Geography and Maps Division*, **86**, 24, 56.

Larsgaard, M L (1978) *Map librarianship: an introduction*, Libraries Unlimited.

Larsgaard, M L (1987) *Map librarianship: an introduction*, 2nd edn, Libraries Unlimited.

Larsgaard, M L (1998) *Map librarianship: an introduction*, 3rd edn, Libraries Unlimited.

Ministry of Defence (1978) *Manual of map library classification and cataloguing*, Mapping and Charting Establishment RE.

Monmonier, M (1985) *Technological transition in cartography*, University of Wisconsin Press.

Nichols, H (1982) *Map librarianship*, Clive Bingley.

Nichols, H (1986) *Map librarianship*, 2nd edn, Clive Bingley.

Parry, R B and Perkins, C R (1987) *World mapping today*, Butterworths.

Parry, R B and Perkins, C R (2000) *World mapping today*, 2nd edn, Bowker-Saur.

Ristow, W W (1967) The emergence of maps in libraries, *Special Libraries*, **58**, 400–19.

Shepherd, I K H and Chilton, S (1980) Computer-based enquiries in the map library: the MAPLIB system, *The Cartographic Journal*, **17**, 128–39.

Stibbe, H L P (ed) (1982) *Cartographic materials: a manual of interpretation for AACR2*, American Library Association, Canadian Library Association and The Library Association.

Treude, M (1972) Location and administration of a map and atlas collection, *Bulletin, Special Libraries Association, Geography and Maps Division*, **89**, 32–40.

Whyment, M (1998) Microsoft Encarta 97 World Atlas versus De Lorme Mappings' Global Explorer – a user's view, *The Cartographic Journal*, **35**, 95–8.

Winch, K L (1974) *International maps and atlases in print*, Bowker.

Winch, K L (1976) *International maps and atlases in print*, 2nd edn, Bowker.

Wishard, L (1997) History of cartographic information society publishing, *Bulletin, Special Libraries Association Geography and Maps Division*, **187**, 44–73.

2
The changing profile of the map user

Carol Marley

> The raison d'être for a collection is map use; all other functions are secondary to this one end.
>
> (Farrell and Desbarats, 1984)

▶ *This chapter considers the traditional uses of maps in libraries and the changing demands and expectations of the user in view of new technologies and the proliferation of computer-generated maps and digital data sets served on the web. Written from a map librarian's perspective, these observations are balanced by other chapters from the user point of view. For the purposes of this chapter a map will be defined as any geographical representation of the spatial environment, including spatially referenced data.*

The analysis of user needs

Map librarians have always expected to have a high level of interaction with map library users, and the traditional medium for understanding users and their needs is the reference interview (Farrell and Desbarats, 1984; Larsgaard, 1998). A reference interview is an exercise in inter-personal relationships. To the users, the library may appear strange, they may not know exactly what they need, and most users prefer to find what is needed on their own. The user is probably not feeling too comfortable. The librarian will need to be approachable, a good listener, and will need to extract information in a sensitive manner. Once the user's need is defined, the librarian will try to find the answer. Usually a librarian will try to enable users to help themselves so that, for example, the next time a geological map is needed, the user feels comfortable using the indexes.

Although each reference interview is unique, sample interviews aid in conveying the range and complexity of user needs. Consider the following interviews which took place recently in a large geographic information centre housing the university map collection and a variety of computer labs.

Interview I

The information services librarian, returning from a data services meeting, picked up the interview from the GIS technician. An undergraduate student working with ArcView was frustrated by not finding a topographic map of San Francisco at an appropriate scale.

'Do you need your map in digital format? Are you familiar with some of the geographic information systems we have on these computers?' [ArcView, MapInfo]

'Yes, I have had an introductory GIS course.'

'I see you have some colour printouts of maps from the *Research Program in Environmental Planning and Geographic Information Systems* [**http://www.regis.berkeley.edu/**]. That's a good place to find information about the Bay Area. How did you find it and what is your project?'

'I am working on the Loma Prieta earthquake. The other librarian suggested that I check the GIS links on your home page. I also found some other good maps. This one shows population density.' [*Digital atlas of California* **http://130.166.124.2/Capage1.html**]

'Have you tried the *GIS data depot*?' [**http://www.gisdatadepot.com/**]

'Yes, I was shown it but didn't find it useful.'

The librarian went back to the site to check under the heading, San Francisco. There she found large-scale maps, categorized as hypsography, for the San Francisco area. The student was unfamiliar with this terminology. When asked if she had ever brought SDTS format into ArcView the student said that she had worked principally with shape files.

'There is a translator here on the depot site, and we have instructions for bringing this format into ArcView. It's easier now with ArcView 3.2. Are you committed to using a GIS, or would you consider looking at a paper map?'

'Well, I don't know how to find them.' [Most of the centre's maps are not in the online catalogue].

'Let's take a look in the drawers at what we have for the San Francisco region.'

We found a satellite view showing the underlying geological formations in various parts of the city.

'This is fantastic. How did they do that? It's a picture, right?'

'Yes, it's an image that has been combined with the geology, and there are some useful graphs at the bottom showing what happened to buildings situated on different formations. Let's take a look at the U.S. 1:100,000 scale topographic maps to see what you think of them.'

Unfortunately San Francisco was missing.

'You can go upstairs to our storage area to see if the 1:24,000 scale maps would be useful.'

The student returned, disappointed that the sheets were too big, and that several were required to cover the region. She preferred her 8.5×11 printouts.

'Why don't we go back to our home page and check one of the major map sites on the web [*Oddens' Bookmarks*, **http://oddens.geog.uu.nl/index.html**]? There is bound to be a lot of useful information on San Francisco.'

'This is perfect. I see some of the other sites here that I found under GIS on our home page. Why didn't I find this site?'

'This site has been grouped with maps and cartography rather than with the GIS databases. Let me know if you need more help.'

'Oh, I do. This is for my hazards course in the Geography Department and I am having trouble finding good articles on my topic.'

'Have you tried the university library's online databases?'

'I'm not familiar with them.'

'You might try *GeoRef*, which is very good for geology.'

'I am an Arts student. I probably wouldn't understand it. It sounds very scientific.'

'Then you might like to try *General science index*, or *Geobase*.'

In the latter we found a book about hazards in California, with a chapter on Loma Prieta.

'This is great. You have been very helpful. I love the web.'

Interview II

A student came to the reference desk, explaining that she was unfamiliar with the geographic information centre, but hoped that we might be able to help her. She was an undergraduate in her final year, working on a project for a biology professor.

'My professor has given me a list of approximately 2000 sponge sightings for North America. He needs to know exactly where these are located.'

'Do you have the coordinates of the sites, the latitudes and longitudes for them?'

'No, but I thought a map might be helpful.'

'Does your professor want a map as the final product?'

'Yes, I think so, although I am wondering if it wouldn't be a huge map and if such a thing would even exist. There are so many points to locate.'

'Probably the quickest way of proceeding is to go to our home page to link to a digital gazetteer [*GEOnet names server* **http://www.nima.mil/gns/html/ index.html**]. You could establish the coordinates of your sites and move this information into a spreadsheet. Are you familiar with geographic information systems?'

'No, I don't know that term.'

The concept of GIS was explained and the student was pointed to the GIS section of the centre's home page for more information.

'You could create a point theme in ArcView using one of our small-scale digital databases. Although we don't teach GIS here in the library, we can get you started. If you are interested in pursuing the matter, you might want to try some exercises through the web [*ESRI virtual campus* **http://campus. esri.com/**] or use one of our basic books and CD-ROMs to learn to use a GIS. Do you know the technician who is responsible for the GIS over in the museum? Maybe he can get you started. He is familiar with ArcView and can probably let you work there if you prefer.'

'Yes, I could talk to him. Maybe I need to talk to my professor again as well.'

What do these interviews tell us about the skills and expectations of the present-day user and the complementary skills required of the map librarian? I would argue that the interviews illustrate the increasing technical sophistication of *some* of our users and of map librarians themselves.

Science students, such as the biologist, have basic computer and statistical skills; often they have very specific research tasks to perform. They expect to use maps or atlases. Many of them have used the web to locate data, but they may not have worked with geo-referenced digital resources nor with GIS. Given some leads on how to get started with GIS, the student can usually get on with solving the problem. Even so these students and their professors have commented on the high learning curve associated with using a 'low-end' GIS such as ArcView. In addition many of them are not familiar with basic cartographic principles; therefore they frequently look to the map librarian for advice on how to produce effective maps for their purposes.

Geography, urban planning and architecture students are conversant with drawing packages and statistical software and have worked with GIS. It is likely that many of our students will have worked with files that we have put up on their LANs, or they will have been directed to library resources such as CD-ROMs with their specific course needs in mind. Some students have followed our links to digital databases and interactive mapping sites. However most students have very little experience in extracting data from the web. No matter how user-friendly the warehouse, the students often need help with terminology, formats and the interpretation of metadata. Invariably they will need to consult a map librarian for help in finding supplementary information stored in a bewildering variety of thematic maps, atlases and imagery on paper.

We don't know what happens with the students who go it alone on the web. Those of us who have built web assignments into professors' courses see that most of the students are unaware of which search engine they are using. Many need help in developing search strategies, evaluating sites in terms of content or bias and in finding reviews of websites.

Experience with those who come to us having failed to find what they want suggests that they are unfamiliar with the university library's web pages, which were designed to get them quick started. They have missed pointers to data-rich collections, in-house or virtual. Despite all, *many* users are taking to the web. For librarians the trick is to maintain a balance between the valuable information that is locked into our paper maps and the increasing volume and variety of maps and data that are being offered on the web. As we perform this balancing act, the difficulty is in understanding where our users are poised in relation to ourselves and a vast array of information resources.

Traditional needs for and uses of maps in libraries

To belabour the obvious, these interviews were time consuming and required a breadth of knowledge and technical skills on the part of both the librarian and user. They conform to traditional needs and uses of maps in libraries in that a high degree of user support has always been a feature of map libraries. Although maps simplify a world that is infinitely complex, they themselves are complicated. However, it should be easier to read a map than a book. After all, it is often said that a picture is worth a thousand words. Reading a map, however, is not an easy task. Users need help and map collection staff have need of specialized subject knowledge, not only to instruct readers in how to use the library, but also in the use and interpretation of the material found in the library.

Map staff need to be familiar with concepts such as scale, projection, symbolization, grids, geodesy and direction, and to be cognizant of the many different types of maps, their subject matter, and methods of reproduction (Larsgaard, 1998). Many map users are not accustomed to examining a map carefully. They may not understand the relationship between maps and gazetteers. They may find it difficult to determine the title of a map sheet or series. Date of survey or publication can be difficult to establish. Users may not be familiar with legends and indexes.

In assessing information needs, it is of prime importance to understand the types of users that come to a map collection seeking information. Winearls (1974), in a classic article on reference in a university map collection, categorized users as follows:

- Many people, the majority perhaps, know little about maps, which makes it difficult to provide information at an appropriate level and in a useful format. The layperson may have simple requirements such as locating parks in a city.
- Then there are students who use maps so infrequently that they are not familiar with the library layout or indexes. They hope that the information desired will be provided on one map, preferably measuring 8.5×11 inches, to be easily incorporated into a paper. This type of user is ill prepared to consult several different maps in order to synthesize information.
- On the next level are academics, specialists who know their subject matter, but are unfamiliar with maps as information sources. The academic is often prepared to do a certain amount of work to achieve goals and is usually easy to work with.
- Finally there is the subject/map expert who really only needs assistance to know how to use the library, to find uncatalogued materials and to be referred to sources that may not be in a particular map collection.

Today these same types of users come to the map collection, a major difference being that they often leave with digital information, in addition to, or in place of, print material.

The types of questions that users ask inform us of their needs. Winearls grouped these into two broad classes:

- Location questions are among the most obvious, eg where is a particular town? Often such questions can be answered by gazetteers, but nevertheless, it may be necessary to consult a map to visualize a location more clearly. Another type of location question concerns boundaries. Some of these questions can be quite complex, such as determining the boundaries of Europe and those of Asia.
- The second most common type of question is for a map of a specific area, containing certain information, such as the current road network in France. Many users need topographic information. Sometimes this information is needed for recreational purposes. Another common user need is for maps comparing different areas, eg land use in Canada in contrast to that in Israel. Many of these comparative uses are generated by class assignments. Sometimes a user wants a specific map, such as the map of Canada that has Thornthwaite climate units on it. These questions often require considerable interpretative assistance on the part of the map librarian.

In many respects, current users continue to fit these profiles and continue to ask similar questions.

Alternative methods of establishing user needs

There are a variety of ways of ascertaining to what extent user needs are changing and how in turn map librarians are responding to these changes.

Surveys

Surveys help to establish user needs but there is very little published literature on map user surveys (Gillispie, 1990). Many surveys done in map collections have been attempts to identify what maps are being used and who uses them. Surveys have most often focused on larger academic and research libraries. Often data have been collected, not by questionnaire, but by circulation records, or staff-recorded statistics about patrons. Few published studies include the actual survey questions. Surveys conducted at map collections apart from a main library, particularly those in close proximity to a geology or geography department, reveal a higher percentage of sophisticated users and more narrowly focused requests than those found in main libraries. Surveys have also looked at which academic departments patronize map collections. The surveys that do exist illustrate the diversity of map users and map use.

In the context of public libraries, a welcome survey of user needs emerged from a recent conference. Gluck (1996) discussed findings from five studies targeted to user needs in public libraries. An underlying assumption of the research is that public libraries have not met the geospatial information needs of their patrons as well as they might, nor have the geospatial needs of the public been systematically analysed. Gluck breaks down user needs into educational, professional, personal and recreational. Another of his breakdowns suggests that slightly less than 60% of user needs pose mapreading tasks, just less than 30% pose analysis, patterns or relationship tasks, and approximately 15% of needs pose interpolation or cause and effect tasks. Gluck contends that the public does not have a real concern for the answer to lie in a particular format, but that people simply want their information in a format that is convenient.

Another important point to emerge is that current formats, content, sources, service and the structure of geospatial information are not to any great extent used, usable, useful, relevant or satisfying to public library patrons. Although the survey gave high ratings to libraries for assisting users to resolve mapreading tasks, low ratings were assigned for help with map analysis and for interpretation task support. Who is responsible for this failure? Gluck argues that it is the inadequacies of spatial information usability and usefulness that are at fault, and it is the library profession's historical solution to train the user to read maps. Gluck calls for more user studies to establish user needs. In addition he recommends that the role that state and federal government, as well as local organizations, may play in the customization of geospatial data for local needs should be examined in the context of making data accessible through public libraries.

Conferences

Conferences provide another means of discerning user needs and document important shifts in information services as new technologies migrate to libraries. In 1993 many of North America's map librarians met in Washington, DC at such a conference, to consider the digital revolution in cartography and its effect on libraries (Wood, 1994). Keynote speaker, Larry Carver of the University of California at Santa Barbara (UCSB), shared his vision of GIS as holding the 'seeds for the electronic library of the future'. The Internet figured prominently in this vision of a future in which it will not matter where data resides. Libraries would fit into the 'big business' of information delivery in terms of standards and a tradition of responsibility for information heritage. Patrick McGlamery, University of Connecticut, asked, 'Will anyone come to the map library anymore?' He encouraged map libraries to begin thinking in terms of spatial data rather than maps. Deborah Lords, University of Utah, was concerned as to whether there is a future for map librarians, commenting that library education is not keeping up with new technologies. Lords outlined another concern, the 'envelope of disenfranchisement' to those who do not have access to any of the new technologies.

Professional journals

Professional journals are quick to pick up on major reconfigurations of information services. A year after the Washington 'summit', Chris Perkins considered the options for the future of map and spatial data collections (Perkins, 1995). He addressed the issues of which aspects of digital mapping were significant for map collections and users of maps and whether services could be delivered to different groups in different societies, not just in the major research collections. Should the traditional map library switch from analogue data to digital? What were the economic implications of change and what about the uneven social and spatial impacts of GIS? Perkins noted the paucity of literature on the use of conventional and digital products in map libraries. No one had yet begun to examine who needs which kinds of digital map data, nor looked at the skills required to use different digital products. Perkins concluded that 'it is unlikely that GIS in a library context will improve access to geographic information for the majority'.

Digital data: a new way of looking at information

User needs studies or not, by 1997 the question was not whether most large university and research libraries in North America would offer digital services, in particular GIS, but how such services were being offered. Two events account for the migration of GIS into these libraries. Firstly, the US Government Printing Office distributed the 1990 census data on CD-ROM. As a result, libraries were forced to consider new technologies to manage and distribute these data. Secondly, relatively inexpensive and powerful microcomputers and software became commonly available in the 1990s. These events led to programmes such as the GIS Literacy Project of the Association of Research Libraries (ARL), which through partnerships with the Environmental Systems Research Institute (ESRI) and others, introduced GIS into many ARL libraries in the USA and Canada.

A growing body of literature attests to these events and to the emergence of spatial data and related services in libraries (see *Current literature on GIS and libraries* **http://www.mcmaster.ca/library/maps/gis_libr.htm**). A key ARL report (*Transforming libraries*, 1997) argues that GIS represents a whole new way of thinking about, or looking at information. Still an emerging technology in most libraries, GIS raises a host of issues. It is expensive, entails a very steep learning curve and requires a solid infrastructure and high-level equipment. At the same time, it is also an enormously attractive technology. One theme that emerged in conversations with the information professionals who contributed to the report is that GIS is nothing without the data 'that bring it to life'. Also the effective use of GIS depends on good problem-solving skills. Both users and librarians now need to know about data, data provenance and data quality. Spatial literacy is predicted to be a term that we will hear more of in coming years, meaning the ability to interpret problems and their solutions in spatial terms, on the part of both librarians and users. The report looks at collections and services, staff and user training, storage and costs.

Expanding upon the ARL report, in 1997 the *Journal of Academic Librarianship* devoted an issue to GIS in libraries. It was pointed out that 'Perhaps no other area of public services relies more on user education' (Argenati, 1997, 465). Users will need assistance in developing an understanding of complex data sets and how data may be manipulated with a variety of software. The difficulty of educating staff and users is a much-visited theme in articles about GIS in libraries. The technically proficient GIS user who does not know how to use numerical data effectively can be as significant a problem as the novice GIS user (Lamont and Marley, 1998). Training, whether for staff or the user, is essential and it must be ongoing. It is not necessary for the library to go it alone; partnerships can be used to mutual advantage. Training requires commitment on the part of library staff as well as the library administration. Out of all GIS efforts 80% fail, and 80% of the failures are due to organizational and management issues, not technology (Peuquet and Bacastow, 1991). Lack of understanding of the necessary commitment of time and resources remains the major impediment to a successful GIS service.

Before implementing GIS services, librarians must assess the resources of the institution for which they work. Services will be a reflection of users, their applications and their data needs. At one end of the continuum a library may collect CD-ROMs and point to valuable data on the web; at the other end of the continuum, will be the clearing-houses and large digital library projects, serving up geographically referenced data and supporting metadata on the web, such as the *Alexandria Digital Library Project* (**http://alexandria.sdc.ucsb.edu/**).

The web: a new means of utilizing digital data

A successful web-based service will be customer driven and based on demonstrable user needs for information and assistance. A case in point are the web initiatives undertaken at the Geospatial and Statistical Data Center, University of Virginia, which were planned in response to user needs for convenient access to spatial data files, spreadsheet maps, digital base maps and reference resources that support direct user query (Stephens, 1997).

Web-based interactive mapping and GIS services are expanding so rapidly that it is difficult to keep abreast. More than 12,500 sites were listed on *Oddens' Bookmarks* (**http://oddens.geog.uu.nl/index.html**) early in 2001. Until recently most maps served up on the web were pre-generated views. Now users can query, plan routes and build customized maps; they can also download an increasing quantity of data.

Musser has created a set of guidelines for evaluating interactive mapping on the web (**http://www.min.net/~boggan/mapping/guides.htm**) which is illustrative of changing user needs. Qualities users look for are zooming and panning features, query functions, control over the appearance of different data layers, data about the data and documentation on how the site was created, cartographic elements such as title, scale or legend, attractive appearance, user-friendliness, the possibility for the user to do spatial data analysis, and the effective use of multimedia.

Subsequently these guidelines have been used to categorize and evaluate online GIS services (Cobb and Olivero, 1997). Certain types of online sites receive such a large quantity of hits that they must be worth looking at to determine changing user needs.

Graphic snapshots are published by servers that hold pre-generated maps. The maps are often generated using a GIS and the results of a query are presented in GIF, TIFF and other image formats; they are simple maps that are not truly interactive or customizable by the user, eg the *Digital atlas of California* (**http://130.166.124.2/Capage1.html**).

Spatial database catalogues provide access to GIS files or spatial data which users can download to manipulate in a standalone GIS. Users cannot always browse or manipulate the data directly from their web browser. These sites often include extensive metadata and graphic previews of the data showing geographic extent. Data are served in commonly available formats, eg *Tools to facilitate access to digital orthophotos* (**http://ortho.mit.edu**).

Map generator services allow the user to request a customized map to be produced on the fly. The user is often provided with a browser form to tick specifications such as location, thematic layers and symbology. The form is sent to the web server, which passes the request to a GIS such as ArcInfo, which then generates a map which is converted to a GIF image. A user does not always have access to the raw spatial data, eg *Virginia 1994 TIGER/line data browser* (**http://fisher.lib.virginia.edu/tiger/1994/**).

Map browser services provide more interactive GIS services, approaching the look and basic functionality of desktop GIS. Users can control location, layers and symbology and, in addition, they often can browse maps, dynamically change displayed layers and custom label, and query and retrieve data. Occasionally they facilitate limited spatial analysis such as buffering, overlay and reclass operations. These sites often rely on off-the-shelf GIS–Internet interfacing software such as the ArcView Internet Map Server or Intergraph's Geomedia, eg the *Irish Environmental Protection Agency's National Freshwater Quality Database* (**http://www.compass.ie/epa/system.html**).

Instead of providing generation and manipulation of existing maps and data, real-time maps and images services supply real-time images, eg *The weather channel* (**http://www.weather.com/**).

Online sites have been developed by business, government agencies, private organizations and libraries. Often the best efforts have been achieved by cooperation. One such project is the University of Connecticut's *Map and Geographic Information Center* (**http://magic.lib.uconn.edu/**), where state and federal GIS data have been subdivided for counties and towns and then made accessible for downloading to the public.

The significance of Internet mapping and GIS lies in the potential radically to change the way people use geospatial information. Already users are able to investigate a range of problems, from the simple to the complex. Soon it won't be necessary to have GIS training or expensive GIS software or hardware to perform data analysis. In the future, problems such as speed of image or data transmission, data conversion and metadata documentation will be resolved as technology improves. Keeping abreast of online GIS resources and services will be a challenge for both librarians and amateur and professional users.

How are libraries responding to changing user needs?

As librarians deal with new technologies and the democratization of digital resources, they find themselves having to develop new skills and to respond to more exacting user expectations. Hamilton (1999) argues that there are real shifts in the profession, brought about by the pressures of a changing environment. There are those who are at the elite edge of offering an integrated spectrum of geospatial information, from print to web. For others there are very real barriers to accessing training, files, equipment and expertise. We can't do it all; there are hard choices to be made. This requires focus on the part of the map librarian and also on the part of the administration that establishes priorities and funding.

Over the last decade, what map collection has not undergone a move or merger or redefined its mission statement? Administrative change in libraries is a constant as we cope with less. Who is working on the reference desk? Who has the time and skills to conserve the maps, let alone to archive the digital maps? Who is there to catalogue the maps? Where is the map librarian in this scenario? The odds are that map librarians are spending less time in one-on-one interviews and more time elsewhere, as their administrative responsibilities have increased.

Time is limited and choices must be made. That these choices are becoming more difficult is certainly one reason why partnerships are emphasized in the literature on GIS and data in libraries. Time is required to develop partnerships. Time is required to formulate grants, to encourage gifts in kind. We campaign in our universities so that all students who have a need can have reasonable access to GIS software. We explain to our systems people why we need top-of-the-line equipment. We work with computing centres to assure that there is space and security for archiving data. We develop digital collection policies, and we administer budgets.

None but the largest libraries will have much geospatial data if they have only their map budgets to rely upon. Data are very often restricted, so map librarians are spending more time on government committees to 'free' the data for the purposes of research and teaching. In Canada, as a result of our efforts, mainly it is the major universities who have access to digital maps. Map librarians negotiate and administer a growing number of licences. As licensing takes precedence over copyright exceptions such as fair use or fair dealing, the typical map user stands to lose rather than to gain access to information.

In yet another sense access is a major issue for map collections. Our collections need to be organized such that users can locate maps. Traditionally map collections relied upon paper indexes to their series rather than the library catalogue. We see the idea of indexes for locating geospatial data being transferred to the web. If users are to search effectively, they will also need metadata. Just at the time when cataloguing departments need to incorporate metadata for numerical and geospatial files, these formats have drifted to the bottom of the priorities list while international standards are being formulated and discussions ensue on metadata. Time is needed to educate users in the creation and use of metadata. Time and a certain level of in-house expertise are required to create metadata for our datasets and to build databases.

The future of map libraries

It seems likely, in view of the capability for direct delivery of electronic information to end-users, that the analysis of information will in the future play an increasingly vital part in the information management process. This will apply as much to users as to librarians. Among the skills librarians will need are new management skills to deal with distributed libraries (and distributed communities of users). The ability to design, use and handle different scenarios will remain essential. Are these skills sufficient for librarians to play a leading role in the information environment of the future? Stephen Arnold, member of the editorial board of the journal *Electronic Library* (1999, 373), thinks that more will be required: 'Purposeful action, not blind reaction, will be increasingly important.'

In the face of changing user needs, map libraries and the librarians who organize them will redefine services. Some will seek to provide access to more digital information, others to archive the past, itself increasingly digital. 'One thing that we know will not diminish is our users' needs for cartographic information' (Gillispie, 1990). Everything suggests that there will be a future for map libraries. The future that many of us envisage for our users is access to a healthy, growing and increasingly vital global information commons.

References

Alexandria Digital Library Project **http://alexandria.sdc.ucsb.edu/**.

Argenati, C D (1997) Expanding horizons for GIS services in academic libraries, *Journal of Academic Librarianship*, **23** (6), 463–8.

Arnold, S E (1999) The future role of the information professional, *The Electronic Library*, **17** (6), 373–5.

Cobb, D A and Olivero, A (1997) Online GIS services, *Journal of Academic Librarianship*, **23** (6), 484–97.

Current literature on GIS and libraries available at
http://www.mcmaster.ca/library/maps/gis_libr.htm.

Digital atlas of California **http://130.166.124.2/Capage1.html**.

ESRI virtual campus **http://campus.esri.com**.

Farrell, B and Desbarats, A (1984) *Guide for a small map collection*, 2nd edn, Association of Canadian Map Libraries.

GEOnet names server **http://www.nima.mil/gns/html/index.html**.

Gillispie, J (1990) Exploiting cartographic resources. In Perkins, C R and Parry, R B (eds) *Information sources in cartography*, Bowker-Saur.

GIS data depot **http://www.gisdatadepot.com**.

Gluck, M (1996) Geospatial information needs of the general public: text, maps and users' tasks. In Smith, L and Gluck, M (eds) *Geographic information systems and libraries: patrons, maps and spatial information*, Graduate School of Library and Information Science, University of Illinois at Urbana-Champaign.

Hamilton, E (1999) Transmutation ? or transmogrification ? Service issues and the future of cartographic information, *ACMLA Bulletin*, **106**, 25–31.

Irish Environmental Protection Agency's National Freshwater Quality Database **http://www.compass.ie/epa/system.html**.

Lamont, M and Marley, C (1998) Spatial data and the digital library, *Cartography and Geographic Information Systems*, **25** (3), 143–9.

Larsgaard, M L (1998) *Map librarianship: an introduction*, 3rd edn, Libraries Unlimited.

Map and Geographic Information Center **http://magic.lib.uconn.edu/**.

Musser, K *Review form* **http://www.min.net/˜boggan/mapping/form.html**.

Oddens' Bookmarks **http://oddens.geog.uu.nl/index.html**.

Perkins, C R (1995) Leave it to the labs? Options for the future of map and spatial data collections, *Liber Quarterly*, **5** (3), 312–29 also available at **http://www.konbib.nl/kb/skd/liber/articles/1perkins.htm**.

Peuquet, D and Bacastow, T (1991) Organizational issues in the development of geographical information systems: a case study of U.S. Army topographic information automation, *International Journal of Geographic Information Systems*, **5**, (3), 303–19.

Research Program in Environmental Planning and Geographic Information Systems available at **http://www.regis.berkeley.edu/**.

Stephens, D (1997) Managing the web-enhanced geographic information service, *Journal of Academic Librarianship*, **23** (6), 498–504.

Tools to facilitate access to digital orthophotos available at **http://ortho.mit.edu/**.

Transforming libraries: issues and innovations in geographic information systems (1997) SpecKit 219, Association of Research Libraries.

Virginia 1994 TIGER/line data browser **http://fisher.lib.virginia.edu/tiger/1994/**.

The weather channel **http://www.weather.com/**.

Winearls, J (1974) Reference work in a current map collection, *Proceedings of the Eighth Annual Conference of the Association of Canadian Map Libraries*, ACML, 11–24.

Wood, A A (comp) (1994) The map library in transition: a joint conference sponsored by the Congress of Cartographic Information Specialists and the Geography and Map Division of the Library of Congress, October 18 & 19, 1993, *Special Libraries Association, Geography and Maps Division Bulletin*, **175**, 29–39.

3
Organizational change

Nick Millea

▶ *This chapter profiles organizational responses to change by institutions holding maps and spatial data. It explores the pressures encouraging local change, detailing the wider context, the role of parent institutions, data suppliers and cartographic agencies, and the varying impacts of technological change. Examples are taken from a global range of map libraries, with comparisons drawn between the variety of responses experienced in different national legal and institutional contexts. It also evaluates the resultant impact on map library personnel, and how these issues affect map library users.*

Introduction

In order to evaluate organizational change, we must first explore why it has become an issue. Asche (1998) pointed out that: 'One thing seems clear, however: if the "new" map library is to flourish in the fully digital cartographic world of the 21st century, redefinition of its aims and functions is inevitable to retain its traditional role', which is seen as 'To efficiently collect and provide the two principal cartographic products – the database and the visualization' – in other words both the cartographic image and the accompanying data without which the map becomes infinitely less useful. However it is not only technology that is driving organizational change: external pressures from parent bodies affect resourcing; and data suppliers and cartographic publishers are themselves changing and influencing map library practice. The wider social and economic environment is of critical importance and users are themselves changing. All of these factors are influencing local practice and are explored in the first section of this chapter, before examples of organizational responses are offered.

External pressures on map libraries
Pressures from wider economic and social contexts

Computer literacy becomes ever greater. Existing map library users are becoming increasingly comfortable using computers, while new, younger users expect to make full use of their computer skills when searching for cartographic data. They also expect more from digital data than from paper maps.

The immediate difficulty confronting the map library is the issue of user support – the more sophisticated the software on offer, the greater the impact on library staff. Learning curves must be factored into library provision, often at the expense of traditional map library services. Map librarians may be forced to decide between 'analogue' services and new digital roles. More conventional tasks may be squeezed, if the library is fully to develop digital services. This assumes that institutions are not financed to fund additional staff to cover cataloguing shortfalls, or to employ digital data specialists in new posts. The issue returns to the question of where these data should be housed. Is the map library their rightful home?

Legal issues also come into play, for example the 1998 change in Denmark's legal deposit legislation, which shifted the emphasis from printed to published material. A similar law was passed in Latvia a year previously, taking into account publications on electronic media (Zalite, 1998). Elsewhere in the Baltic Region, both Estonia and Finland now include data sets under the terms of their respective legal deposit arrangements. Sweden's Kungliga Biblioteket (Royal Library) has been making use of GIS, especially since the 1994 legal deposit legislation for electronic documents in hand-held form. Legislation moving in favour of the deposit of digital data is therefore necessitating the incorporation of GIS technology into the legal deposit libraries as a matter of urgency (Millea, 1999b). Beyond the realms of legal deposit, GIS permits the display of statistical and numerical data. This is an important part of the visualization function, integral to life in the academic, business and local authority communities that act as host institutions of many map libraries. A modern map collection has to offer both traditional and digital material, as demonstrated by the ETH Bibliothek (**http://www.ethbib.ethz.ch/ ks/karten_e.html**). Bühler (1999) expands to state that 'Only in this way may the profession of map librarianship justify its existence in the coming Millennium'.

On the social side, the 1993 US Government Printing Office Electronic Information Access Act has ensured that even computers are deposited to libraries in order to enable users to access information in depository institutions, thus promoting computer literacy (Lamont, 1999).

Pressures from parent bodies

Aside from technological developments, libraries are being challenged to respond to shrinking budgets, staff cuts and rising user expectations – all of which are leading librarians to assume new roles and responsibilities by way of reorganization and restructure (Pinnell, 2000). However it is not always the map librarian who is responsible for collecting spatial data. Within the institution, digital map data might well come under the control of a GIS specialist or a data librarian. Pinnell points out that the University of Toronto has a Data, Map and Government Information Services Division, far removed from the traditional map library. Harvard's Geospatial *Liboratory* was created to access geographical digital data, and cuts across traditional faculty, departmental and library boundaries (Parris, 1999). Such examples indicate how institutions may be led to respond to change. Remaining within the academic world, Fleet (1998) notes that an institution may be following a predetermined information technology strategy, far beyond the influence of the map library; thus a strategy will be imposed from above. Despite understanding these advantages and disadvantages, many map libraries find that decisions concerning computer technology are dictated by the institutional framework within which they operate.

The political role of the map library within the institution is also likely to influence decisions (Fleet, 1998). Because of their specialization, map curators are sometimes beyond the mainstream of library life because they identify themselves more with their subject and its content (Smits, 1999). Map curators therefore need to promote themselves as experts in the handling of spatial and spatially related data sets (Parry, 1995). To counteract the marginalization of the map library, Pinnell (2000) cites the example of the University of Waterloo in Canada, advocating the formation of a 'geodata advisory group', with membership drawn from university-wide users in the library, academic and administrative fields. Within such an organizational framework, mechanisms can be implemented to address some of the more fundamental issues that might arise, for example formalizing structures to enable purchasing of data across institution-wide boundaries, and combining to place any licensing arrangements under a single coordinating body.

Pressures from data suppliers and cartographic organizations

A growing problem for map libraries is that not all maps are routinely published as printed items. Many national survey departments are concentrating their attention on the production of digital data rather than paper-based maps (Parry, 1995). This section draws upon examples from Britain, Europe and North America and contrasts the increasingly targeted strategies used by data suppliers for different library markets.

Great Britain's Ordnance Survey (OS) is no longer committed to providing printed copies of its largest scale material: since the map of Great Britain became fully digital in 1995, these data do not fall within the remit of the 1911 Copyright Act. The UK's legal deposit libraries have been forced to focus their attention on the need to provide continued access to large-scale OS mapping, traditionally published at scales of 1:1250, 1:2500 and 1:10,000, which have now ceased publication. Since 1986 discussions have been ongoing between BRICMICS (the British and Irish Committee for Map Information and Catalogue Systems) and OS on providing copyright libraries with large-scale maps. The agreement, whereby OS supplied copies of the mapping on aperture cards, ceased in 1999, but a draft consensus was reached in April 1997, ratified in August 1999, and was yet to be implemented towards the end of 2000. Essentially this new agreement confirmed that, from 1999, OS would supply its National Topographic Database as an annual snapshot to each of the six legal deposit libraries. This enables OS's large-scale digital data to be supplied to the libraries, which can therefore provide continued access for their users (Ordnance Survey, 1999). The libraries can provide on-screen viewing facilities and also regulate plotting for non-commercial private research purposes. This final condition is however likely to hold significant repercussions for library staff, who will be obliged to *police* users in an unprecedented manner, monitoring both users and their usage of the data.

A wider range of OS data is now available to the UK academic community via the EDINA Digimap service. In October 1997 a Java-based trial service, accessible via the world wide web, was released for use at six trial sites across the country, enabling users to browse the mapping database, and produce hard copy mapping, or download files for use on their own machines, beyond the library (Millea, 1999a). Details are available at **http://digimap.ed.ac.uk/**. So successful were the trials that a full national service was launched to 43 academic institutions in January 2000, with access to these data financed by an affordable annual subscription. Again, there are hidden, perhaps unforeseen, implications for the map library, whereby once the user has registered for Digimap, there is little need for that user to return to the library – Digimap can be accessed from anywhere within the institution.

Since 1994 Sweden has experienced legal deposit for electronic documents in a fixed form, such as CD-ROMs and floppy disks including maps, but not databases. Relevant material comprises mainly the Statens Lantmäteriet (National Land Survey) small-scale topographic maps, but also a few route planners (Bäärnhielm, 1999). More specifically, in August 1998 a State Commission report was published with proposals for the legal deposit of online electronic documents, which will eventually result in an amendment to the law on legal deposit. Estonia saw its first digital cartography workstation for public use in the National Library in 1995, a good example of the cooperation with Estonian map producers, who made a gift to the Library of software and digital maps (Tang, 1996). In Denmark, a new law came into effect on 1 January 1998 covering all published works, regardless of the medium used for the production of copies, including Internet material. A 'work' is defined as 'a delimited quantity of information which must be considered a final and independent unit'. The main shift in emphasis in the law is a move from *printed* material to *published* material. Denmark eventually hopes to see website snapshots deposited in the future, following a model initiated in Finland (Dupont, 1999; Jacobsen, 2000).

In the USA, the US Government Printing Office has been developing online-only products, leading to the question of whether items will be available for sufficient time to warrant making a record of their existence. If so, the item is catalogued (with a URL included in the catalogue record) and circulated via the online US Government Publications Catalog. The distribution of Statistics Canada's numerical and statistical data via the Data Liberation Initiative (DLI) has resulted in many more library staff becoming involved with spatial data (Pinnell, 2000).

Globally, the trend for digital as opposed to hard copy has been increasingly evident in the case of thematic mapping, where the use of digital data in GIS form has reduced the need for expensive print runs of conventional soil, geological and other kinds of thematic maps (Parry, 1995).

For those institutions charged with maintaining a historical record of cartographic information a key issue is how change itself should be archived. This was highlighted as early as 1992 in Great Britain, where the problem lies with continuously updating databases, and was acknowledged by the Future History of the Landscape Seminar (Board and Lawrence, 1994). The problem is whether to archive by period of time, or amount of change. Historically, new editions of printed paper maps were published after a certain number of house units of change. The UK legal deposit libraries have moved away from accepting new editions of map sheets every '20 units of change', to an annual digital snapshot of data – the entire database refreshed each year (Perkins, 1995; Fleet, 1999).

The preponderance of the Internet has seen global digital data sources become readily available worldwide: digital maps, map data, and geographic information retrieval services in national mapping agencies, map publishing houses and map libraries. Details can generally be traced using the excellent Utrecht-based *Oddens' Bookmarks* at **http://oddens.geog.uu.nl/index.html**. A case study of change in the national mapping agency of Great Britain, Ordnance Survey, illustrates how change in cartographic organizations can itself greatly influence map library practice.

Ordnance Survey has long been keen to make its digital data available to the British education sector, but the main problem has been pricing policies. During the 1980s and 1990s OS has aimed for full cost recovery, and high-cost data has represented a means of recouping a substantial proportion of OS's financial outlay. Willing buyers in the 'marketplace', for example, commerce, public utilities (such as gas, water and electricity) and local government have enjoyed greater resources than the education sector and were able to buy in to digital services. A change of emphasis was brought about in 1999 by the UK government's award of a National Interest Mapping Service Agreement (NIMSA). This has encouraged OS to strive for 'maximizing usage', and must be viewed with enthusiasm by those in the UK map library world. The Digimap deal is now helping to deliver in the educational sector. Local authority map collections are benefiting from service level agreements negotiated between OS and UK local government, and make it possible for digital data to be available to public libraries. OS has also reached agreement over digital deposit. Together these measures comprise a very significant change from the paper emphasis apparent in British map libraries only a decade earlier, and all are directly related to change in the publishing agency itself.

Pressures from technological change

The USA has been at the forefront when responding to technological change. In November 1993 James Madison Council, a private sector adviser to the Library of Congress, provided $30,000 to investigate corporate support for the Geography and Maps Division. A Center for Geographic Information (CGI) group was set up, initially convening in 1995, with eight firms committing themselves to the project: Autometric Inc, ESRI, the Harvard Design and Mapping Company, Gousha, Intergraph, Magellan Geographix, MapInfo and Tangent Engineering (Mangan, 1997). The CGI's intention was to:

• advise, train and financially support the transition towards digital data
• facilitate sharing the Library's rich cartographic heritage
• promote the use of electronic spatial data
• encourage the deposit of digital data sets
• advance the Library's outreach programme.

Technological change may hinder the development of the traditional map library. As demand for digital resources increases, so, in an age of vulnerable budgets, the hard-copy map collection may become subject to financial neglect. Perkins (1995) suggested the existence of a perceived threat that map libraries could become dying archives for the period up to the Millennium, with spatial data responsibilities transferring elsewhere within the institution. Map libraries may choose to extend their scope; as digital map data require computer environments for display and use, the provision of hardware and software is an essential requirement in retaining the map library's central function for map usage (Asche, 1998).

Antonelli (1999) asks 'What is digital spatial data? What information do we need to store in order to be able to access that data? In order to meet the needs of users in the 21st century we clearly need a different approach.' Meanwhile, Smits (1999) observes how changing activities are encroaching on the map librarian's role. From the analogue age, five key areas can be identified: acquisition, accessing, conservation, collection management and public services. However, additional functionality brought about by new media will see the map librarian drawn away from the more traditional disciplines of cartography, geography and history. New responsibilities in data use and management will increase, so as to exploit the value of digital mapping. To accommodate such a transition, the map librarian's five key functions are being augmented by continuous study to keep abreast of developments, data analysis and the representation of data. Hence 'Map curatorship comes closer to "geoinformatics", that is a discipline concerned with the modelling of spatial data and the processing techniques in spatial information systems' (Smits, 1999).

A positive American angle is taken by Cobb (1999):

> By not offering GIS services, libraries are restricting the use of their data sets and not allowing their users to take full advantage of the analysis and display of spatial data. We are relying less and less on the paper maps produced by [map publishers] and are following their digital data products. We must also plan for the change from analogue reference to digital reference and yet not lose sight of the value of our historical paper collections.

A further issue concerns the underlying advantages of incorporating digital data into the map library. For example, developments in telecommunications and mass storage have permitted new digital technology to help integrate data from widely ranging sources, and facilitated cooperation and data sharing. Recent illustrations of this can be seen in the National Spatial Data Infrastructure in the USA. New digital cartographic media have been provided at a basic level, for example electronic atlases, whilst at a more advanced stage other libraries have allowed access to digital mapping and statistical data for the creation of maps by users (Perkins, 1995; James, 2000).

In the USA the 1990s saw the arrival of CD-ROMs in the map library, especially with the US government distributing data such as census material in digital form. In 1994 the Alexandria Digital Library was set up, its remit being to: 'design, develop and evaluate a distributed, high-performance digital library of spatially-indexed information that includes collections of maps and images in digital form' (Larsgaard, 1999). In Switzerland, the ETH Bibliothek Zürich elected to integrate digital maps into its collection as early as 1993 (Bühler, 1999). By 1996 the National Library of Estonia was employing a part-time librarian whose responsibility was to maintain a workstation and to be available to answer all digital cartography questions (Tang, 1996).

At the Württembergische Landesbibliothek in Stuttgart, web technology has been incorporated to devise a system of *hot* indexes detailing a chronological breakdown of map series holdings within the Library. As a result of the Internet becoming increasingly important as an additional means for librarians to collect and distribute information, the Library chose to exploit the technology for carto-bibliographical purposes. A visual catalogue of various map series has been provided, moving one step ahead of a standard OPAC-based retrieval system. In effect the Württembergische Landesbibliothek has created a web-based version of that conventional map library tool, the graphic index, except this version is capable of describing holdings in a method far more detailed than could be reasonably expected from a paper index. Such a system provides the map user with an instant history of the institution's holdings of a particular sheet (Crom, 1999; Millea, 1999b).

Responses by libraries

In different sectors/contexts

A broad-brush approach towards accommodating GIS in the map library has been outlined by Boxall (1999), citing his Canadian experience. He believes it is essential to include internal institutional or agency departments alongside external partners, who should be able to provide support and guidance, and may become integral collaborators. Any such collaboration will benefit from an alliance beyond the immediate vicinity of the host institution to reap the greatest rewards.

Examining data usage on a sector by sector basis, differing practices can be identified. In government-funded libraries, Antonelli (1999) describes the response of the UK's Defence Geographic Centre, which has contemplated severing the conventional map library understanding of the series/sheet relationship. The library's MODMAP database held just 3000 series records as opposed to 860,000 sheet records. Subsequent improvements to the computing power of MODMAP switched the emphasis away from series towards sheet-based enquiries. Therefore, maintaining both the sheet and series records became a burden and hence a template on which MODMAP summarized data from all sheets within a series was devised. Series level metadata were effectively rendered redundant. Apart from cataloguing, the rigid application of the classification rules for atlases was also revised.

In the education sector, many map libraries have tended to purchase modestly but practically, selectively acquiring data on CD-ROM or disk (see Chapter 6). Such items function in a manner familiar to librarians – they can be catalogued and used as substitutes for paper maps, and perhaps of greatest relevance, their natural home is the map library, not the computing laboratory (Parry, 1995).

At the Bodleian Library in Oxford, the Map Room invested in MapInfo Professional, launching GIS to readers late in 1999 – this course of action has been the direct result of student demand, but in turn has placed sizeable demands on staffing to the detriment of other map library duties. If GIS is offered within the range of map library services, then users will need much more support. It could be argued that users should be required to attend training courses, rather than relying upon time-consuming individual training from library staff during a GIS-related inquiry (Perkins, 1995). A more structured GIS approach, in a research environment, has been employed by the map library at Cambridge's British Antarctic Survey, whereby mapmaking and geographical information are closely linked. The mapping division's function is to provide maps to order from the Antarctic Digital Database, hence stretching the role of the map library (Millea, 1999b).

International responses: analysis of differences

In contrast to the USA, European spatial data are not generally in the public domain. It is argued that the cost of spatial data should be paid for by the user. Data sets are viewed as cost-recovering assets for the spatial information producers (Bäärnhielm, 1999). As a consequence, Europe lacks the basic preconditions for freely available digital data dissemination (see Chapters 12 and 13).

Having justified the need for electronic or digital maps in map libraries, how might this need be met? Parry (1995) outlines two kinds of approach: one radical, and the other more cautious. The radical model, or North American-style of approach, can be seen in the examples cited by Boxall (1999), Cobb (1999), Larsgaard (1999), Mangan (1997), Parris (1999) and Pinnell (2000). In the USA active attempts to implement a cartographic laboratory in the map room have been made in the more important libraries. The resultant model visualizes a map library invigorated by free and frequent supplies of electronic data. How does the conventional map curator fit into this environment?

The more cautious of Parry's models is apparent in UK map collections, where constraints on ownership and distribution of digital mapping have proved to be something of a hindrance. High prices and prohibitive copyright restrictions have reduced the incentive for libraries to adopt digital mapping with the same energy and enthusiasm as their North American counterparts. European map libraries are well aware of where their future might lie; the constraints, however limit their freedom of action. An intriguing e-mail posted to LIS-MAPS, the UK-based map librarianship listserver, illustrates this point (Castleford, 1998). Castleford suggests that university map libraries in the UK may well be in decline, and questions the future of the paper map. However he also recognizes that users require customized mapping and questions who should supply it. He hints that a move towards a GIS-friendly map librarian was a natural evolutionary step.

An initial view of the role of GIS in European map libraries was aired by Smits (1999) who argued that: 'most map curators, with the exception maybe of those in the United Kingdom and Scandinavia, do not want to learn a technology which will be predominant in the future spatial library'.

There is, therefore, much learning required before GIS finally breaks through into mainstream European map librarianship in the new Millennium.

Changing networking within and between institutions

Data conversion issues were to the fore when the UK legal deposit libraries brokered their arrangement with OS. Rather than each library performing the task alone, the British Library agreed to undertake the work on behalf of others, effectively employing institutional networking to address the problem of unnecessary duplication (Fleet, 1999).

Digital formats make true data sharing possible, so it may therefore be more appropriate not to acquire digital data sets, but rather to access them when required over a network, to acquire collaboratively and share resources. Data sharing, cooperative purchase and remote access may be the only viable economic route for map libraries to follow if they wish to continue to allow access to current cartographic data (Perkins, 1995). Cooperative purchase of digital data sets in the UK by CHEST (Combined Higher Education Software Team) already allows the research community to use Bartholomew digital databases, and various OS data sets. Smits (1999) endorses this view by arguing that map libraries must try to create national infrastructures and negotiate agreements with publishers to make digital sources mutually available, or available through distributed licences. Canada's equivalent is DSI (Ridley, 1998), while there is also the GIS in Canadian Libraries Initiative, designed to support collections and software negotiation, and training. Canada can also point to the success of the TriUniversity Group of Libraries – a confederation of institutions (the Waterloo, Guelph and Wilfrid Laurier Universities) acquiring data on a collaborative basis.

Beyond the multi-institutional framework, there is scope for networking within individual libraries. As map libraries consider moving from cartographic displays to the acceptance of digital spatial data in the GIS environment, then Smits (1999) argues that virtual integration between library or institutional departments should be encouraged. The Alexandria Digital Library Project at **http:// alexandria.sdc.ucsb.edu/** is a good example of this practice (Larsgaard, 1999).

Library users may also benefit from networking, by accessing metadata without physically visiting the library, or indeed, consulting library staff. Accessing the Internet renders searching for digital cartographic data relatively straightforward. Gateway sites such as *Oddens' Bookmarks* or the Swiss *Die Welt der Karten* site at **http://www.maps.ethz.ch/maps3.html** provide classified portals to the rich variety of Internet-based map sources and are discussed in more detail in Chapter 8.

Institutional responses to the changing business of mapping

The Finnish national survey, Maanmittauslaitos, launched its map service on the web in June 1996. *MapSite* contains cartographic material of Finland at four different scales: 1:8,000,000, 1:800,000, 1:160,000 and 1:50,000, and is open to everyone with an e-mail address. The service is free of charge at **http://www.kartta. nls.fi/index_e.html**. Larger-scale mapping was made available from a second site in 1997, and is a fee-paying service (Korttinen, 1996).

The United States Geological Survey, the Automobile Association and even OS all now have websites from which digital spatial data may be downloaded. Sweden's Lantmäteriet runs a web service, with cadastral mapping extracts and property register details deliverable by fax or e-mail. Originally free of charge, this service has levied a fee since 1998. The role of the map library changes when web-based services are available: facilities such as a computing station, colour printers and skilled staff to assist in the printing out of on-demand maps have to be provided (Bäärnhielm, 1996).

Publishers often need to regulate access and monitor data security in such systems. For example the arrangement between UK legal deposit libraries and OS has considered the importance of storing OS data securely to ensure that there is no danger of data leakage, and data are only accessible via standalone workstations (Fleet, 1999).

Responses of institutions to changing map dealing

While there are numerous high-quality sources for hard-copy maps, for example GeoCenter in Germany and Omni Resources in the USA, there has not been sufficient time for digital data vendors to establish a lasting reputation. The Internet offers possibilities, but nothing with the repute of the established map dealers. Chapter 11 reviews these acquisition or accessing issues in greater detail. Conventional wisdom errs towards personal contact, or else sharing the collective experience of relevant listservers such as Carta, Carto-Soc, LIS-MAPS or MAPS-L. Web-based spatial data clearing-houses are emerging, for example Natural Resources Canada's CEONet, as are commercial data vendors such as MapInfo and ESRI. Map curators are, however, frequently unable to rely on objective product reviews – aspects such as data format and resolution may not be readily discernible (Pinnell, 2000).

Another consideration is price. Data costs may involve not only buying the data, but also paying for the medium used to deliver them, data preparation costs, updates, royalties, licences and annual subscriptions. Further payments may be necessary in order to prevent data leakage.

Responses of institutions to changing users

The Bodleian Library's early assumption that Oxford's Archaeology and Geography Departments would account for the majority of Digimap use has proved to be significantly adrift of what has now transpired. These disciplines account for just 9% and 13% of registered users respectively. The genuine surprise has been the number of different academic disciplines now using digital cartographic data.

However, the traditional map user does not seem to be benefiting as much from Digimap as the computing experts. It is the computer-literate who are gaining most from digital data, not the cartography-literate. Traditional map users are finding the computing skills necessary to exploit Digimap's range of options somewhat complicated, while those with the necessary computing talent are unlikely to possess the cartographic know-how to produce the maps that would support their research to the maximum capability (Millea, 1999a). Expanding on this theme, Fleet (1999) notes that whether digital data are easier to use than paper maps depends very much on the user and their priorities. Academic research increasingly uses spatial data, but the more eclectic and unpredictable reference use of the map library still requires a mix of digital and analogue solutions. Most map libraries' effectiveness or 'reach' will be judged by quantity of use rather than quality of use, which in turn has implications for the map library's profile within the institution.

Conclusion

There are issues for which little guidance or precedent exists when considering the incorporation of digital data in the map library. What about the interpretation of existing map library standards and their application to digital products? Or the cataloguing of digital holdings? Or the handling and provision of metadata? Or cataloguing standards (Perkins, 1995)?

In November 2000 BRICMICS set up a group to gather information about potential, proposed and actual cessation of scheduled paper map publication by producers worldwide. This will establish national informant contacts and bridge the gap between the conventional map library and Parry's (1995) 'radical model'.

The final word should, however, be left to the map library user:

> Prospective users of spatial information will need to have someone behind the virtual counter to act on their behalf. In the 'good old days' that meant going to the map store and pulling out the appropriate sheets. In short then, map librarians have traditionally been paper map people. Are they, as a community, willing and able to take on the role of a middleman required by digital data users and providers?
>
> (Castleford, 1998)

Seemingly, the answer to Castleford's question is geographical. Much depends on the physical location of the map library, its organizational, social, economic and political context and the emphasis of national legislation. Technological change alone is a necessary part, but is not sufficient to answer the question.

References

Antonelli, S (1999) Breaking with conventions: what does digital spatial data require? *LIBER Quarterly*, **9** (2), 149–61.

Asche, H (1998) Mapping and map use in the age of information technology, *LIBER Quarterly*, **8** (2), 127–35.

Bäärnhielm, G (1996) *National progress report Sweden 1994–1996* available at **http://www.kb.nl/infolev/liber/progress/19941996/sweden.htm**.
Bäärnhielm, G (1999) Digital cartography in the Royal Library – the National Library of Sweden, *LIBER Quarterly*, **9** (2), 162–6.
Board, C and Lawrence, G R P (1994) *Recording our changing landscape: the proceedings of the seminar on the future history of our landscape held at the Royal Society on 16th October 1992*, Royal Society and the British Academy in association with the British Cartographic Society.
Boxall, J (1999) Developing a geomatics alliance and community: increasing map library association status, cooperation and effectiveness, *Association of Canadian Map Libraries and Archives Bulletin*, **106**, 32–6.
Bühler, J (1999) Electronic maps – a new library service, *LIBER Quarterly*, **9** (2), 228–34.
Castleford, J (1998) E-mail to LIS-MAPS, 28 July.
Cobb, D (1999) GIS: Its impact on library services, *Meridian*, **16**, 5–8.
Crom, W (1999) A map collection on the Internet, *LIBER Quarterly*, **9** (2), 222–7.
Dupont, H (1999) Legal deposit in Denmark – the new law and electronic products, *LIBER Quarterly*, **9** (2), 244–51.
Fleet, C (1998) The role of computer technology in the future map library, *LIBER Quarterly*, **8** (2), 136–45.
Fleet, C (1999) Ordnance Survey digital data in the UK Legal Deposit Libraries, *LIBER Quarterly*, **9** (2), 235–43.
Jacobsen, G (2000) Unpublished paper presented at 12th Groupe des Cartothécaires de LIBER Conference, Copenhagen, 28 June.
James, N (2000) MapInfo professional: an easy guide, *Western Association of Map Libraries Information Bulletin*, **31** (2), 133–47.
Korttinen, P (1996) *National report of Finland 1994–1996*, available at **http://www.kb.nl/infolev/liber/progress/19941996/finland.htm**.
Lamont, M (1999) Past, present and future? The question of access to spatial data in the U.S., *Association of Canadian Map Libraries and Archives Bulletin*, **106**, 37–41.
Larsgaard, M L (1999) Toward a catalog for The Millennium: digital geospatial metadata and data in the Alexandria Digital Library, *Meridian*, **16**, 29-36.
Mangan, E (1997) LC/G&M's scanning program: where we are and how we got here, *Meridian*, **12**, 37–42.
Millea, N (1999a) Delivering digital data into the library: the Digimap Project and its impact on the Map Room – the Bodleian Library experience, *LIBER Quarterly*, **9** (2), 189–200.
Millea, N (1999b) GIS in libraries at the Millennium: a European perspective, *Meridian*, **16**, 27–8.

Oddens' Bookmarks **http://oddens.geog.uu.nl/index.html**.

Ordnance Survey (1999) *Historical map data*, Information Paper 19/1999, Ordnance Survey.

Parris, T M (1999) The Harvard Geospatial 'Liboratory', *Meridian*, **16**, 9–18.

Parry, R B (1995) The electronic map library: new maps, new uses, new users, *LIBER Quarterly*, **5** (3), 262–73.

Perkins, C R (1995) Leave it to the labs? Options for the future of map and spatial data collections, *LIBER Quarterly*, **5** (3), 312–29.

Pinnell, R H (2000) Data acquisition issues: the Canadian map libraries' perspective, *Association of Canadian Map Libraries and Archives Bulletin*, **107**, 16–22.

Ridley, M (1998) Data Liberation Initiative (DLI) and the GIS in Canadian Libraries Initiative (GCLI): policy issues and implications for libraries and universities, *Association of Canadian Map Libraries and Archives Bulletin*, **103**, 14–19.

Smits, J (1999) The necessity and nuisance of survival, or how to keep to our senses, *LIBER Quarterly*, **9** (2), 140–8.

Tang, E (1996) *National progress report of Estonia 1994–1996* available at **http://www.kb.nl/infolev/liber/progress/19941996/estonia.htm**.

Zalite, A (1998) *National progress report of Latvia 1996-1998* available at **http://www.kb.nl/infolev/liber/progress/19961998/latvia11.htm**.

4

New technologies in the map room

Patrick McGlamery

▶ *This chapter reviews the development of automated cataloguing and online retrieval of map records, the use of technology for internal housekeeping and administration, and the impact of different formats of digital mapping on the nature of map library services. It also discusses the significance of CD-ROM and web-based mapping. It introduces ways in which digital map data have been used, explores the significance of communications technologies and highlights the arrival of the Internet and the web as an alternative to hard-copy publication. Finally it points to the metaphor of sharing and to the role of the library as an institution in this process.*

Introduction: maps in libraries

The impact of computing in libraries has had profound effects, to say the least. Transforming the catalogue record to a machine catalogue record in the 1960s and 1970s has made possible our current integrated library systems, efficiencies in sharing materials through interlibrary loan and automated materials processing. However, the impact of computing in map libraries has been sublime, changing the very nature of spatial information media. Mapping is a wholly different endeavour at the beginning of the 21st century than it was a decade ago, and the library science required to manage these emerging mapping sciences is new as well.

Maps in research libraries in the USA gained the status of collections following World War 2. Few universities or public libraries had significant collections of maps until the US Army Map Service (AMS) distributed an extensive collection of their topographic maps of areas of national interest. Between 1946 and 1950 about 150 libraries each received over 20,000 maps (Stevenson 1979, 119). By the end of the 1960s some 194 libraries had received map collections of about 24,000 individual maps and other publications including gazetteers. The impact on libraries was significant as the US Army made a condition that these collections be curated. The expense of storing maps in file drawers, of indexing and of providing reference services to these maps brought map collections to the attention of library administrations. These research collections reflect the emergence of the USA as a nation with international interests and concerns in the era of the Cold War, and depositing maps in public universities and libraries expanded on the democratization of higher education in the USA. There was a boom not only in the number of new map collections but also in the material produced by the federal and state governments. Because of efficiencies in the mapping sciences as a result of World War 2, the development of a National Guard, the Corps of Army Engineers civil engineering projects, and the US Geological Survey, map collections blossomed in the 1950s. While the USA has had a Federal Depository Library Program since the 1930s, deposit of maps only really happened with the boom in the post-war economy.

By 1960 in the USA collections numbering over 50,000 sheets were prevalent and primarily part of libraries, not academic departments. Courses in map librarianship, though not widespread, were being taught regularly.

Development of automated cataloguing and online retrieval of map records

While the history of cataloguing maps extends into the late 19th century, the development of automated cataloguing and online retrieval of map records is over 50 years old. Mary Larsgaard provides an excellent history of the need to automate the indexing of map sheets, describe maps and integrate those records into library systems (Larsgaard, 1978, 1987, 1998).

Remarkably, by 1948 the AMS map sheet card catalogue was on punched cards and by 1951 their map library had begun to use a UNIVAC I mainframe computer. It was not for another dozen or so years that other projects used processing equipment for maps, and these efforts were in public universities and not national agencies. The map library at the University of California at Los Angeles began to plan for automation in 1963. In 1966 studies were underway at the University of Washington in the USA, and McMaster University in Canada, and in 1967 the Map Library at the Illinois State University at Normal worked cooperatively with the University Computer Center to code 5000 maps. In 1968 Simon Fraser University decided to work on map library automation and that spring one of Larsgaard's 'giants', the Library of Congress, lumbered into the arena with a grant for a pilot project to develop automated controls for single sheet maps. By 1970 several universities were exploring the use of computers to automate the control of map (and other bibliographic) records; the old AMS, now named the Defense Mapping Agency, had added about 120,000 maps and texts to its master file (DMA) and the Library of Congress was working on planning and implementing MARC Map. *Maps, a MARC format, specifications for magnetic tapes containing catalog records for maps* was published in 1971.

By the 1980s MARC had become the standard format for maps. Though other systems emerged, some better suited for handling cartographic material, the cataloguing giant of LC Geography and Map Division assured the primacy of the MARC Map format. In the spring of 1980 the Library of Congress added its MARC Map records to OCLC, raising the number of records to 63,393. Early in the 1980s the publication of the second edition of the *Anglo-American cataloging rules* (AACR2) marked another major developmental step in map cataloguing and the automation of map records. Among other things (Larsgaard manages to give an exciting account of these events), AACR2's Chapter 3, Cartographic Materials, expanded and elucidated AACR's Chapter 11, Maps, Atlases, etc. More to the point, AACR2 provided the philosophical underpinnings for cataloguing in general, using punctuation as markers for data fields, preparing the cataloguer to consider the record not simply as a card in a card catalogue, but as a record in a database. ISBD, with its primary concerns of order of and punctuation between elements in a catalogue or a database record, was an integral part of this thinking. For maps, and other cartographic materials, this inclusion of ISBD Cartographic Materials (ISBD(CM)) provided richer and more complex opportunities for representing the map record. The revised Chapter 6 of AACR2 became the cartographic cataloguing standard, designated as ISBD(CM). AACR2 and ISBD(CM) are best interpreted by *Cartographic materials: a manual of interpretation for AACR2* (Stibbe, 1982).

In 1980 this librarian left the Geography and Map Division for the University of Connecticut and joined that generation of map librarians who could search OCLC for 'acceptable' copy and catalogue and add the University's map collection to a growing union catalogue of map holdings. Over the course of a decade, the University of Connecticut's one full-time staff member succeeded in bringing control to the Library's map holdings and adding original cataloguing for maps of Connecticut and southern New England. This activity was duplicated by other map librarians in libraries around the nation, and the world. In January 1983 there were 107,966 map format records in OCLC. By January 2000 the number of map format records had grown to 552,420; 197,789 had been created by LC, 347,885 by participating libraries and 6746 input by members using LC copy (OCLC, 2000).

The use of technology for internal housekeeping and administration

In many libraries the MARC record is now, to all intents and purposes, the fundamental unit of a library's Integrated Library System. It forms the foundation for acquisition through purchase and through interlibrary loan. The half-million map catalogue records in OCLC go a long way toward assuring the user of the hope of procuring a copy of a map through interlibrary loan. It is the primary form of the record for reference query, discovery and access to information in the library's Online Public Access Catalogue (OPAC).

While the MARC Map format has become a *pro forma* for maps, it has not been particularly well adapted for cartographic material. In the early 1980s the MARC Map format was amended to include fields particularly significant for spatial querying. In particular the 034 field, for describing mathematical data, was added. This MARC field codes the scale or scales of the map, and the northern, southern, eastern and western extents of the map's sheet in degree, minute, seconds: its 'bounding box'. The information is echoed in the 257 field, encompassing scale. While standard author, subject, title, keyword searching provides the user with the ability to search for a word, map users really need spatial access based upon these mathematical fields. Algorithms supporting spatial searching of MARC records were described in the 1970s (van de Waal, 1974), and were adopted in a number of European systems in the 1990s, eg by the British Ministry of Defence in the MODMAP system (Antonelli, 1999). The mainstream North American applications of spatial querying have, so far however, been elusive.

In the final years of the 20th century, NIMA, the National Image and Mapping Agency, having evolved from the US Defense Mapping Agency and the Army Map Service, succeeded in converting its database of sheet level cataloguing into MARC format. Endeavor's Voyager, an Integrated Library System, formally debuted its 'GeoSpatial Search Engine' at the 2000 American Library Association annual meeting in Chicago. For the first time a major library systems vendor had developed a way to extract records based on a mathematical query. Admittedly limited to a latitude/longitude query (and not a place name query) it points the way to what we can expect in the new millennium. That is, a true spatial query of our library catalogues, perhaps even a graphical interface, enabling the library user to draw a box around their area of interest and pull all the records, regardless of the geographical name in the subject field.

The impact of different formats of digital mapping on the nature of map library services

In the late 1980s, debate raged over the definition of cartography and maps and the International Cartographic Association (ICA) invited redefinitions in light of innovations in computer technology. Two camps emerged, stressing the importance of the map on one hand, and the spatial database on the other. Visvalingam (1989) articulated a middle ground, focusing not on product, but on content:

> If cartography is concerned with the making and use of maps, then it is not just concerned with visual products: it is equally concerned with the processes of mapping, from data collection, transformation and simplification through to symbolism and with map reading, analysis and interpretation. These intellectual processes are expressed in terms of prevailing technologies and computer-based Information Technology is fast becoming the dominant technology of the day.

Since that ICA meeting, and in spite of the wisdom of Visvalingam's logic, there continue to be distinct boundaries drawn between cartographic products and spatial data in Geographic Information Systems (GIS), by both geographers and librarians. Maps are carriers of spatial information, but GIS is a tool for analysing and presenting spatial data, sometimes in a cartographic format. In the USA the ubiquitous nature of federally produced and distributed spatial data in the public domain has blurred the boundary lines. While electronic atlases and maps thrive in libraries, few map libraries have embraced the systems approach of the 'processes of mapping' delineated by Visvalingam by collecting and providing access to digital spatial data. The general trend, so far, is to provide access only to cartographic products, that is images of maps stored as graphic files. This trend overlooks the importance of GIS as the natural successor of the paper map in the 'dominant technology of the day', computing technology. The map as a 'report' of the underlying database is the more dynamic model used by a GIS.

GIS has been a real part of the mapping sciences since the 1960s when it was developed in Canada (Tomlinson, 1998). But GIS is defined by computer technology. Evolutions in hardware from ENIAC to the PC, in data management from databases to Relational Data Base Management Systems (RDBMS) and Object-oriented DBMS, in software and programming from FORTRAN and BASIC to Java and C++; and evolutions from standalone computer to local networks to LANs, WANs, the Internet and intranets and in media from punched cards to 9-track tape to CD-ROM have each had profound effects on the development of GIS and spatial information. Sharing spatial data, which is what, after all, libraries do, has also been profoundly affected. These agents of change have affected how libraries look at spatial information, including maps, aerial photography and tabular data. While hardware and software facilitate access to spatial data, it is *data* that drive GIS evolution, and experts tell us that perhaps 80 to 90% of data collected have a spatial component (Foresman, 1998). Chapter 5 discusses the implications of the awesome responsibility this data explosion poses for map librarians who just wanted a quiet career building a college map collection.

The transition in geographic information has been there to see, for those who dared to look. In the UK Lord Chorley's report, *Handling geographic information,* was published in 1987 and provided a concise listing of the issues (Department of the Environment, 1987). Most important to libraries is Section III, Removing Barriers, and particularly Chapter 5, Availability of Data:

> 5.1 Two main problems experienced by users trying to obtain or use spatial data – other than Ordnance Survey (OS) digital data – are:
>
> 1   obtaining spatial data in a form which permits linking to other data sets; this problem is most evident with Government data suppliers; and
> 2   trying to locate and access data from a variety of sources.

This report made several liberal recommendations, which taken as a whole would have made spatial data in the UK, if not free, certainly affordable. Copyright and intellectual property issues were well articulated. Finally, issues relating to the library's role were mentioned with pointed considerations: the need to include libraries in the long-term archiving of geographic or spatial data through legal deposit or increased funding to purchase the data, the development of storage facilities, and finally archival selection policies. Subsequent development of the UK data market continued to be influenced by official attitudes to public sector cost recovery, however, and a quite restrictive interpretation of intellectual property rights (see Chapter 12), but Chorley remains a key source of information about data issues.

In the USA, guidance has come from the National Academy of Science's Mapping Science Committee. The Committee serves as a focus for external advice to federal agencies on scientific and technical matters related to spatial data handling and analysis. The purpose of the Committee is to provide advice on the development of a robust national spatial data infrastructure for making informed decisions at all levels of government and throughout society in general. A significant contrast developed to the more market-oriented British information policy.

The concept of a National Spatial Data Infrastructure (NSDI) was first advanced in *Toward a coordinated spatial data infrastructure for the nation* (National Research Council Mapping Sciences Committee, 1993). Subsequent MSC reports have addressed specific components of the NSDI, including partnerships (*Promoting the National Spatial Data Infrastructure through partnerships* (National Research Council Mapping Sciences Committee, 1994)), basic data types (*A data foundation for the National Spatial Data Infrastructure* (National Research Council Mapping Sciences Committee, 1995)), and future trends (*The future of spatial data and society* (National Research Council Mapping Sciences Committee, 1997)). Most recently *Distributed geolibraries* directly links issues of spatial information dissemination and the library mode (National Research Council Panel on Distributed Geolibraries, 1999).

When the NSDI was defined in 1993, few users or producers of geospatial data made much use of the Internet or the world wide web at the time. Although there was emphasis on digital geospatial data, the primary method of dissemination was by magnetic tape. There were virtually no digital online catalogues of geospatial data or methods for searching for data across computer networks. Moreover, since most useful geospatial data were produced by a small number of federal agencies, there was little problem locating the appropriate source. Today, the web has grown into an enormously successful tool and has had a profound impact on the entire environment for geospatial data acquisition (see Chapters 7 and 8). At the same time, it has presented a growing problem as the number of potential suppliers has mushroomed, and the web has been unable to deal effectively with the task of discovering what geo-information exists and of locating an appropriate source.

The latest Mapping Sciences Committee report, *Distributed geolibraries*, can be understood, therefore, as an updating of the Committee's concept of the NSDI in the era of the web. In organizing this effort and producing this report, the Committee expressed its view that the web has added a new and radically different dimension to its earlier conception of NSDI, one that is much more user-oriented, much more effective in maximizing the value of the nation's geospatial data assets, and much more cost effective as a data dissemination mechanism. Distributed geolibraries reflect the same basic thinking about the future of geospatial data, which emphasizes sharing, universal access, and productivity but in the context of a technology that was almost impossible to anticipate prior to 1993.

The report makes extensive use of the traditional library as a framework for discussion because it is so familiar and well understood. Undoubtedly, much future work in researching and developing distributed geolibraries will occur within this framework, but the framework will also be constraining in some respects. Exactly how distributed geolibraries develop and how closely they follow the metaphor of the library remains to be seen.

The activities of the Committee have served to guide the user's access to spatial information in the USA by affecting policy. For example, in order to develop the NSDI, a spatial metadata standard was needed. The Federal Geographic Data Committee's (FGDC) Metadata Working Group, an initiative of the first Committee report, worked closely with the library community, inviting Elizabeth Mangan, one of the authors of the MARC Map format and Head of Cataloguing at the Library of Congress Geography and Map Division, to participate in the working group. Drafts of the standards were freely distributed to the extended library community for comment. The interest and response were extensive, indicating serious professional attention at the state and local level. FGDC cooperative grants have helped to fund metadata creation and NSDI nodes at state and local levels. Metadata issues are discussed in greater detail in Chapter 9.

Coincidentally the Association of Research Libraries (ARL) began its GIS Literacy Project. In 1992 ARL managed the cooperation of 25 American libraries with ESRI, a major GIS software developer. The cooperation focused libraries' interest on spatial data and offered training at ESRI annual meetings. In two years 25 more libraries were added and in 1996 20 Canadian libraries joined the project. The ESRI training opportunity provided librarians with an opportunity to meet and share concerns and to develop GIS skills. ESRI has established a K-12 Educational/Library Coordinator who attends major library conferences, speaks regularly and supports library needs. IFLA's Geography and Map Section has also held day-long training sessions in Copenhagen and Bangkok, distributing ESRI software and introducing GIS in libraries. ARL has reported on its project with good case studies from the field and a summary of future trends (Soete, 1997). Italics represent this author's comments on the state of the trends late in 2000.

- GIS will only grow and become an increasing part of our information consciousness. Our users will become more familiar and skilled with the technology, and they will become more data and spatial-literate. *The inclusion of computer mapping in Microsoft Office's Excel software since 1995 has led to a standalone mapping package, MapPoint 2001, as part of Microsoft Office 2000 family of applications.*
- Standards of all sorts will become increasingly important, especially standards for metadata (the description of GIS and other data). *ISO standards for metadata and XLM spatial DTD have emerged; a coverage element of the Dublin Core is being established, and a MARC field for reporting metadata variables has been established (see Chapter 9).*

- Storage will become less of a problem as space becomes cheaper and compression techniques become more widely used. One factor may be the possibility of a pervasive ability to create one's own CD-ROMs. *Writeable CD-ROMs have become pervasive, and the cost of hard drive storage continues to decline.*
- GIS will begin to appear in standard packages, such as spreadsheets, and GIS software will itself probably evolve into off-the-shelf products that practically anyone will be able to master. *See the comments on the growth of GIS.*
- Internet GIS capabilities will grow tremendously – not only the ability to access static information, but also the ability to interact with and manipulate the data online. *ESRI's ArcIMS, an Internet map server, is proving to be a success. Of even more interest is MapServer, **http://mapserver.gis.umn.edu/index.html**, an open source map server that is configurable and programmable, particularly from the library's point of view. The Open Source software movement has the potential to enable communities, like libraries, to directly effect program development (see Chapter 8 for further discussion of web resources).*
- Distributed collections will be aggregated under projects like Alexandria and USC's Integrated Data Archive. Such projects will make enormous amounts of geo-referenced information available over the Internet. *This prediction has not yet been realized, though the research agenda developed by the Committee for Mapping Sciences will build it.*
- Librarians will take more managerial roles in the design and provision of GIS services, leaving the technical aspects to specially trained technicians. *In the past year at least five libraries have advertised for a GIS librarian position that augments the map librarian's responsibilities.*

The significance of storage and communication technologies

CD-ROM

Until the emergence of CD-ROM in the late 1980s, spatial data were provided on 9-track tape, requiring a tape-drive and a mainframe computer. In fact, digital spatial data have been around since the 1960s, though few libraries in North America either collected spatial data or made them available. Notable among the early adapters are the University of California–Santa Barbara, Davidson Library's Map and Imagery Laboratory and the University of Florida, George A Smather's Map and Imagery Library, both of which hold large collections of digital satellite imagery. The introduction of CD-ROM as a computer technology freed computer mapping and GIS from the constraints of mainframe computing and enabled it to take advantage of the remarkable evolution in personal computing.

In 1986 CD-ROMs for data seemed immediate to three applications: libraries, law and medicine, archive and research and geographic applications (Lambert and Ropiequet, 1986). Don Cooke, while noting the important distinction between maps as pictures and maps as databases (a distinction that Visvalingam put into its proper perspective in 1989), concentrated on the database method of computing maps. He forecast the emergence of CD-ROM based mapping applications both in vehicles, as navigational tools, and on desktops (Cooke, 1986).

One of the earliest CD-ROM mapping programs, DeLorme's *Street atlas USA*, came out in 1991. It quickly became a best seller. Marketed with a GPS unit, *Street atlas USA 7.0* now comes with over three million 'points of interest', hotels, restaurants, churches, transportation services, gas stations, real estate agencies, pharmacies, office supply stores, schools, colleges, government offices, banks, public services, malls, video rental stores, fitness centres, hospitals and much more. Such electronic atlases are described in more detail in Chapter 6, but a simple illustration here shows that the technology has come a long way in a decade! *Street atlas USA 7.0* now includes the new Back-on-Track GPS feature that helps you get back on course if you stray from your chosen route while using a GPS receiver. With a multimedia laptop, one can even hear spoken directions and updates about upcoming exit services (**http://www. delorme.com/StreetAtlasUSA/**).

The use of CD-ROM is representative, not so much of a transfer or storage technology, but as a marketing and publishing device. DeLorme is, first and foremost, a map publisher. The CD-ROM products augment the DeLorme atlas and gazetteer paper publications. At only $44.99 *Street Atlas USA 7.0* is a reasonably priced cartographic product. The CD-ROMs provide the cartographer with a method of projecting a style and the ability to 'lock it down' by distributing it in a read-only format. One of the frustrations for libraries has been the standalone nature of these products. Running them in a networked environment has been difficult. Cartographers like DeLorme are beginning to recognize the power of networking information and in the new millennium are delivering their products network-ready.

Digital spatial databases have always been 'large' data. In fact, they fall into the realm of VLDB or 'very large databases'. The 676 Mb capacity of the CD-ROM seemed providential. The size of the file is proportional to the detail of spatial data, just as the number of sheets in a set of maps is proportional to the detail. As more detailed spatial data have been made available, the CD-ROM was able to provide a storage and distribution solution . . . to a point. Recently the medium has not been able to keep pace with the detail demanded. The move seems to be towards DVD and networked data delivery over the web.

Internet

The ultimate network (for now) is the Internet. Spatial data on the Internet run the gamut from the interactive web tool such as MapQuest, which includes maps, driving directions in the USA, Canada and Europe, live traffic reports with traffic cams and accidents by city, yellow and white pages to find businesses and find people, and a travel guide with rated restaurants, rated hotels, travel deals, city guides, news, 'Best of the City' and entertainment, (**http://www.mapquest.com/**) and offers the FTP download of digital spatial data. Chapters 7 and 8 document the potential of the Internet and web in greater detail.

For libraries, the Internet has, so far, been used primarily for information about the map library and its collections, but also for online exhibitions, digital atlases and digital data distribution. The Osher Map Library (**http://www.usm. maine.edu/~maps/**) has an excellent programme of online exhibitions. The Harvard Map Library's *Massachusetts electronic atlas* (**http://icg.harvard.edu/~maps/**) is a map viewer of demographic data. The *Massachusetts electronic atlas* does a fine job of enabling the user to view cartographic information. The University of Connecticut's MAGIC site (**http://magic.lib.uconn.edu/**) is a library of digital spatial data. There is little cartographic information available on MAGIC, but an enormous amount of spatial data that are downloaded by the user community to use in a GIS program.

The other map data that are finding their way on to the Internet are scanned images of historical maps (described in more detail in Chapter 10). The Library of Congress's American Memory Project is not the first of these, but is, perhaps, the most extensive. The Geography and Map Division (**http://lcweb2.loc.gov/ ammem/gmdhtml/gmdhome.html**) is very aggressively adding maps which have been identified in its various carto-bibliographies. One of the technological innovations that are enabling these historical map images is wavelet compression, but this is only one of a series of innovations that make managing a map library in the 21st century a challenge.

Conclusion

Map libraries have indeed made good use of computers, both through standard library operations such as cataloguing and interlibrary loan, but also with digital spatial data. The ARL GIS Literacy Project has shown that resources can clearly make a difference. Attention from library administration in the form of resources is good. However, the issues of intellectual properties and copyright, fitness for use and data quality and the authenticity of the data are more problematic and enduring for libraries. These are not so much technological as social issues and have to do with *sharing*. Sharing is always hard; we've known that since kindergarten, yet libraries are first and foremost sharing institutions. They even go so far as to 'ration' information by circulating material to a limited community for prescribed time limits in order to share fairly. 'Sharing of geographic information is important because the more it is shared, the more it is used, and the greater becomes society's ability to evaluate and address the wide range of pressing problems to which such information may be applied' (Onsrud and Rushton 1995, 502). Map libraries have a role, perhaps even a mission, in assuring that spatial data are shared equitably through our society.

References

Antonelli, S (1999) Breaking with conventions: what does digital spatial data require? *LIBER Quarterly*, **9** (2), 149–61.

Cooke, D F (1986) Maps, optical discs, and vehicle navigation. In Lambert, S and Ropiequet, S (eds) *CD-ROM, the new papyrus: the current and future state of the art*, Microsoft Press, 553–62.

Davie, D K (1997) *The ARL Geographic Information Systems Literacy Project*, ARL Office of Leadership and Management Services, 1997.

DeLorme Mapping Company **http://www.delorme.com/StreetAtlasUSA/**.

Department of the Environment (1987) *Handling geographic information: the Chorley Report*, HMSO.

Foresman, T W (1998) GIS early years and the threads of evolution. In Foresman, T W (ed) *The history of geographic information systems*, Prentice Hall, 3–17.

Harvard Map Library **http://icg.harvard.edu/~maps/**.

Lambert, S and Ropiequet, S (1986) *CD-ROM, the new papyrus: the current and future state of the art*, foreword by William H Gates, Microsoft Press.

Larsgaard, M L (1978) *Map librarianship: an introduction*, Libraries Unlimited.

Larsgaard, M L (1987) *Map librarianship: an introduction*, 2nd edn, Libraries Unlimited.

Larsgaard, M L (1998) *Map librarianship: an introduction*, 3rd edn, Libraries Unlimited.

Library of Congress, Geography and Map Division **http://lcweb2.loc.gov/ammem/gmdhtml/gmdhome.html**.

Map and Geographic Information Center **http://magic.lib.uconn.edu/**.

MapQuest **http://www.mapquest.com/**.

National Research Council Mapping Sciences Committee (1993) *Toward a co-

ordinated spatial data infrastructure for the nation, National Academy Press.

National Research Council Mapping Sciences Committee (1994) *Promoting the National Spatial Data Infrastructure through partnerships*, National Academy Press.

National Research Council Mapping Sciences Committee (1995) *A data foundation for the National Spatial Data Infrastructure*, National Academy Press.

National Research Council Mapping Sciences Committee (1997) *The future of spatial data and society*, National Academy Press.

National Research Council Panel on Distributed Geolibraries (1999) *Distributed geolibraries: spatial information resources: summary of a workshop*, National Academy Press.

OCLC (2000) OCLC, *Bits and Pieces, Electronic support news for OCLC users*, **235** available at
http://www.oclc.org/bit/235/00Jan.htm.

Onsrud, H J, and Rushton, G (1995) *Sharing geographic information*, Center for Urban Policy Research.

Osher Map Library **http://www.usm.maine.edu/~maps/**.

Soete, G (1997) *Issues and innovations in geographic information systems: transformation libraries; 2*, ARL Office of Leadership and Management Services.

Stevenson, R W (1979) Map collections and map librarianship in the United States, *Special Libraries*, **70** (3), 117–26.

Stibbe, H P (1982) *Cartographic materials: a manual of interpretation for AACR2*, American Library Association.

Tomlinson, R (1998) The Canada Geographic Information System. In Foresman, T W (ed) *The history of geographic information systems*, Prentice Hall, 21–32.

Visvalingam, M (1989) Cartography, GIS and maps in perspective, *The Cartographic Journal*, **26** (1), 26–32.

Waal, H van de (1974) The application of geographical co-ordinates for the retrieval of maps in a computerized map-catalogue, *International Yearbook of Cartography*, **14**, 166–72.

5

The changing role of GIS in the map room

Jennifer Stone Muilenburg

This chapter introduces the nature of Geographic Information Systems (GIS) and explores the use of digital map data by map libraries. It focuses upon the results of a survey carried out in the spring of 2000 and discusses the takeup of the technology by libraries and the nature of use being made of the software. The diffusion of GIS amongst different types of collections is considered and the relative significance of different software and hardware is discussed, along with a consideration of data and their use. The implications of moving towards providing a GIS-related service are also evaluated along with ways of integrating digital data with hard-copy traditional mapping. It is concluded that profound changes in the nature of map library services will follow in the wake of the shift towards GIS.

Introduction

> The question is no longer whether libraries should provide geospatial data and GIS but how.
>
> (Lamont and Marley, 1998)

One of the most recent of the new technologies to change the way the map room operates is Geographic Information Systems, or GIS. While GIS has been around for more than 20 years, its use by libraries is more recent, having started in the late 1980s and early 1990s. The number of libraries currently offering some kind of GIS service, whether custom maps, data provision or data creation, is growing steadily, and an increasing number of new job descriptions are requiring or preferring existing knowledge of GIS and digital mapping technologies, as well as a general fluency with information technology and digital data. The increase in demand for libraries' involvement with GIS is not only changing the skills of library staff, but also affecting the patron base, collection development, services and map use in general. This chapter will look at the current state of GIS in libraries, and consider how the use of GIS in the map room has changed the role of the collection, the patron and the librarian. A survey of some current library GIS users was made in April 2000; results of this survey will be used as an illustration.

Key concepts

A Geographic Information System (GIS) is a database management system for the display and analysis of digital geospatial data. It combines mapping capabilities, databases of geographical and feature information, and spatial analysis to allow users to look at an area in relation to other areas, in relation to changes over time, and in relation to various factors. The technology itself is several decades old (the company Environmental Systems Research Institute, the GIS industry leader, was founded in 1969; ArcInfo, the company's first commercial software, was released in 1981), but the techniques of spatial analysis themselves are much older. Prior to the computerization of spatial analysis, people used maps and mylar overlays to compare different 'layers' of one particular area – for example, soils, building outlines, slope and existing landslide areas could be overlaid to see how close previous landslides came to existing buildings. Soil type and slope in those slide areas could be compared to non-slide areas, and similar areas not yet affected by landslides could be characterized as 'potential slide areas'. All of this analysis could be accomplished with paper, pens, mylar, rulers, a calculator and mathematics. GIS provides not only a dramatic increase in speed of analysis, but the ability to create databases of feature and attribute information, as well as the ability to map those areas and the accompanying feature information at the same time (see Figure 5.1). The analysis and mapping is what makes GIS such alluring software, but some people use the software primarily as a cartographic tool, again replacing the pens and pencils and inks of several years ago. Traditional GIS users include government, urban planners, foresters, geographers and geologists, but as GIS software becomes less expensive and more available to the desktop computer user, the demographics of the GIS user group are changing.

There are a few libraries that have been offering some kind of GIS service for many years but many libraries have only recently begun their involvement with GIS. The major push to offer GIS in libraries came from a few changes in the 1990s. A primary factor was the dramatic increase in US government data being offered in digital format, delivered to American libraries as part of the Federal Depository Library Program. With the expanded availability of 1990 census information

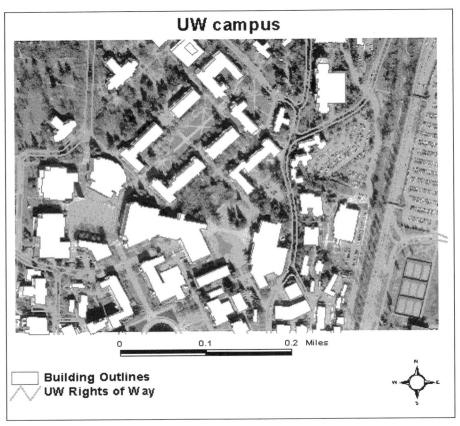

Fig. 5.1   *University of Washington campus. Map created by Jennifer Stone; data copyright 2000, City of Seattle. Map shows an example of raster data (the digital aerial photograph), and vector data (building outlines and rights of way).*

delivered on CD-ROM, TIGER files and digital aerial photography, government publications departments and map collections began dramatically to increase their holdings of digital data. Building on the momentum of increased data and more available, less expensive GIS software, the Association of Research Libraries began the Geographic Information Systems Literacy Project in 1992. The goal of the project was to 'introduce, educate, and equip librarians with skills needed to provide access to spatially referenced data in all formats and to provide effective access to selected electronic information resources in library collections' (Adler, 1995, 234). This project partnered the Environmental Systems Research Institute, or ESRI (makers of ArcView and ArcInfo software), with other public and private entities to bring GIS software and data into libraries, and to provide librarians with GIS training (Soete, 1997). The project recognized that providing GIS services in a library setting would necessitate a commitment to several things, including:

> the development of staff expertise and training on a continuous basis; provid[ing] hardware and software to meet the significant demands of an analytical tool which can be characterized as a "data hog," with constantly growing requirements, thus pressing on the need for higher end systems; the evaluation of data and the information needs of the user community; and the development of new collaborative relationships with a variety of communities to access data resources and to engage clientele in these services. Such efforts can place new demands on how staff interact with and meet user information needs.
>
> (Adler, 1997, 447–8)

The increase in digital data in their collections was the spur for many libraries to offer GIS services, but without the software and accompanying expertise to use that software, viewing and interpreting the digital data within the libraries was next to impossible. Expecting users to take data home for use or interpretation was unrealistic, and counter to the ideal that libraries provide information for use by anyone within their buildings. With the addition of GIS and spatial analysis to many academic curricula, and the growing data holdings in libraries, the idea of the library as a GIS resource began to take shape. Adler recognized the logic of offering GIS services in libraries, and stressed certain skills that were necessary to offer the service:

> GIS requires an understanding of computers and the ability to work with visual representation of data, in addition to the knowledge and skills typically found in libraries relating to organization of data, knowledge of information retrieval systems, reference services, and collection development. To implement GIS, as a strategic direction for a library, requires a commitment to developing this special combination of strengths.
>
> (Adler and Cline, 1995, 114)

There is no set formula for establishing GIS services in a library. Lamont and Marley (1998) found that 'There will be as many types of implementations of GIS and data services in libraries as there are institutions, because each has a different service mission and user base'. There are several key components of GIS services, many of which will differ between institutions. Funding, which affects all of the items in the list below, will vary from institution to institution. More funding will mean more staff, better trained staff, a more in-depth collection, better hardware and software, and the ability to offer multiple types of GIS services. Other components include:

- Collection development. Companion to the federally deposited data in many libraries must be data appropriate to the local library's user group. The best place to start when beginning to collect data is by understanding the local library's user community, which will be the basis for the data that are collected (Stone, 1999). Local and regional governments, commercial providers and free data all have different foci, potential uses, metadata, formats, licence restrictions and cost. The policies and data holdings for each library will vary with the potential user group, funding, staffing and community involvement of the library. As an example, a partial collection development policy for the University of Washington Map Collection and Cartographic Information Services unit is online at **http://www.lib.washington.edu/maps/colldev.html**, and shows that the GIS data collection policy is based on the policy for traditional materials.
- Managing data. Not only are time and cost associated with gathering the data, but once the data are in hand there are issues of formatting, data cleaning, tutorials, and archiving and updating to be considered. Again, staff expertise, software and hardware availability and funding will affect how each library handles these issues.

In addition to the skills and challenges listed above, Cox (1995) lists several other challenges to GIS use in libraries, including data accessibility; 'resistance to change while introducing new technology'; 'mystery data' lacking documentation or metadata; technical challenges such as computer maintenance, storage space and multiple database maintenance; time for data selection; information distribution and copyright issues; and learning digital map and spatial analysis concepts. The greater diversity of local organizational factors is considered in more detail in Chapter 3.

2000 survey

Several surveys of GIS use in libraries were undertaken in the 1990s (Barrow, 1995; Baruth, 1993; Kollen and Baldwin, 1993; Soete, 1997). Building upon the knowledge gained by these past surveys, and to understand the current use of GIS by libraries, another survey was undertaken by this author in April 2000. Two e-mail discussion lists were chosen to announce the web-based survey: MAPS-L (Maps and Air Photo Systems forum), a list for map collectors, librarians, vendors and aficionados; and GIS4LIB, a list geared toward users of GIS in libraries. The number of people subscribing to the lists at the time the survey was announced was 1310. The web-based survey form consisted of a variety of questions about GIS in libraries, including who is using GIS, what services are being provided, and some demographic information about the respondent's institution. The two lists were chosen for their maps- and GIS-focused missions, and offered the most specialized lists for librarians using maps and GIS. Sixty-seven people responded, and the responses are detailed below to illustrate the current state of GIS use by the libraries surveyed (Stone, 2000).

Who is using GIS and who is being served?

Starting with the ARL GIS Literacy Project, and building on the increase in the number of academic departments utilizing GIS for research and instructional purposes, many academic libraries in North America are currently offering some kind of GIS services. Public libraries are increasingly offering some kind of GIS service, branching out from the distribution of public-domain mapping software such as LandView, provided by the US Census Bureau. Unfortunately, from an international perspective, in the several surveys of GIS use by libraries, the majority of respondents have always been academic libraries, and mostly from North America (Barrow, 1995; Baruth, 1993; Kollen and Baldwin, 1993; Soete, 1997).

For the April 2000 survey, 85% of respondents were from academic libraries: 3% each from public, corporate/private, and non-profit; 4% from government; and 1% from state libraries; 2 participants did not respond to this question. Personal identification was optional on the survey, but most respondents included at least an institution name. Most were from the USA and Canada, with one from the UK, and one from Australia.

Traditional users of GIS come from forestry, urban planning, geology and geography, but an increasing number of users are coming from disciplines such as business, health care and education. On an academic campus, departments such as fisheries, oceanography, music, English and history are all beginning to show interest in using GIS for research and educational purposes. In academic libraries, users include faculty, staff and students, and sometimes the general public, who are more often directly served by public libraries. Public libraries tend to offer services to the majority of their users, with occasional restrictions or appointment-only policies. Special libraries tend to offer GIS services in conjunction with their other services, and mainly to their primary constituency.

Appropriate to the high number of academic responses in the respondent pool, the most-often-served clientele for the April 2000 survey was university-based. Of the libraries responding, 85% serve university students, 79% university staff; and 84% university faculty; 72% also serve the general public and 75% serve fellow library staff; 21% provide services to institutional staff (such as colleagues within a private company) and 12% serve paying customers; 3% are serving other groups, including local, state and federal government officials, small businesses and non-profit organizations, and 3% serve anyone who requests the service.

Most respondents report a small number of patrons seeking GIS assistance: 57% report that one to five patrons seek assistance with GIS projects in a typical week. From there, the numbers begin to drop: 16% report questions from six to ten patrons a week; 7% report for both 11–15 patrons in a week, and 16–25 patrons in a week; 6% of respondents report 26 or more patrons in a week. Four did not respond to the question. These numbers are surprisingly small, given the growing number of GIS staff being hired internationally, the amount of data being acquired, and the amount of discussion given to the topic of GIS in libraries. There are several possible reasons for the low numbers in this survey: it was not a comprehensive survey of all libraries offering GIS services; the survey was heavily weighted with academic respondents; it is possible that a high number of respondents are relatively new to offering GIS services. A more comprehensive survey could be administered with more directed questions about the number of users, the types of questions asked, and the type of assistance requested, to try to provide a better answer to this question.

How long have GIS services been offered?

The majority of respondents have been providing some kind of GIS-based services for one to four years, with 28% offering services for one to two years, and 31% offering services for three to four years. Eight and a half percent of respondents reported that they are just getting started with GIS services or have been offering them for less than six months. Twenty-one percent have been offering GIS for five to seven years, and 9% have been working with GIS for eight or more years.

One of the problems for libraries offering GIS services is working to define what, exactly, those services will entail. Some libraries have enough funding and staff to be able to offer custom mapping and analysis on demand; others offer quick- or ready-reference with GIS data, software and hardware. The level of service in one institution can change, too, as staffing and funding levels wax and wane throughout the years. In the April 2000 survey, the majority of respondents reported offering data provision (87%) and technical assistance with hardware and software, including one-on-one software training (75%). Forty percent are providing custom maps-on-demand, and 42% are working on analysing geographical problems, either for themselves, their patrons, or their institutions. Thirty-one percent are offering formalized instruction through workshops and classes, and 34% are offering online mapping applications, where interactive mapping capabilities are provided through a website using such software as ArcView Internet Map Server or something similar. Eighteen percent are offering other services, including reprojecting and reformatting of data, large-format plotting, collaborating with faculty research, and administering software site licences (see Figure 5.2).

Maps and government publications units are the most likely library units to offer GIS services, the figures being 58% and 28% respectively. Sixteen percent of respondents have GIS services offered in the reference department, and 18% have a separate GIS unit or department on campus or within the libraries. A few respondents said GIS services were offered in health sciences (3%) and geography (4%). Sixteen percent cited the 'other' category, which included special collections, microforms, the computer department, electronic resources and a combined maps/GIS/data unit. Of all respondents, 56% had GIS services offered in only one department; 33% offered services in more than one department, with

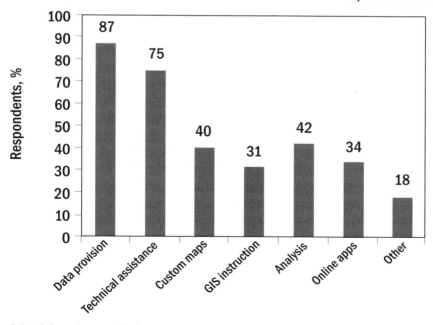

Fig. 5.2   *GIS services provided*

a very small number (6%) having GIS services in three to five departments.

Hardware and software

ESRI (**http://www.esri.com**) is the most used software vendor of the group surveyed. The desktop package ArcView is the favourite, with 90% of respondents reporting it being used by their library. Only 27% are using ESRI's powerhouse package, ArcInfo, and 31% are using other ESRI products such as BusinessMap and Atlas GIS. MapInfo, ESRI's main competitor, is used by 25% of respondents – the low turnout most likely the result of the ARL GIS Literacy Project and ESRI's strong partnership programme offering software, data and training to universities and libraries. Other products being used include Wessex, Maptitude, Landview, IDRISI, various drawing programs, ERDAS, ERMapper, and AutoCad.

The platforms being used by the libraries to offer GIS services are dominated by Microsoft: 51% are using Windows 95 or 98; 55% are using Windows NT; and only one respondent is using Windows 2000 (still very new at the time of writing). Eighteen percent are using UNIX-based systems, and only 7% are using Macintosh – not surprising, since ESRI, the software vendor of choice, stopped updating ArcView for Macintosh with version 3.0a, in the late 1990s (the current version of ArcView at press time is 3.2).

Companion peripherals are standard for many GIS stations: 84% of respondents offer colour printers, 69% offer black and white printers, and 27% offer plotters. Sixty-seven percent offer some kind of external storage drive such as a zip or jaz drive. Data creation can play a large part in some GIS projects, especially those concerning historical analysis. Fifty-one percent of libraries offer a scanner, and 12% offer a digitizer, for those wishing to create their own data, and other uses in conjunction with GIS. Thirty-six percent utilize a CD burner, and 7% checked the 'other' category, including in their lists items such as tape drives, digital cameras, and DVD drives (see Table 5.1).

Table 5.1   *Peripherals*

Peripheral	Respondents, %	Peripheral	Respondents, %
Digitizer	12	B&W printer	69
Scanner	51	CD burner	36
Plotter	27	External storage drive	67
Colour printer	84	Other	7

Data

Digital data on a variety of scales are being collected and used by GIS users in libraries. Nearly all libraries are collecting US government data and international commercial data from ESRI (often included as part of the university or library site licence), at 82% and 61%, respectively. Thirty-six percent are collecting other official county government data, and 58% are collecting data from vendors other than ESRI. City/county data and state data are also popular, with 73% and 66% of respondents collecting those data sets. Thirteen percent cited the collection of other data, including international health and education sources, data produced by university departments/staff/faculty/students, regional planning association, intergovernmental organizations (FAO, World Bank, etc), remote sensing data and provincial data.

Of the data that are collected, the survey inquired as to the frequency of the use of different types. For US government and national data, 22% said they use them daily, 22% said they use them at least once a week, 22% said they use them a few times a month, and 18% said they use them a few times a year. Ten people did not respond. For international commercial data from ESRI, 6% said they use them daily, 16% use them at least once a week, 24% reported using them a few times a month, and 25% reported using them a few times a year. Nineteen people did not respond. For other official county government data, 6% said they use the data daily, 9% said they use them at least once a week, 16% said they use them a few times a month, and 19% said they use them a few times a year. Thirty-three people did not respond.

For data from other commercial providers, 12% said they use the data daily, 18% reported at least once a week, 21% said they use them a few times a month, and 15% said they use them a few times a year. Twenty-three people did not respond. City and county data are used by 19% on a daily basis, 19% use them at least once a week, 22% use them a few times a month, and 16% use them a few times a year. Fifteen people did not respond. And for state data, 18% reported daily use, 15% reported at least once a week, 27% said they use them a few times a month, and 12% said they use them a few times a year. Nineteen people did not respond.

This list of numbers shows that the data sets used most frequently (daily or weekly) by the largest number of respondents are US government data, data from other commercial providers than ESRI, city and county data, and state data. For data formats and types, raster data such as aerial photographs, remote sensing data and digital elevation models are provided by 78% of respondents; vector data such as streets, boundary files and rivers are used by 88%; and attribute data such as census data, business data, and spending data, by 88%.

In addition to offering data on CD-ROM, 69% of respondents said they provided information about their GIS services on their web pages. Thirty-four percent provide GIS data for downloading, and 73% link to other data sites for downloadable data. Three percent said they don't yet have a web page; six people did not respond to the question. Twenty-three respondents said they were offering some kind of interactive mapping application on their web sites (see the earlier question on services).

How is GIS being integrated with traditional mapping?

As GIS has been introduced into libraries, many questions have developed about how GIS affects not only staff skills and requirements, funding and equipment, and collection development, but how GIS is being integrated with traditional mapping, and how users are reacting to the newer, digital information. Whereas some digital data cannot be interpreted without the use of GIS software, an increasing number of applications are being produced that provide an interface for the lay user to interpret the data behind the application. One example is the *National atlas of the United States* (**www.nationalatlas.gov**). This current incarnation of the *National atlas* is an update to the version published in 1970. With this version, however, the US Geological Survey, ESRI and other partners have worked together to provide access to various national data sets via an online mapping application available to anyone with web access. GIS expertise is not needed – the site includes instructions on how to make on-screen maps, as well as directions on printing the maps from a local printer. For GIS users, the site also includes the raw data used in the online mapping application. The data and its associated metadata are available for download and use in a variety of GIS software packages. No print version of the atlas is being produced in this round, though some single-sheet maps are being produced and distributed. This is a site where users without GIS experience can benefit from an online mapping application that utilizes GIS.

Microsoft's foray into the digital mapping world is also bringing spatial literacy and mapping capabilities to a new set of non-GIS users. Beginning with MapPoint 2000 and continuing with MapPoint 2001, Microsoft has geared its software toward the lay user who has data with a geographic component, either a street address or latitude/longitude coordinates. MapPoint can take that geographic component and map the user's data (currently only available for the USA), and has bundled demographic and some consumer data inside the product, for quick views and maps of local areas. No spatial analysis can be completed inside MapPoint, and data cannot be extracted for use in another program, but simple maps can be made and linked with information about that geographic location. With this product, Microsoft is aiming to capture the market that lies between the electronic atlas user described in Chapter 6 (eg Microsoft's *Encarta*, DeLorme's *Eartha global explorer* or *Street atlas USA*) and the GIS user (eg, ArcView, ArcInfo, Map-Info), and is especially interested in targeting business users, a growing segment of the GIS user population.

The increase in digital cartographic data that is non-GIS specific, as well as the growth in affordable software and hardware, is creating a greater number of non-GIS users who are literate in multiple cartographic data formats. A printed map is one option, and where an online mapping application exists, a digital map often also suffices. This is affecting users who come into a map library, in that they can use a variety of formats to answer their geographic questions. They can use a combination of paper maps, CD-ROM atlases, and websites to find the information they need (see Chapter 6).

The April 2000 GIS survey asked respondents to think about their last few patrons, and answer whether or not those patrons were looking for format-specific types of information. Twenty-four percent of respondents said their most recent patrons were looking for digital information only. Nine percent said that users were seeking paper or traditional formats only. And the majority, 63%, said that their users were not seeking format-specific information – they were interested in either paper or digital materials. As to what those patrons ended up using, 28% said their patrons walked away with digital information only, 12% said they used paper information only, and 55% said their patrons were using a combination of paper and digital cartographic information. An interesting follow-up to this study would be to investigate what types of paper and digital products are used most often, and which are used in conjunction with each other.

How is the map librarian's role changing in light of using GIS?

In 1993, Wong stated that 'The versatility of digital cartographic data and analytical capability of automated mapping systems warrant an increased level of operational and technical skills of a cartographic materials librarian' (Wong, 1993, 2–14). This increased level of skills is evident when looking at current job descriptions for maps/GIS librarians, which in addition to map library-related skills include desired skills such as experience with GIS software like ArcView, ArcInfo and Map-Info; systems design and administration; server management; web skills; remote sensing; programming with AML, Avenue, and/or Visual Basic; relational database use and programming; and Windows NT and UNIX environments.

The growing number of GIS applications has also necessitated an increased number of staff in the library who work with GIS on a regular basis. In the April 2000 survey, 67% respondents reported one or two individuals working with GIS on a regular basis, 24% reported three to four people working with GIS, and 4% reported five to six people working with GIS on a regular basis. Sixty-five percent reported that one to two of those staff members working with GIS on a regular basis also had an MLS or equivalent professional degree; 24% said that none of the GIS staff members had an MLS or equivalent. The subject specializations of those degrees are much the same as for those working in map libraries: 30 respondents reported staff members with bachelor's degrees in geography or geology, 15 reported staff members with a master's degree in geography or geology, and one respondent reported a staff member with a PhD in geography.

Many staff members are receiving GIS training on the job, through a variety of methods (see Figure 5.3). Fifty-four percent have received formal commercial instruction from sources such as ESRI, a local training firm, or MapInfo. Sixty-six percent have received in-house training in GIS, 40% have used online training methods, and 45% have taken formal academic instruction in GIS.

Perhaps the greatest indicator of the growth of GIS in libraries is the increase in the number of librarians being hired to spend 50% or more of their time working with GIS. In the April 2000 survey, respondents were asked to list their job titles, and to say how long they had been in their current position. Eleven respondents had the word 'GIS' in their job titles, such as GIS/Data Librarian, GIS Librarian, GIS Administrator, GIS Specialist, GIS Coordinator, and Map and GIS Librarian. Other relevant titles included Reference Librarian for Digital Spatial Data, Coordinator of Digital Mapping, Electronic Documents Librarian, Cartographic/Graphic Assistant, and Team Leader of Electronic Resources. The mean number of years that respondents were in their current position was 6.8 years, with a median of 3.6. The mode, or most frequently cited number of years in the current position was one, suggesting that many of the respondents to this survey are relatively new to their current job. Sixty-six percent said GIS was included in their formal job description, 31% did not have GIS as part of their job description, and two people did not respond to the question.

Conclusion

The increase in the number of libraries offering GIS services has grown dramatically throughout the last decade. This growth has caused changes in the kind of collections and services being offered by map libraries, and has also caused changes

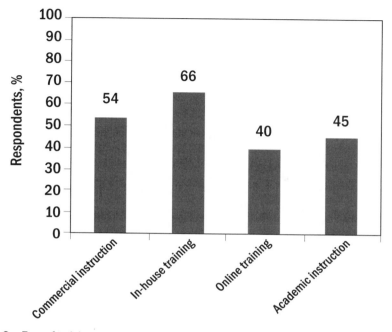

Fig. 5.3 *Type of training*

in the types of library staff being hired and the kinds of skills they need for the job. As GIS and desktop mapping become more accessible, greater numbers of traditional and non-traditional GIS users are turning to their libraries for GIS assistance. More staff training is necessary, and more librarians need to be well versed not only in traditional cartographic information formats, but also in the new digital forms. Even though the April 2000 survey reports low numbers of patrons requesting assistance with GIS, anecdotal evidence from several campuses and public libraries shows that the numbers have been growing over the last few years, and continue to grow. The increased availability and use of cartographic information by businesses, websites, and academia reported in Chapter 8 would suggest that GIS services by libraries will continue to grow in the next millennium, further changing the role of the map librarian and map collections internationally.

References

Adler, P S (1995) Special issue of geographic information systems (GIS) and academic libraries: an introduction, *The Journal of Academic Librarianship*, **21** (4), 233–5.

Adler, P S (1997) An introduction – where are we heading? *The Journal of Academic Librarianship*, **23** (6), 447–8.

Adler, P S and Cline, N M (1995) GIS and research libraries: one perspective, *Information Technology and Libraries*, **14** (2), 114.

Argentati, C D (1997) Expanding horizons for GIS services in academic libraries, *The Journal of Academic Librarianship*, **23** (6), 463–8.

Badurek, C (2000) Managing GIS in academic libraries, *Western Association of Map Libraries Information Bulletin*, **31** (2), 110–14.

Barrow, W C (1995) *Follow up survey to Congress of Cartographic Information Specialist Associations (CCISA) 1992 survey*. (Personal correspondence).

Baruth, C (1993) Digital data survey, *Special Libraries Association Geography and Map Division Bulletin*, **172**, 67–8.

Buttenfield, B P (1998) Looking forward: geographic information services and libraries in the future, *Cartography and Geographic Information Systems*, **25** (3), 161–71.

Cox, A B (1995) An overview to geographic information systems, *The Journal of Academic Librarianship*, **21** (4), 237–49.

Davie, D, Fox, K J and Preece, B (1999) *The ARL geographic information systems literacy project: a SPEC (systems and procedures exchange center) kit*, ARL Spec Kit **238**, ARL.

Deckelbaum, D (1999) GIS in libraries: an overview of concepts and concerns, *Issues in Science and Technology Librarianship*, **21**, available at **http://www.library.ucsb.edu/istl/99-winter/article3.html**.

Kollen, C and Baldwin, C (1993) Automation and map librarianship: three issues, *Special Libraries Association Geography and Map Division Bulletin*, **173**, 24–38.

Lamont, M and Marley, C (1998) Spatial data and the digital library, *Cartography and Geographic Information Systems*, **25** (3), 143–9.

Moulder, C (2000) Current literature on geographic information systems and libraries, available at **http://www.mcmaster.ca/library/maps/gis_libr.htm**.

Soete, G J (1997) *Transforming libraries: issues and innovations in geographic information systems*, ARL Spec Kit **219**, ARL.

Stone, J (1999) Stocking your GIS data library, *Issues in Science and Technology Librarianship*, **21**, available at **http://www.library.ucsb.edu/istl/99-winter/article1.html**.

Stone, J (2000) *GIS in your library survey*, available at **http://faculty.washington.edu/jnstone/gis**.

Wong, M K (1993) Exploring the impact of digital cartographic data on map librarianship using data use models, *Special Libraries Association Geography and Map Division Bulletin*, **173**, 2–14.

6
Offline digital maps

Bob Parry

This chapter is concerned with offline digital map data and mapping packages, with a principal focus on the CD-ROM. During the 1990s, and before the growth of the Internet, the CD-ROM supplanted the floppy disk and magnetic tape as the prime medium both for storing spatial data and for the development of digital mapping packages. The chapter outlines the advantages and limitations of this medium in the context of map libraries, discusses the different kinds of CD-ROM package that have become available, and considers the likely future for the medium.

Introduction

Barely more than a decade ago the author attended a road show of CD-ROMs for business use and was disappointed to find no examples of maps or mappable data in this medium. Now, as we enter the new millennium, and the Internet notwithstanding, we are overwhelmed with CDs providing every kind of spatial data, sometimes in relatively raw form, but more often packaged with interactive mapping programs, or at least with simple viewing software.

It might be argued that within that short time span the CD-ROM has already served its purpose, with most of its advantages superseded by the wealth of data now available on the Internet. Certainly this must be true of many applications. A few years ago, for example, the author's map collection acquired the *GEOname* gazetteer of the world on CD-ROM, which concentrated the contents of many shelf-metres of printed gazetteers onto a single disk. Now this same gazetteer is readily accessed on the web, and its availability as a standalone package has ceased. In view of the intermittent demand for place name searching, the Internet provides a more convenient means of access, and can obviate the need for the user to visit the map room. (However, we are still in transition: our map collection often receives telephone inquiries relating to the location of places, most of which come from people with desktop access to the answer!)

At the outset, one must acknowledge a distinction between, on the one hand, the use of CD-ROMs primarily as a medium for the distribution and storage of data, and on the other, their exploitation as multimedia devices providing the electronic equivalent of a world, road, national, state or thematic atlas. The distinction is not clear-cut, however, as increasingly, CD-ROMs intended for data distribution have incorporated software to allow the user to view and manipulate the data.

As an offline storage medium for data, both spatial and non-spatial, the convenience and low cost of the CD-ROM were quickly recognized by government organizations, especially in the USA, and through the US government's depository programme many libraries have amassed as many as a thousand or more CD-ROMs over the last decade, and have had to face the daunting task of providing catalogue data and access to this relatively new medium. This has been a stimulus for the provision of GIS facilities in those libraries (Chapter 4).

The advantages of CD-ROMs for multimedia have also been well rehearsed (for example, Spiess, 1995; Borchert, 1999), ranging from economy in storage to the interactive potential of the medium. Many of these advantages apply equally well to maps on the web. For mapping packages that are used as tools for research, however, the CD-ROM retains, at least for the time being, a useful role. Extended periods of research involving the manipulation of census statistics, and design of graphic output in the form of maps and graphs, for example, can often be better done with data and software stored locally, and the CD-ROM provides an easier way to control and service the use of such data.

The development of CD-ROMs and related media

Many digital map resources designed for general public distribution, and for use on PCs, began life on floppy disk during the 1980s, but by the end of the 20th century, almost all had migrated to CD-ROM or to the Internet. Concurrently, a number of other promising technologies were developed but these, generally, failed to survive. One of the most unfortunate examples in Britain was the BBC Domesday project, developed in the mid-1980s by the British Broadcasting Corporation with numerous collaborators. This has often been cited as an early example of a multimedia package. The two, high-capacity Domesday videodiscs included maps (the whole series of Ordnance Survey *Landranger* maps), searchable gazetteer, text, photographs, surrogate walks through selected environments, video and, most importantly, a huge database of thematic data from which maps and graphs could be constructed interactively. This was indeed a true multimedia package which also included maps and spatial data of considerable value to geographers and other thematic map users (Maguire, 1989). However, the system was platform-dependent, requiring several thousand pounds-worth of dedicated hardware comprising a Laservision videodisc player specially developed by Philips linked to a BBC microcomputer. The technology died, and with it the prospect of maintaining the system or extending the products.

Another development that has failed to survive in spite of its early promise is CD-i (Compact Disk Interactive). This was developed by Philips Electronics and Sony in the mid-1980s and comprised a multimedia player that could be plugged into a television set. It was easy to use, designed mainly for showing videos, and had a point-and-click interactive capability. Although more flexible than the more recent DVD, and despite many thousands of players still being in use, it has been supplanted by the latter as a device for showing high-quality videos, and Philips ceased manufacture in 1999. The author reviewed a CD-i disk of early maps produced by On/Q Corporation, Montreal, in 1994, and found great difficulty in locating a player on which it could be used (Parry, 1994)! These examples serve as cautionary tales of the danger of technological redundancy.

Other media for the electronic storage of data have also been developed more recently than the CD-ROM, and include DVD and, most recently, FMD data disks. While standard DVD disks hold 4.7 Gb of data, the use of fluorescent multiple layer technology for FMD disks can increase the storage capacity of a single disk to as much as 140 Gb stored in as many as 30 data layers. It may even be possible to increase this capacity to a terabyte. Although these media are not yet widely used for the storage of spatial data, it is clear that the CD-ROM must be seen as only part of the evolving technology of the 'new media'. Moreover, although these newer products are currently mainly seen as vehicles for high-definition TV film viewing (a standard DVD disk can hold one full-length feature film), there is a clear potential for FMD as a medium for spatial warehousing, as is recognized on the manufacturer's website (Constellation 3D at **http://www.c-3d.net/**). Other storage media such as CD-R, CD-RW and zip drives are used mainly for the transfer or temporary residence of data, rather than for commercial products.

Among the advantages of CD-ROMs over earlier electronic data storage media are their high capacity (over 650 Mb per disk), the relatively fast data retrieval (ie compared with the Internet), their durability and their security (Unwin, 1991). The data are secure in the sense that they cannot be wiped or altered, but they can also be kept relatively secure for data protection purposes, since, if necessary, they can be kept physically under lock and key in a map library. CD-ROMs also offer the significant advantages shared by all digital products in that they can give access to hyperlinked data of various kinds, that not all data layers of a map have to be displayed at any one time, and that they can incorporate built-in interactive programs.

After CD-ROM technology took off in the early 1990s, many electronic atlases and route planners originally launched on floppy disk migrated to the superior storage capacity and durability of the CD-ROM. So, for example, the early route planning package for Great Britain, *AutoRoute*, grew to occupy five floppy disks before being transferred first in part and then in its entirety to CD-ROM. Electronic atlases also continued to be issued on multiple 5¼ in. or 3½ in. disks well into the 1990s. Meanwhile, government organizations in the USA, such as the United States Geological Survey, the National Geophysical Data Center, the Census Bureau and the National Climatic Data Center began to distribute numerous spatially encoded data sets on this medium.

For the publisher, CD-ROMs are cheap to produce. Moreover, as the authors of the *Atlas of Arkansas* stressed, their contents can also be updated quickly and inexpensively, and this has been a feature of many CD-ROMs, such as route planners (though not, as it happens, the *Atlas of Arkansas*). If printed maps are required, they can be produced at the user's expense, rather than the publisher's. For the map library, CD-ROMs have the advantage of saving space and being relatively easy to file and catalogue.

What kinds of CD-ROMs are of interest to map libraries?

A map library's interest in CD-ROMs is not restricted exclusively to contemporary maps or spatially encoded statistical data. Catalogues (such as the *British Library map catalogue*), archival material (maps from the past issues of the *National Geographic Magazine*, for example), encyclopaedias and travel guides, dictionaries, gazetteers, computer software and learning packages can also be included.

CD-ROMs that are primarily concerned with mapping may be grouped in a number of ways. One important distinction, already made, is between those developed as user-friendly multimedia products packaged with their own dedicated software, and those whose function is more simply the cheap and effective delivery of spatial data. The former include electronic world atlases, such as Microsoft's *Encarta world atlas* and DeLorme's *Eartha global explorer*, and increasingly, route planners, which now usually include a range of additional tourist and recreational information. The latter include collections of raster images of modern topographic or historic maps, and files of spatially encoded statistical data, such as census and environmental data. Some items in this second group may require additional software in order to view and manipulate the data.

More elaborate classifications of such mapping packages can be made according to the functionality of the package, ie the degree of *interactive* use of the data made possible by the included software. At their simplest, electronic maps and atlases are little more than screen-based analogues of their printed equivalent, typified by the *Atlas of Arkansas* (University of Arkansas Press), in the introduction to which it is stated: 'This atlas works like a book, except the pages are turned with a mouse instead of by hand'. At their most complex, they work almost like a fully functional GIS, but with data included. Most contemporary electronic mapping packages fall somewhere between these extremes. Many in fact are targeted at a specific user group with software designed to perform appropriate but limited functions. The most obvious example is the route planning package, with software dedicated to calculating best-fit routes within constraints specified by the user (eg fastest, shortest, avoiding certain road categories). In the USA a number of CD-ROM based maps have also been launched for use in hiking, and are designed to display routes and route profiles, or provide for live, on-screen GPS tracking. Examples are *TOPO! Interactive maps* and *TOPO! GPS USA* from National Geographic Maps, or *Take a hike* and *Terrain navigator* from MapTech Inc. These are all based on scanned images of US Geological Survey topographic quadrangles. A rather different example is the use of maps in real estate management. A UK product called *Promap*, available on licence, uses the very detailed Ordnance Survey Land-Line™ data and provides software to enable the user to highlight buildings and property boundaries and to measure areas and perimeters. *DemoGraphics '96*, developed by Gerhard Heilig in association with The Netherlands Interdisciplinary Demographic Institute, enables the user to study future world population scenarios by viewing maps, graphs and population pyramids, and animating time series data using different demographic growth models (Heilig, 1994).

Clearly, the view-only type of package provides the greatest ease of use for both the map curator and the map library patron. Such packages do not require an extensive tutorial, and the only problems will be to supply suitable printing hardware and software, together with mechanisms for providing and charging for printouts. More demanding are those packages that do not hold ready-to-print, 'cartographic-quality' maps, but provide map creation software for combining a reference base map with statistical data. These may also enable users to influence the structure and design of the map, by manipulating scale and class intervals, and choosing colours, line widths and point symbols. Interactive packages of this kind raise the issue, one central to the theme of this book, of the extent to which the curator should intervene when the patron needs assistance in using the package.

Borchert (1999) has explored more detailed classifications of so-called 'multimedia atlas concepts'. Like all atlases, they can be classed according to their thematic and topographic content and target user group. But they can also be classified with regard to production concepts (such as the computer platform and the programming language), media concepts (ie the kinds of graphic products and their sources), information retrieval concepts and map interaction concepts. Where a package fits under these various headings will have implications for how useful it will prove in a map library. However, in terms of map library convenience it is appropriate to consider map-related CD-ROMs mainly in terms of their thematic and regional content and their primary function. An ad hoc scheme would be multimedia electronic atlases (world, national and regional), route planners, street level atlases, topographic map collections, historic map collections, demographic data sets, earth science and environmental data sets, and gazetteers. As categories outside this classification, one could also add library catalogues on CD, and learning packages. These categories, with some examples, are discussed below. As will be seen, there is often overlap between these groups.

The multimedia atlas

The term 'electronic atlas' is sometimes used in a broader sense to include most of the categories described below, but is here used more restrictively to mean electronic multimedia packages that have been deliberately developed as digital equivalents of (or complements to) printed atlases, whether general, national or regional. Kraak and Ormeling (1996) have suggested that conventional atlases are structured in such a way as to have a narrative role, or by map sequencing to enable the user to explore possible causal relationships, but in a way determined by the atlas authors. While it is doubtful whether general atlases are often used in this way, there is no doubt that a well-designed electronic atlas extends the navigational opportunities for the user. New access structures give new freedoms of opportunity to explore data (Ormeling, 1993), and although a view-only electronic atlas offers the user only limited freedoms, many multimedia atlases now allow disparate maps to be called up and compared side by side on the screen, or to be hyperlinked to other information. The user may also be able, by zooming, to view maps at different levels of resolution, or to view different combinations of data layers. Increasingly too, such atlases are linked to a website that can supply updated or real-time information. However these kinds of atlases generally lack the more sophisticated analytical tools associated with GIS or with some of the statistical packages discussed below. In this author's experience, most of the multimedia world atlases have proved of limited value in the map library. Regional and state atlases, with their richer thematic content, are more worthwhile acquisitions. Examples of the latter include the *Atlas de la República Argentina multimedia*, published by the Instituto Geográfico Militar, Buenos Aires in 1999, or the *Interactive atlas of Georgia*, produced by the Institute of Community and Area Development, University of Georgia, Athens (1996).

Route planners

The first mass-market route planner to be released in the UK, and possibly the first mass-market package of this kind in the world, was *AutoRoute* in 1987, pioneered by a company called NextBase using the then recently digitized Ordnance Survey vector data set at 1: 625,000 scale (Perkins and Parry, 1996). In North America, the earliest example was an innovative program from DeLorme called *Map'n'Go*, which like *AutoRoute* has subsequently passed through numerous editions, and is now called *AAA Map'n'Go*. *AutoRoute* has become a product of Microsoft, and now provides European cover as well as cover of Great Britain. Today, however, there is a superabundance of route planners at the national, continental and even global scale (*AND Route '99 world route planner*). For Britain alone, in spite of the stringent copyright restrictions on use of government mapping data, there were (late in 2000) competing packages from at least six commercial providers.

Street level atlases

The first nation-wide electronic street atlas was *Street atlas USA*, launched by DeLorme in 1991. As increasing detail has been added to route planners, these two categories have tended to merge: both usually provide route planning and distance/time measuring software, as well as location to the level of individual street names. Canada has several street-level CD-ROMs, including the recent *Canada street locator* from MapArt, which has street-level maps for every community with a population in excess of 30,000. More sophisticated electronic urban atlases also now exist for many of Europe's capital and other major cities, from Budapest to London to Riga, and some of these include additional thematic content, such as the CD-ROMs of European cities by the Spanish company VisualGIS Engineering. There are also some purely thematic urban CD-ROMs, such as the *Digitaler Umweltatlas*

Berlin (published by Senatsverwaltung für Stadtentwicklung Umweltschutz und Technologie, Berlin).

Archives of topographic and historic mapping

Many national survey organizations have issued their basic topographic map series on CD-ROM, sometimes including additional data or a route planning facility. These series are usually stored in raster format and so can provide carto-graphic-quality screen or printed images. Examples, from what could be an enormous list (Parry and Perkins, 2000), include *TOPOmap*, offering 1:50,000 scale cover of the settled areas of South Australia on CDs, Denmark's topographic series which are available on ten CDs, cover of Latvia at 1:200,000 scale, and CDs of the 1:25,000-scale topographic sheets of many of the German Länder. Depending on the pricing formula, they may offer a map library the opportunity to acquire complete topographic-scale cover of a country at an economical price. However, patrons of the map collection will generally require colour-printed output, and this will not be able to emulate the high print resolutions of good quality litho-printed maps (see Chapter 10).

However, the digital environment presents opportunities as well as limitations. DeLorme's *Topo USA*, version 2.0, offers in addition to two-dimensional medium-scale topographic maps of the whole of the USA, 3-D renderings that can be scaled horizontally and vertically, and rotated and tilted to give different viewing angles. Many national topographical data sets have been incorporated into multimedia products that include additional material such as air photographs and satellite imagery, and additional functions such as route planning. The Danish survey organization (Kort- og Matrikelstyrelsen, Copenhagen), for example, issued all its topographic series on multiple CD-ROMs in 1993; these were followed in 1995 by a CD for Windows which provided just 1:100,000 and smaller scale topographic cover but with satellite images, tourist information and a quiz. Subsequently this was further upgraded as *Det levende Danmarkskort* to include route planning software.

In 2000, historical map archives are appearing increasingly both on the web and on CD-ROM. Among the latter is the recent appearance of the Royal Geographic Society's archive collection of Ordnance Survey 1:10,560-scale maps of Great Britain, issued county by county as raster-scanned images on CD-ROM by a commercial company, Sitescope (**http://www.sitescope.co.uk**).

Demographic, earth science and environmental data sets

Of particular value as a map library resource has been the distribution of spatially attributed thematic data on CD-ROM. This has made it possible to map and therefore visualize spatial distributions as never before. Such data sets do of course require viewing software and also, depending on the nature of the data, reference mapping stored in raster or vectorized format, and outlines of the areas – counties, enumeration districts, zip codes etc – to which the data values are attached. Some of the earliest CD-ROMs in this category made use of the availability of population census data in digital form using Supermap software (Rystedt, 1995), resulting in census CD-ROMs for the UK (*The 1991 Census on CD-ROM*), Australia (*CDDATA91*), and France (*CD-Atlas de France*), and *Regiomap* for European Union statistics.

Large amounts of relief, climatic, geophysical and other environmental data emanate from the NOAA National Data Centers in the USA (**http:// ngdc.noaa.gov/**) and can be viewed using shareware programs included on the disks, or GeoVu software downloadable from the web. These US government data are provided at marginal costs only, or distributed free to public and institutional libraries. However, the data are sometimes not easy to use and benefit from being repackaged by commercial publishers who provide a better user interface and management software, or data compliance with major GIS systems. *ADC WorldMap* is an example of such repackaging applied in this case to the US National Imagery and Mapping Agency's *VMap* 1:1,000,000-scale world topographic database. Demographic data from the US Census Bureau has also been repackaged on CD-ROM, for example by GeoLytics Inc.

Gazetteers

A name searching function is incorporated in most electronic atlases (in the sense used above), route planners and topographic map data sets. Many national survey organizations have also released their names databases on CD-ROM, although these are sometimes only plain text files, and do not include full search routines, for example the Australian *Master names file* or the Ordnance Survey *Landranger* names database. Some gazetteers of the geographical dictionary type have also been transferred to CD-ROM, for example the *Diccionario geográfico de Colombia* (published by the Instituto Geográfico Agustin Codazzi, Bogotá). However, as mentioned above, the web has also become an important tool for place name searching.

Library catalogues

A number of map library catalogues are now directly accessible on the web, but the catalogue of at least one major historical map archive, that of the British Library Map Library, has been released as a self-contained package on CD-ROM, and provides new research possibilities for cartographic historians as a result of the re-keying of 19 volumes of printed catalogues. In contrast to some other categories of CD-ROM, this has been carefully reviewed in several periodicals (eg Fox, 1999; Archer, 2000; Whistance-Smith, 2000), an important consideration when purchasing high-cost (and high-value) CD-ROMs.

Educational and learning CD-ROMs

Many of the examples cited under other categories are educational in the sense that they can be used effectively as learning tools (Dymon, 1995). However, there are also many CD-ROMs that are specifically designed as learning packages, or that provide maps intended as a learning resource for a specific age group. Examples of these would include *Axion cartographic map projections of the world*, *AFIM Africa interactive maps*, or the already mentioned *DemoGraphics*. Ordnance Survey has an *Interactive atlas of Great Britain*, published in association with Attica Interactive, and this is clearly aimed at a schools' market in the UK. The acquisitions librarian has to be especially cautious in acquiring these kinds of package to ensure that target users of the package are found among the map library's own patrons.

Issues

As a relatively new medium, packaged digital data raise many problems that are less commonly encountered by map curators in the provision of printed paper maps. Issues of the availability, suitability and reliability of maps and data sets on CD-ROM provide the map curator with new challenges for which satisfactory solutions are not easy to find.

Availability

Five years ago it was possible to create useful lists of CD-based mapping packages that a map library might aspire to hold (eg Perkins, 1995). More recently, Larsgaard has compiled a list of holdings from the Map and Imagery Library, University of California (Larsgaard, 1998). Interestingly, Larsgaard's list reflects strongly the way in which American libraries have received data on CD-ROMs through federal depository arrangements, rather than a list based on what a map library might most need out of a more global assessment of what is available. However, no list can remain valid for long, and a list posted by MAGERT on the web (**http://www.sunysb. edu/libmap/brill.htm**) extends to only eight items! Much more useful are web listings of CD-ROM collections held by map libraries, such as that of the Pennsylvania State University Libraries (**http://www.libraries.psu.edu/crsweb/maps/ cdcoll.htm**). The second edition of *World mapping today* (Parry and Perkins, 2000) includes numerous references to available digital mapping, but does not always indicate the medium on which it is distributed. Moreover it still provides a necessarily very partial listing: for example for Poland, a CD atlas of Poland and a multimedia atlas of Warsaw are listed, but not the multimedia atlases of several other Polish cities, nor a large range of route planners. A recent paper about Polish electronic atlases on CD lists no fewer than 36 examples (Andrzejewska, Baranowski and Okonek, 1999).

Information posted on the web by map dealers is useful in being current and including prices. For example, Omni Resources in the USA have a separate listing of digital maps on their excellent website (**http://omnimap.com/**). In the UK, Elstead Maps have a good stock of CD-ROMs in the categories of electronic atlas and route planner, and offer impartial advice to prospective purchasers. The Elstead Maps website is worth visiting (**http://www. elstead.co.uk/**), and includes a tabulated comparison of the specification, price and interactive features of UK CD-ROMs.

Evaluation

A map collection acquiring CD-ROMs for its patrons is also faced with a problem familiar to map curators when acquiring conventional maps from commercial publishers: that of evaluating the product. In the case of CDs however, the problem is exacerbated by the multimedia (i.e. 'popular') nature of many packages and the general lack of advice about the quality and utility of the products. CD-ROM mapping packages are commonly reviewed in computer magazines, but such reviews often lack an awareness of the cartographic and data quality criteria that are so important to cartographers and to serious map users. Reviews appear somewhat less commonly in the cartographic press, and even these are often unhelpful, or insufficiently thorough, especially from a map curator's point of view. For example, a comparison of world electronic atlases from Encarta and DeLorme in *The Cartographic Journal* said little or nothing about the scale, content, design or provenance of the maps (Whyment, 1998). Clearly map curators need access to much keener reviews of such products, and this is an area where they could be more active themselves. One way of soliciting views of a product is to put a message on a special interest listserver such as MAPS-L or LIS-MAPS. Such messages do appear from time to time, but more often they concern hardware or software problems rather than data quality.

Many CD-ROM products have been designed for a popular audience and at best provide 'edutainment' (Taylor, 1999) rather than more serious and focused applications. Because they depend on a large mass market for their success, attempts to develop more serious GIS-type applications risk being abandoned. Thus *Map-Base*, a spin-off from *AutoRoute*, was dropped when Microsoft acquired ownership of the product from its original developer, NextBase, while DeLorme's *MapExpert*, based on the route planner *Map'n'Go*, was also discontinued (although the recently launched *Xmap business* by DeLorme bucks this trend).

Quality control

Quality of content applies as much to CD-ROMs as it does to conventional maps and books. However, many digital mapping packages, especially in the electronic atlas or route planning categories, are coy about stating their sources. Marketing hype is concerned mainly with the innovative things the software will do, and the amount and level of map detail included. Detailed examination of some CD-ROM atlases and route planners has revealed many examples of inappropriate selection of place names, and of places mislocated, and route planners have often been deficient in incorporating intelligence about one-way streets and problems of cross-town navigation (although these are being rectified by the capture of attribute data for in-car navigation systems). When the maps are generated from vector data, electronic atlases often fail to construct an acceptable *cartographic* image: place names may overlap and a proper visual hierarchy is often lacking.

In many cases the quality and utility of a CD-ROM product will only become apparent with use, and so expensive acquisition mistakes may have been made.

User control

With an interactive atlas, the maps that emerge are only as good as the data quality, the built-in intelligence of the mapping program, and the knowledge, experience and intelligence of the user! Potentially therefore, there is an important role for the map curator to educate the user on the importance of scale in relation to data resolution, or the choice of colours and class intervals when producing choropleth maps for example. A common weakness of packages on CD-ROM is that default settings often not only produce cartographically poor quality maps, but in the case of statistical maps fail to give a meaningful representation of the statistical distribution of the data. Map curators have always been closely involved in the education of the map user, but digital data make new demands (see Chapter 2).

Map library control

As with all digital data, CD-ROMs raise new issues of responsibility concerning intellectual property rights and their implications for copying, data modification and data use (Chapter 12). Map curators may find themselves liable to ensure that digital data are only used in an educational context, for example. Most CD-ROM packages provide documentation on terms and conditions of use (either in printed form, on disk or both). These are often extremely lengthy and complex. How far is it the curator's responsibility to ensure that the user abides by any restrictions on use? When CD-ROMs are networked, how can licensing controls be enforced? The CD-ROM has also presented new problems for the cataloguer, and has stimulated the drive to produce metadata standards (Chapter 9).

Cost

CD-ROMs are cheap to make and distribute, with the burden of hard-copy production (if required) being placed upon the user. There is therefore an expectation that prices of CD-ROM mapping should also be low. This expectation is further sustained by the knowledge that similar data are often available at zero cost on the web. At first sight, however, there seems to be no logic to the pricing of the CD-ROMs that a map library might seek to acquire. Prices range from a few pounds or dollars for route-planning disks to a thousand pounds or more for the UK census or the British Library map catalogue. Moreover some purchases are not restricted to a one-off payment, but involve licensing and networking fees, or charges for frequency of use. As with other digital data, the price of data on CD-ROM can be affected by governmental attitudes to data ownership and cost recovery (Chapter 12), the cost of data collection, and the nature and size of the target market. Many route planners, for example, are in a very competitive market and prices have been forced to low levels, but in some countries topographic and census data are marketed at a high price to facilitate full cost recovery. Issues concerning the educational and research use of such data at reasonable cost have not always been resolved.

CD-ROMs and the map curator's task

A recurring theme of this book is the map curator's place (assuming he or she still has a place) amidst the plethora of new technology. The introduction of map data on CD-ROM has brought with it many tasks and duties which also relate to digital data in general including those served on the web (Spiess, 1995). Users may need to be registered to have access to certain data, licences may be required, the pricing structure of data acquisition may restrict access to a single point of delivery, leading to potential congestion at the terminal and the need to book sessions in advance. Charges may have to be introduced to cover licence fees, or printing and hardware costs. Users may need to be shown how to download data on to other media, or how to save and print maps. Staff may need to serve as troubleshooters when there are hardware or software problems. The more sophisticated the package, the greater the learning curve and the level of instruction required. Tutorials, demonstrations and help menus may be provided on the disk, but often it is left to the map room staff to write or present something more closely adapted to user needs. Working against this necessity, however, are the increasingly user-friendly and intuitive characteristics of computer programs. Long gone are the days of the black screen and DOS interface.

Unfortunately for the map curator, the most useful CD-ROMs in a map library are likely to be the ones with the more complex programs, such as census mapping or climatic and terrain modelling and mapping packages, rich both in thematic data and software for exploratory data analysis and for map creation. As Slocum (1999) observes, with a sophisticated electronic atlas 'users can explore data in an interactive graphics environment', and it is this facility that most commends their use in an academic environment.

CD-ROMs and the Internet: is there a future for the medium?

In spite of the advantages of CD-ROM as a medium for maps and spatial data outlined earlier in this chapter, many of these advantages may already have been eclipsed by the Internet. Indeed, many new electronic atlases are being released on the net rather than as CDs, as for example the *Internet atlas of Switzerland* (**http://www.karto.ethz.ch/~an/atlas/**), and it is possible to find Internet equivalents of most of the kinds of CD outlined above. However, just as rumours of the death of printed paper map have proved premature, so this medium is likely to persist for some time yet. Many publishers are maximizing sales by producing both online and CD-ROM versions, vide the launch in 2000 of a commercially packaged CD-ROM version of the new *National atlas of the United States*. There are also hybrid productions in which core data stored on CD-ROM can be enhanced or updated from a complementary website.

One must always be cautious, however, about the longevity of a 'new' medium, such as the CD-ROM, which requires specific hardware and software to become operational. Already in the author's own institution, we have had to dispose of electronic maps on 3½ in. and 5¼ in. disks, and now find that some of our very latest CD-ROMs will not run on newly installed NT software.

To a degree, the CD-ROM could be regarded as a bridge connecting traditional paper-based mapping with the fluid and ever-changing medium of the web. It is also a medium that has helped (and can continue to help) the map curator enlarge his or her skills base. Conventional routes to a career in map librarianship have not usually involved an advanced training in computing or GIS, although recently many libraries in the USA have been advertising for GIS specialists, and established map curators have been retraining in certain GIS skills (Chapters 2, 4 and 5). But GIS is principally a tool for information processing and analysis, and not inherently a tool for creating good maps. In the digital environment, map library users may need a range of specialized help to get what they require from a digital product, whether offline or online, and this includes not only technical knowledge of GIS, but a firm grounding in how maps work. Self-contained mapping packages on CD-ROM still have a part to play in providing a gentler introduction to thematic map creation than having to import data into a fully functional GIS. Nevertheless they still call for an education in map design and the theoretical underpinnings of graphical representation. The introduction of offline mapping packages in the map library has been a pointer to expanded and challenging roles for the map curator in the new millennium.

References

Andrzejewska, M, Baranowski, M and Okonek, M (1999) Electronic atlases in Poland: concepts, development and the present status. In *The Polish cartography* 1999, Head Office of Geodesy and Cartography, 165–75.

Archer, D (2000) [Review of] The British Library map catalogue on CD-ROM, *Sheetlines*, **58**, 29–37.

Borchert, A (1999) Multimedia atlas concepts. In Cartwright, W, Peterson, M P and Gartner, G (eds) *Multimedia cartography*, Springer, 75–86.

Dymon, U J (1995) The potential of electronic atlases for geographic education, *Cartographic Perspectives*, **20**, 29–34.

Fox, J (1999) [Review of] The British Library map catalogue on CD-ROM, *Bulletin of the Society of Cartographers*, **33** (1), 41–2.

Heilig, G (1994) DemoGraphics: a graphical database and tool for population education, *Options*, Autumn, 8–9.

Kraak, M J and Ormeling, F J (1996) *Cartography: visualization of spatial data*, Longman.

Larsgaard, M L (1998) *Map librarianship: an introduction*, 3rd edn, Libraries Unlimited.

Maguire, D J (1989) *Computers in geography*, Longman.

Ormeling, F (1993) Ariadne's thread – structure in multimedia atlases, *Proceedings, 16th International Cartographic Conference, Cologne*, International Cartographic Association, **2**, 1093–100.

Parry, R B (1994) [Review of] Charting new worlds: maps of discovery, *Bulletin of the Society of Cartographers*, **28** (1), 56–7.

Parry, R B and Perkins, C R (2000) *World mapping today*, 2nd edn, Bowker-Saur.

Perkins, C R (1995) The electronic atlas, *GeoCal*, **13**, 10–15.

Perkins, C R and Parry, R B (1996) *Mapping the UK: maps and spatial data for the 21st century*, Bowker-Saur.

Rystedt, B (1995) Current trends in electronic atlas production, *Cartographic Perspectives*, **20**, 5–11.

Slocum, T A (1999) *Thematic cartography and visualization*, Prentice Hall.

Spiess, E (1995) Some problems with the use of electronic atlases, *LIBER Quarterly*, **5**, 235–44.

Taylor, D R F (1999) Future directions for multimedia cartography. In Cartwright, W, Peterson, M P and Gartner, G (eds) *Multimedia cartography*, Springer, 315–26.

Unwin, D (1991) CD-ROMs for teaching geography, *CTICG Newsletter*, **3**, 6–10.

Whistance-Smith, R (2000) [Review of] British Library map catalogue on CD-ROM, *ACMLA Bulletin*, **109**, 41–3.

Whyment, M (1998) Microsoft Encarta 97 World Atlas versus DeLorme Mappings' Global Explorer – a user's view, *The Cartographic Journal*, **35**, 95–8.

7
Maps and the Internet

Michael P Peterson

▶ *Maps are now transmitted from place to place over a network of computers called the Internet. Although in existence since the late 1960s, the introduction of the world wide web in the early 1990s made the Internet accessible to millions of people. The growth in the use of maps through the Internet has been particularly dramatic in the second half of the 1990s, but a variety of problems remain in making the Internet a suitable medium for cartography. For example, finding a particular map is still very difficult for the average user. The printing of large format maps is also a problem, as is the transmission of large files.*

Introduction

The medium of the Internet is redefining how maps are used. No longer restricted to paper, maps are now transmitted almost instantly and delivered to the user in a fraction of the time required to distribute maps on paper. Maps are viewed in a more timely fashion. Weather maps, for example, are updated continuously throughout the day. Most importantly, maps on the Internet are more interactive. They are accessed through a hyperlinking structure that makes it possible to engage the map user on a higher level than is possible with a map on paper. Finally, the Internet is making it possible to distribute more easily different kinds of cartographic displays such as animations. The Internet presents the map user with both a faster method of map distribution and different forms of mapping (Peterson, 1995, 1997a, 1997b, 1999).

The exact number of maps that are distributed through the Internet is difficult to determine. The electronic distribution of maps has increased drastically with the introduction of the world wide web in the early 1990s. A single web server operated by MapQuest.com, formerly GeoSystems and now a subsidiary of AOL Time-

Warner, responded to an average of over six million requests per day for user-defined maps during 1999. Web servers that distribute maps number in the tens of thousands. Given the rate at which maps are downloaded and the number of world wide web map servers, the web has become the major form of map distribution. The new medium has already had a major impact on the methods employed in digital mapping, especially methods of interactivity in the display of maps.

Examining how maps are distributed and used is important in understanding trends affecting cartography. Through the Internet, map users are interacting with maps in entirely new ways. The traditional cartographic products may have little meaning to these 'new' map users once they have been exposed to interactive mapping through the Internet. As cartographers and map librarians, it is important to understand how maps are used and the changing attitudes about maps and map-related products. For many applications, this new form of map distribution may serve as the best medium to communicate spatial information in an economical and efficient manner. Libraries, as storefronts to information, serve an important role in this new way of disseminating geographic information.

This chapter provides an overview of the Internet and the range of cartography-related uses that are provided by this new medium. It begins by examining the development of the Internet, the growth in its use and the current extent of worldwide usage. This is followed by an overview of the types of maps available through the Internet. The third section looks at the use of specific Internet technologies in cartography. This includes the use of search engines, map listings, online databases, methods of printing and the distribution of large format maps, as well as non-web Internet applications associated with mobile phones.

Development and use of the Internet

Background

The Internet has been described in many ways. In the simplest sense, it may be thought of as a system for transferring files between computers. These files, manipulated as numbers and ultimately stored and transferred in binary 0s and 1s, may consist of text, pictures, graphics, sound, animations, movies, or even computer programs. Defined in terms of hardware, the Internet may be thought of as a physical collection of computers, routers and high-speed communication lines. In terms of software, it is a network of computer networks that are based on the TCP/IP protocol. In terms of content, the Internet is a collection of shared resources. Finally, and most importantly, from a human standpoint, the Internet is a large and ever-expanding community of people who contribute to its content and who use its resources.

The beginnings of the Internet can be found in ARPANET – a computer network created for the Advanced Research Projects Agency and funded by the US Department of Defense. The initial purpose of the network was to help scientists work together and also to create a network with a redundantly linked structure that would continue to work even after a limited nuclear attack. The initial Network Control Protocol (NCP) was first implemented in 1969 between Stanford University, the University of California at Santa Barbara, and the University of Utah. ARPANET switched from the NCP protocol to the currently used TCP/IP (Transmission Control Protocol/Internet Protocol) on 1 January 1983. Many view this date as the beginning of the Internet.

The ARPANET model specified that data communication always occurs between a source and a destination computer. Further, the network connecting any two computers is assumed to be unreliable and could disappear at any moment. Sending data from computer to computer required that it be put in an 'envelope', called an Internet Protocol (IP) packet, with an appropriate 'address'. The computers – not the network – had the responsibility for routing the messages. All computers could communicate as a peer with any other computer. If a certain connection between two computers was inoperative, the computer would re-route the message to another computer that would attempt to 'deliver' the message.

Increasing demand on the network throughout the 1980s forced the US government to commission the National Science Foundation (NSF) to oversee the network. NSFNET was primarily designed to distribute the power of five research supercomputers that were located at major universities. More research and educational institutions were connected on a high-speed Internet 'backbone'. Eventually, Internet service providers expanded the network to include telephone access from homes, and more recently from mobile phones.

The Internet consists of a number of protocols including: 1) File Transfer Protocol (FTP) – for exchanging files between computers; 2) Telnet – a remote log-on procedure for accessing programs on remote computers as though they were local; 3) e-mail – an electronic mail system whereby one can exchange mail messages across the Internet; 4) newsgroups – discussion groups which distribute information to groups of users providing a forum for researchers; and 5) the world wide web – a graphical distributed hypermedia system that incorporates most aspects of the previous four services and delivers files with multiple media, including text, pictures, sound and animation.

The Internet does not rely on a single computer nor is it managed by any one entity. Rather, it is a system of computers and networks based on the single TCP/IP protocol that are linked together in a cooperative, non-centralized collaboration. The major Internet protocol, accounting for approximately 70% of Internet traffic, is the world wide web. Conceived at the European Particle Physics Laboratory (CERN) located near Geneva, Switzerland, in 1989, the web was intended to assist researchers in high energy physics research by linking related documents. Tim Berners-Lee played a large role in designing the system. The developers wanted to create a seamless network in which information from any source could be accessed in a simple and consistent way. Before the web, accessing the needed information required the use of many computer programs because of the incompatibility between different types of computers. The web introduced the principle of 'universal readership', which states that networked information should be accessible from any computer in any country with a single program. A prototype of the new protocol was finished in 1991 and was largely accepted by 1994. The system was quickly embraced because the web browsers could support the previous protocols for file exchange, including FTP, newsgroups and mail.

The popularity of the web can be measured by the quick adoption of the Mosaic web browser. Released in September 1993 for a variety of computer platforms by the National Center for Supercomputer Applications (NCSA) in Urbana, Illinois, the program was widely used in a matter of months. Implementing the hypermedia file-access structure, the program incorporated hypertext and hyperimages, to create links to other documents, either text or graphic. Mosaic has been superseded by other browsers but the basic hyperlinking, multimedia model that was implemented by the program remains the same.

The dramatic increase in the use of the Internet is also apparent in the growth of world wide web servers. In June of 1993 there were only 130 web servers. By mid-1995 there were 23,500 web servers and this had grown to 230,000 by 1996. In June 1998 there were 2.4 million web servers. Measured in terms of unique domain names, there were 29.7 million in January 1998. This had grown by 45% to 43.2 million by January 1999 (Thompson, 1999).

Internet use

The number of Internet users is growing rapidly as well. A report from April 2000, estimated that fully 106 million US adults, or 53% of the adult population, are connected to the web (Strategis Group, **http://www.thestandard.com**). This is up from approximately 80 million during 1998 (independent surveys performed by **www.intelliquest.com**; **www.mediamark.com**; **www.mediamatrix.com**). Usage

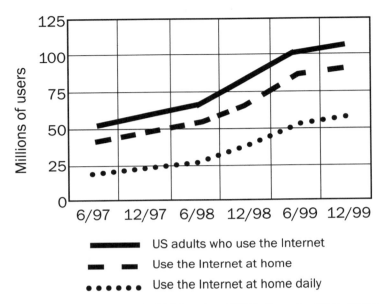

Fig. 7.1 *Growth of web usage in the USA from June 1997 to December 1999. Adoption of the Internet slowed somewhat during the second half of 1999 (after www.thestandard.net).*

continues to increase but has slowed since mid-1999 (see Figure 7.1).

The number of Internet users around the world is also growing. The Computer Industry Almanac has reported that by the year 2002, 490 million people around the world will have Internet access (**http://www.c-i-a.com/**). This is up from 61 million in 1996, 148 million in 1998 and 327 in 2000. Estimates for 2005 are 720 million. The top 15 countries will account for nearly 82% of the world-wide Internet users (including business, educational and home Internet users). It has been estimated that by the year 2000 there would be 25 countries where over 10% of the population were Internet users (**http://cyberatlas.internet.com/big_picture/geographics/**).

Access to the Internet varies considerably by country. A common definition of 'Internet access' is use of the Internet in the past week, but this is not consistently used for all countries. Table 7.1 shows the approximate populations that have Internet access. The percentage of people that have access to the Internet for the countries listed here varies from 70% in Iceland to 0.05% in Vietnam.

Table 7.1 *Internet access by country. Number of users is given in millions. The percentage of users is specific to the population of each country. Updated May 2000.*

Country	Number of users	Users, %	Country	Number of users	Users, %
Australia	4.20	25.00	Japan	32.40	27.00
Austria	0.50	4.90	Malaysia	0.25	1.10
Belgium	1.40	17.50	Mexico	1.00	1.05
Brazil	7.50	4.60	Norway	2.20	61.00
Canada	11.40	44.00	Netherlands	2.30	18.60
China	8.90	7.40	Portugal	0.20	1.90
Denmark	1.75	33.00	Saudi Arabia	0.10	0.50
Egypt	0.40	0.60	Singapore	0.25	6.40
Finland	2.10	43.00	Slovak Rep.	0.51	9.50
France	4.00	7.00	South Africa	1.80	9.40
Germany	24.00	30.00	Sri Lanka	1.00	5.30
Iceland	0.19	70.00	Sweden	3.50	50.00
India	1.00	1.00	Taiwan	3.00	14.30
Ireland	0.60	2.00	UK	18.80	32.00
Israel	0.50	10.00	USA	135.70	50.30
Italy	9.00	15.00	Vietnam	0.04	0.05

Internet maps

The major reason that maps have found their way on to the Internet is cost. It is simply less expensive to make maps available through the Internet than it is to print them on paper. When the additional costs of colour printing and distribution of the maps are factored into the printed product, the cost advantages of sending maps through the Internet become even more apparent.

In addition to cost, a major advantage of the medium for cartography is that it allows more interactive forms of mapping (Peterson, 1995). Among the different types of maps on the web, it is the interactive sites that have gained the most interest and financing. Interactive mapping sites allow the user to change the scale or otherwise alter the view. The most popular of the interactive sites are those that make street or road maps (see Figure 7.2). These sites make it possible to create a customized street map of a city centred on a user-specified address, or plan an itinerary for travelling between cities.

Another advantage of the Internet for cartography is the distribution of maps

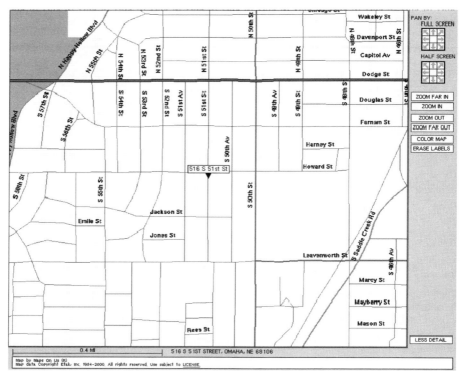

Fig. 7.2 *An example of a street map from an interactive mapping website (from* **www.mapsonus.com**).

that are frequently updated. Among these are weather maps, maps depicting the current sun position relative to the earth, and traffic patterns. These maps indicate the potential of the medium to display maps that are always current. The web also supports the distribution of animated maps that can depict change over time or simulate flying over a terrain.

Internet map use

Monitoring map use on the Internet is difficult. There is no coordinated method for counting the number of maps that are downloaded. Beyond this, of course, there is no way to determine if the maps are effectively utilized once downloaded. A centralized 'counter' has been proposed to at least keep track of all maps that are distributed through this new medium, but it would be difficult to coordinate the thousands of sites that distribute maps (Peterson, 1997a).

Commercial map sites that accept advertising represent a major source of data on web map usage. These sites maintain accurate statistics on the number of 'hits' their sites receive and independent auditing companies verify these numbers. The reason that these data are maintained is to attract advertising revenue. The more hits a site receives, the more it can charge a potential advertiser. However, these hit data are now themselves a commodity and are sold to companies that will only share the information with potential advertising customers.

Non-commercial sites are more open with the amount of usage that they receive. The Xerox Parc mapping site (Xerox Parc, 1999), an early example of interactive mapping on the web, maintains a page that has tracked usage since it began operating in 1993. A single Sun SPARCstation 2 computer averages over 90,000 map requests daily (see Figure 7.3). Usage has levelled off since 1996, most likely because of slow server response and competition from other interactive map sites. One can also notice a somewhat cyclical trend based on the school schedule. A decrease in usage corresponds to the summer vacation months in North America.

Other popular interactive mapping sites also report a considerable amount of

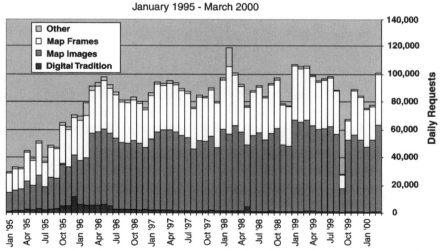

Fig. 7.3   *Xerox Parc site usage from January 1995 to March 2000. Usage has levelled off since 1996. This may be because of server response times, due to a combination of a slow computer and slow Internet access (after* **http://pubweb.parc.xerox.com/mapdocs/ usage.html**).

95

usage. The Tiger Mapping Service operated by the US Census Bureau responds to 70,000 map requests a day (Stuber, 1999; US Census Bureau, 1999). The Earth-View site produced an average of 68,000 maps a day during 1999 (Walker, 1999). Monitoring Internet map usage is an indication of the types of maps that are in most demand by users.

Finding maps

There are three basic tools for finding maps on the Internet: search engines, lists and databases. The use of all three takes a certain amount of training in the use of the Internet. More lists and databases also need to be developed so that maps can more easily be found.

Search engines

A search engine is a method of indexing and finding material on the web. It consists of two basic programs. The first program examines web pages and creates an index based on a defined set of keywords. The second program responds to user 'keyword' requests to this index. A particular keyword may return a large number of matches. The matches are sorted based on a variety of criteria but are usually a function of how often the particular keyword is included in the document.

Search engines work continuously. One of the most powerful search engines on the web is AltaVista, originally developed by the Digital Equipment Corporation. By the mid-1990s its search engine indexed material – 'crawled the web' – at a rate of three million pages a day. The debut for AltaVista was December 1995. At the time it had indexed 16 million web pages. Five months later the index had grown to more than 30 million pages and the site was receiving 12 million daily keyword requests. By early 1999, it had indexed 150 million pages. The purpose of the search engine is not only to find new material but also to update the location of existing pages. The use of search engines can be frustrating, particularly for people who are accustomed to the relative order of a library, but they represent the only automated approach to indexing the large number of pages that make up the web.

Depending on the keyword entered, a search engine may return a large number of documents. For example, a search with the keyword 'maps' in 1999 using AltaVista returned over five million matches. This means that the search engine found this number of text documents that contained the word 'maps'. There are many ways of limiting the search to a more specific topic but the syntax for doing so varies between different search engines. In AltaVista, for example, a search on 'maps&world' (also in 1999), in which only documents are found that contain both words, resulted in only about 1000 hits. Effectively 'surfing the web' requires a good working knowledge of several search engines.

Search engines have yet to index all of the pages on the web. Northernlight.com now claims it has indexed the largest number of pages. However, it estimates it has only found 37% of web pages that are in existence (cf Chapter 8).

Another problem with search engines is that they key on text documents. Some search engines include an option to find only files that are in the picture file formats of GIF and JPEG. However, there is no specific file format associated with maps. A solution to finding maps on the Internet is to require that all maps on the web be accompanied by a metafile that both describes the map and points to its location. A special search engine could then index all of these metafiles. Map libraries could have a major role to play in the metafile process. An incentive to making the system work would be for search engines to index only those maps that were accompanied by a metafile.

Map lists

A list is a manually compiled set of resources that are provided in a hyperlinked format. An example is the page that was originally developed by Mark MacLennan for the University of Iowa Center for Global and Regional Environmental Research (**http://www.cgrer.uiowa.edu/servers/servers_references.html**). The page categorizes a list of maps by region (USA, World, Foreign Countries) and map type (Interactive, Historical). The US maps are sub-categorized by national, state, regional and city maps. The 'Foreign Countries' link is divided into national and city maps. Interactive maps are sub-categorized by type (General, Java, VRML, Animations). There are also links to map libraries, historical map exhibits and collections, tutorials about maps and mapmaking, map stores and resellers, online atlases, geographic references and gazetteers, and searchable bibliographies.

The major problem with lists of this type is that they need to be constantly maintained. New material is added every day to the Internet and other links become inactive. Maintaining such a page is a tedious and time-consuming process. Programs are available to identify dead links but few other resources help make the job easier. Of course, the use of search engines is necessary both to find new links and determine the new address for a site that has been moved.

In one sense, the personal bookmark listing of a web browser can also be viewed as a links page. Categorizing these links and making them available is a way of both organizing the web for yourself and communicating about available resources to others. Assembling a large number of personal links pages into one large page is a way of sharing information. This type of 'shared bookmarks page' could be done among professionals in any particular field, and many map libraries are already doing this.

Online map databases

The best-known example of an online map database is the one compiled by Roelof P Oddens, the map curator at the Faculty of Geographical Sciences at the University of Utrecht in the Netherlands (**http://oddens.geog.uu.nl/ main.html**). Early in 2001, the site had over 12,500 cartographic links. As opposed to a list, the user can search an online database. An integrated search function accepts a key-word and the user is allowed to limit the search by the following categories: region or country, maps and atlases, sellers of cartographic material, map collections, carto- and geoservers, cartographic and geographical societies, departments of cartography, government cartography, libraries, literature, gazetteers and tourist sites.

What is most amazing about the Oddens site is that it is done with fairly easy-to-use computer software and hardware. FileMaker Pro is used for the database on an Apple Macintosh computer. It is important when setting up an online database to use software and equipment that are not overly complex and can be easily maintained. While much more sophisticated and expensive equipment is available to support this type of online database, it will not be functional if it is too complex to set up and maintain.

Internet maps for printing

The printing of maps from the Internet is necessary because of portability. A major use of maps is for outside activities such as fieldwork or hiking and mountaineering. Because of the Internet, fewer maps are being printed and the real possibility exists that suitable printed maps may no longer be available, or only available at much higher prices.

The printing of maps obtained through the Internet presents several problems. The major problem is that the resolution required for the screen (72 dpi) is far less than that required by printers (300 dpi or higher). Any map designed for the screen will not make a suitable print and vice versa. Another problem is that the size of the printed map can vary between printers. As a result, scale cannot be maintained and the numeric scales including the representative fraction and the verbal scale are rendered meaningless. The bar scale is the only type of expression of map scale that can still be used. Colours also appear differently on different printers, raising similar concerns about maintaining the integrity of the map.

These problems are not unique to cartography. Online stores that sell clothes, for example, will certainly want a system that shows the colours of garments correctly so that customers are not disappointed when they receive the item. Some high-end printers already incorporate colour calibration software. Depicting the size of objects correctly will be another concern in the commercial sector. Market forces will demand better standards for the display of their products, which will, in turn, benefit the display of all types of graphics, including maps.

The printing of large format maps presents another problem. Small colour printers are common and are used extensively for the printing of maps, but printing large-format maps is difficult. The Remote Replication System from 3M Corporation (**http://www.mmm.com/front/bosnia/index.html**) solves this problem by combining a large-format, ink-jet printer, specialized paper and a print engine. This system was developed by 3M for the Defense Mapping Agency to produce detailed maps for military and other uses. It uses an alternative to full colour screen-printed graphics to produce highly accurate, computer-generated maps in a short amount of time. However, the rasterized file required by the system is enormous and cannot be easily transmitted through the Internet. Plans are being made to maintain the basic information on CD-ROM or DVD and only transmit the changes by Internet. The system demonstrates that high-quality, large-format maps can be printed one at a time, and this method of printing can at least be aided by the Internet.

File compression methods have been introduced to make the distribution of large raster files more possible through the Internet. A format that is already being used for the compression of scanned maps is MrSID, a software product that both reduces the size of rasterized files, and makes these files viewable through the Internet. The MrSID encoding technology patented by the Seattle-based LizardTech company (**www.lizard-tech.com**) significantly reduces the size of large high-resolution images to a fraction of their original file size while maintaining the original image quality and integrity. The compression achieved by MrSID is in the order of approximately 50:1. A 23 Mb file can be reduced to 513 Kb. The free browser plug-in makes it possible to zoom, pan and print the image. This technology may make the printing of large format maps possible through the Internet.

This technology makes a totally digital map library conceivable, where users can peruse the collection via computer monitor and then select which maps to print (or which maps to save in a digital format). The conversion of maps to digital formats is advantageous for both the preservation and distribution of maps. In addition, it makes an all-digital map library more possible – a library of maps that can be viewed by anyone with an Internet connection.

Mobile mapping

There has been a dramatic increase in the use of mobile phones since 1990, and the Wireless Application Protocol (WAP) now provides Internet access from mobile phones. Begun by Unwired Planet, and the mobile phone manufacturers – Motorola, Nokia and Ericsson – WAP is a standard for wireless content delivery on the next generation of mobile phones that include a small screen. The advantage of WAP is that you don't need a computer to access the Internet. WAP phones have been designed to allow users to read news and monitor share prices. Other intended uses are television and cinema listings, cash machine locations and information about traffic congestion or train times. Gartner (2000) has suggested that a combination of maps and verbal instructions to assist in wayfinding could be delivered from WAP sites.

Industry estimates are that within a few years there will be more people using WAP phones to access the Internet than are using computers through a wired network. This is partly due to cost. It has already been noted that it is less expensive to build up a wireless telephone network than a wired network. It is forecast that there will be 1.2 billion mobile phone users in the world by 2003, with about half using phones to access the Internet. In comparison, there will be about 550 million computer users. Internet access is bound to migrate to phones.

WAP includes a set of protocols that covers the whole process of wireless content delivery: from the definition of WML (wireless markup language) and WMLScript for creation and layout of the actual content. It also incorporates the specification of security measures. Its Wireless Transport Layer Security (WTLS) allows full strength security in WAP client and server applications.

WAP has many similarities to the Internet set of technologies. For instance, the Wireless Markup Language used to create WAP pages is very similar to the HTML used to create web pages. Similarly, the WMLScript is based on JavaScript. It should be noted that both WML and WMLScript are adapted and optimized for a wireless environment (eg compression to save bandwidth).

There are still a limited number of computers that specifically distribute documents for WAP phones using the Wireless Markup Language. Attempts have been made to convert HTML documents to WML automatically, but human involvement is still necessary to design text and graphics properly for small displays. The primary challenge here is to miniaturize maps in such a way that they remain a useful display. The secondary challenge is to support the establishment of WAP-specific map servers. Map libraries may have a role to play in making maps available to the public using this technology, and WAP servers within libraries could distribute maps of the local area.

Conclusion

More than any other technological development in the past century, the Internet forces us to examine the purpose of cartography and our means of map distribution. The Internet has changed how maps are distributed and used on a world-wide basis, and it is apparent that the Internet has already improved the distribution of maps. If done properly, the Internet also has the potential to improve the quality of maps as a form of communication, thereby influencing both the mental representations that people have of the world and how people mentally process ideas about spatial relationships. The increased access to spatial information has implications for all countries (Crampton, 1998), even those with limited connections to the Internet, but a considerable amount of work still needs to be done to expand the network and improve methods of map distribution and map interaction.

The Internet, and particularly the web, have established themselves as a major form of map distribution. It is vital to understand how these maps are being used and whether map usage will become more interactive. Certainly, the possibility exists that users will eventually not accept the use of static maps, but it is also possible that the use of static maps on paper will increase after people have become accustomed to using maps on the Internet.

References

Crampton, J (1998) The convergence of spatial technologies, *Cartographic Perspectives*, **30**, 3–6.

Gartner, G (2000) *WAP phones for mapping*, paper given at Workshop on Internet Mapping, 15 March 2000, Munich, Germany. Not published.

Peterson, M P (1995) *Interactive and animated cartography*, Prentice Hall.

Peterson, M P (1997a) Cartography and the Internet: introduction and research agenda, *Cartographic Perspectives*, **26**, 3–12.

Peterson, M P (1997b) Trends in Internet map use, *Proceedings of the 18th Interna-*

tional Cartographic Conference, Stockholm, Sweden, **3**, 1635–42.

Peterson, M P (1999) Trends in Internet map use: a second look, *Proceedings of the 19th International Cartographic Conference, Ottawa, Canada*, 571–80.

Stuber, C (1999) Personal communication, 10 March.

Thompson, M J (1999) Spinning an ever-widening web, *The Industry Standard*, (1 March) available at **www.thestandard.net/metrics/display/0,1283,848,00.html**.

US Census Bureau (1999) *Tiger mapping site FAQ*, available at **http://tiger.census.gov/faq.html**.

Walker, J (1999) Personal communication, 1 March.

Xerox Parc (1999) *Parc map site FAQ*, available at **http://pubweb.parc.xerox.com/mapdocs/usage.html**.

8
Web resources and the map library

Menno-Jan Kraak

The world wide web offers many opportunities for disseminating and accessing maps and geospatial data, and has changed the nature of map use. This chapter discusses the nature of maps on the web, and outlines their advantages and current limitations. They offer a freedom to interact with geospatial data that is not available in the traditional map library. The map library must engage in these changes. Although the web can operate as a virtual map library, it needs organizing. Ways of finding maps and geospatial data on the web are discussed. Map libraries have a role in providing organized access to web mapping, supplying metadata about data sets, and linking their traditional resources to web data.

Introduction

The world wide web has become a new and highly important medium for disseminating and accessing geospatial data. It offers data providers a relatively cheap method of distributing their products, including geospatial data sets and maps. The product needs to be created only once, while many users can access it. If necessary, access can be controlled, limiting it to subscribing customers only, for example. It is also possible for providers to produce an incomplete product that can be finished according to user demands. Through the web, users can have relatively easy access to interactive maps and geospatial data sets.

Here the words 'geospatial data' and 'maps' have to be clarified. In literature the terms can sometimes be used interchangeably; in this chapter they cannot. Maps are visualizations of geospatial data. This chapter will explain the function maps can have on the world wide web in general as well as in the context of a map library. In today's world of geospatial data handling and in map libraries there is an increasing demand for geospatial data sets, both in addition to and instead of maps, since these can be used in GIS software directly.

Why is the web an interesting medium for presenting and disseminating geospatial data? The answer is that information on the web is virtually platform-independent, unrivalled in its capacity to reach many users at minimal costs and easy to update frequently. Furthermore and more particularly in relation to maps, it allows for a dynamic and interactive dissemination of geospatial data, offering new mapping techniques and possibilities of use not seen before with traditional printed maps, such as multimedia integration.

What is the function of a map library in this context? Why would someone visit a map library or query its catalogue, if one can, somehow, consider the web to be a global map library accessible from any computer linked to the Internet? Answers to these questions are needed if one wants to evaluate the role of the web with respect to a map library. Do we still need map libraries, as we know them? Web maps could be considered virtual map library items. They save storage and the map library catalogue system could offer a structured access to the map jungle in cyberspace. Additionally the map library might give information on their usefulness and quality.

Map libraries have to recognize the changing nature of map use in this context. The web can be characterized as a medium associated with interaction and dynamics and map users now have different, more time sensitive questions to ask (Elzakker, 2000). From this perspective it should also be noted that most maps on the web are created on demand. Contents change depending on the nature of the questions asked, and users have a great flexibility in creating and re-creating their own maps by browsing the data available. This freedom is less likely to be found in a traditional map library which comprises mainly paper maps stored in drawers, and which probably restricts users from browsing these drawers themselves.

Maps on the web can play multiple roles (see Figure 8.1). They can function as they have always done and, as an abstraction of geographic reality, be used to explain geospatial relations and patterns. This can be done by the presentation of a static map, or by offering an interactive framework for exploration (MacEachren and Kraak, 1997; Kraak and MacEachren, 1999). They can also be used as a metaphor, and as such function as an index to other information. The hyperlinked nature of the web allows this information to be of a geographical or non-geographical nature. To particular map elements one can link other, more detailed maps, geospatial data sets, drawings, photographs, text, and videos or animations. The location of this additional information can be anywhere in cyberspace. With respect to geospatial data, the maps can be used as a preview to the data to be acquired.

Alternatively the map can also be used as part of a search engine. This is especially relevant in a geospatial data infrastructure (GSDI) where users look, for

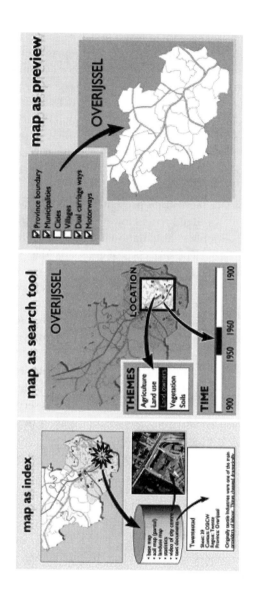

Fig. 8.1 The role maps can play on the world wide web

instance, for agricultural data from a particular geographical region for a specific time period. Using the map to add the locational part of the search criteria will be helpful to the users, while the actual search takes place based on metadata descriptions (see Chapter 9). This type of map use can be found in some traditional map libraries as well, where the map functions as the prime element in the map library's user interface to its cataloguing system. In a web environment, search results could be references to either internal map library items or external items; an example of this use is the Alexandria Digital Library (see below).

The web could be regarded as the new face of the map library, allowing in most situations more user interaction than in more traditional systems. However, traditional map libraries might have a more organized access mechanism available, and a combination of services will probably point to the future of map libraries.

One of the claims for disseminating maps and geospatial data via the web is that they can be more up-to-date than when presented on other media. From a technological perspective this is indeed true. However, simply putting their products on to the web will not suddenly enable national mapping agencies, for example, to make them more up-to-date! The processes of geospatial data collection and map production have to be adapted so that those organizations can indeed offer timely information. Web users, of whom many are new map users, may not be impressed when a website indicates that the age of the data is only two years old!

Some disadvantages of web maps that any environment has to consider are limitations due to current technology. Among these are problems with the physical size of the geospatial data sets and maps, and access to the websites. The size of screens and the design of web pages are limiting factors, and one also has to consider the size of the files to be downloaded, because Internet bandwidth is still limited (see also Chapter 7). The technological environment used, such as server–client concepts, plays an important role as well, but goes beyond the remit of this chapter (Köbben, 2000). Access to the web is globally rather unbalanced with good connectivity in North America, Western Europe, Japan and Australia, and a less favourable situation in the rest of the world.

Interactivity might be described as part of the democratization of cartography (Morrison, 1997), but because of this, geospatial data and map providers cannot be sure how their map product will look at the site of the user. The web cannot guarantee an effective cartographic product. This is due, for instance, to the display of colours in web browsers: and only when the limited web-safe colour palette is used can one be certain how the end-user will see the map colours. Since the products are increasingly offered in accordance with user demands, providers allow the users to create or design their own maps by offering them a wide selection of symbols and tools to choose from. The book *Web cartography* gives an overview of all these aspects and their implications (Kraak and Brown, 2000, **http://kartoweb.itc.nl/webcartography/webbook/**).

Appearance and nature of web maps

To be able to play the roles shown in Figure 8.1, maps on the web require a specific environment and functionality. Based on the way they can be used, they can be classified into two main categories as shown in Figure 8.2.

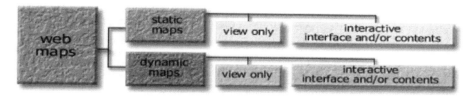

Fig. 8.2   *Web map classification system (Kraak and Brown, 2000)*

The scheme distinguishes between static and dynamic web maps. Each of these categories is further subdivided into view-only and interactive maps. The map most commonly found on the web is the static view-only map. Often the sources for these web maps are original cartographic products, which are scanned and put on the web as bitmaps using formats such as GIF and JPEG. This form of presentation can be very useful for map libraries to show their treasured items (eg **http://www.nls.ac.uk/digitallibrary/map/frame_map. htm**), such as old maps; or maps could be selected to highlight the particular specialization of the library, such as items from regional collections or items that demonstrate the library's thematic orientation. This approach can also be used to make historical maps more widely accessible, as at a site where rare maps by the famous Dutch cartographer Blaeu can be viewed (**http://odur.let.rug.nl/~welling/maps/blaeu.html**) or at the site of The Netherlands Royal Library (**http://seagull.konbib.nl/atlas**). Often maps like these can otherwise only be seen and studied in the archives of libraries and map collections. The web offers these institutions the opportunity to share their cartographic heritage. Similarly, map sellers, auctioneers or national mapping agencies can show samples of their products on the web, and sell them via e-commerce (see Chapter 16). A problem with many of the static view-only maps is that they have not been designed for the web, but have been scanned from atlases or other paper maps. Because of this their information density will be high and the maps may not be readable or the files will be large and will be slow to download to the user's site.

Static maps can also be interactive. With these so-called 'clickable' maps, the map can function as an interface to other data. Clicking on a geographic object can lead to other information sources on the web (eg **http://www.nationalgeographic. com/mapmachine**). These might be other maps, images or other web pages. In a map library the clickable maps could be a digital version of the index maps or be part of the regional entry to the catalogue. Interactivity could also mean the user has the option to zoom and pan, or it could allow the user to define the contents of the web map by switching layers off or on (**http://tiger.census.gov/cgi-bin/mapsurfer**). The images on display are still in GIF or JPEG format. If a map library stores geospatial data sets this could be a means of allowing visitors to get an impression of the data available. Many GIS vendors offer web-mapping solutions that allow users to look at the data and execute simple operations as just described (eg *Autodesk* **http://www3.autodesk.com/adsk/** and *ESRI* **http://www.esri.com/**).

The world wide web has several options for displaying dynamic data via animations. The so-called animated GIF can be seen as the view-only version of the dynamic maps. Several bitmaps, each representing a frame of the animation, are positioned after each other and the web browser will continuously repeat the animation. Famous (or notorious) examples are the commonly used spinning globes (**http://www.geog.fu-berlin.de/globes/index.html**). Other applications are maps to depict the aspects of the weather for example such as radar maps of rainfall (**http://weerkamer.nl/radar/**), or other time-sensitive topics. Slightly more interactive versions of this type of map are those to be displayed by media players, in AVI, MPEG or Quicktime format. Plugins to the web browser define the interaction options, which are often limited to simple pause, backward and forward operations. An application in the map library, although rather laborious, could be to show for some areas a time series of map detail of, for instance, available city plans or topographic map sheets. This would allow the user to get an idea of historic developments.

Interactive dynamics can be created by Java, JavaScript or via virtual environments in VRML or QuicktimeVR. VRML especially offers opportunities to define the travel path, or to make decisions on directions and height in a three-dimensional data set (eg **http://flightinfo.schiphol.nl/engine/index_def.html?lang=en&page_nr=590?**). A map library application could be to provide a model of its rooms and layout, allowing potential visitors to take a simulated walk around the place before a visit. Furthermore, such an interactive map can incorporate links and thus becomes a more interactive 'clickable animation'.

Most of the web maps discussed above are delivered in bitmap format, but this is not necessarily a disadvantage. Since they are based on digital geospatial data, links can be maintained with the original and other data. The map image can be kept relatively simple, and as such will be easier to download, but behind the map's symbols a whole world of geospatial data can be hidden. For instance mouse-over techniques allow text or imagery to appear only when the mouse pointer is moved over a particular symbol (**http://www.waterland.net/rikz/waterstand/**). Geospatial data sets can be downloaded fully for subsequent use in a GIS. Large format paper maps can be downloaded as well, if map providers prepare their maps in PDF format. This format ensures that printed output looks like any other printed map. Maps in PDF format can of course also include links to other web pages or data sets. The National Parks Service of the United States offers maps like these (**http://www.nps.gov/carto/data.html**).

What are typical web map applications? Browsing the web reveals that these are often related to time-sensitive topics such as weather and traffic, and to topics that provide maps for quick one-off use. There are maps that give answers to questions such as 'Where is?' or 'How do I get from A to B?'. Tourism is one of the sectors that have many, still simple, web map applications that are designed to answer these kinds of questions.

Where to find (web) maps and/or geospatial data sets

Assuming the web can be considered a map library, how would one find a particular map or geospatial data set? A number of different solutions may be identified: using search engines, browsing maintained lists and databases, visiting digital map libraries, querying dedicated sites or using the national geospatial data infrastructure.

Finding and using search engines

If someone tries to find something on the web it is very likely a search engine will be used. The most common engines use programs like spiders or crawlers to hunt for keywords to index the web, while others rank websites based on the number of hits or authority. This last approach is based on the number of pointers referring to that particular website. Table 8.1 gives the results of a query to several cartographic items using different general search engines. The keywords were 'maps', 'atlas', 'map library', 'digital map library', 'geospatial data', 'clearinghouse', 'cartography' and 'gis'. From the table it becomes clear that there are differences between the search engines. The table shows that simply using a single keyword like 'map' will not be very helpful, since the number of hits will also include non-cartographic products or services that use the word; think of the mathematical meaning of mapping or its metaphorical use in 'sitemap' referring to the website contents. Of course, results can be improved if more advanced queries are composed.

Table 8.1   *Using search engines to find maps and geospatial data (as of 25 May 2000)*

Search term	Northern Light[1]	AltaVista[2]	Google[3]	Lycos[4]	Infoseek[5]
maps	10,965,477	6,073,460	564,998	850,264	1,378,821
atlas	821,869	1,578,530	245,000	171,435	144,645
map library	16,134	17,715	16,100	207,070	2,413
digital map library	1,336	640	431	25,047	247
geospatial data	20,501	20,684	12,398	6,185	3,367
clearinghouse	351,994	352,425	10,800	79,458	71,855
cartography	77,829	95,150	37,999	14,038	26,035
gis	556,493	1,119,280	195,999	9,335	112,308

[1] http://www.northernlight.com   [2] http://www.altavista.com   [3] http://www.google.com/
[4] http://www.lycos.com/   [5] http://infoseek.go.com/

The problem remains that search results point you to particular websites, but without sufficient indication of how useful they will be. An interesting task for map librarians would be to provide metadata about the sites, to give the searcher a better chance to judge their utility (see Chapter 9).

Another limitation of search engines is that, despite more intelligent search and indexing methods, they keep track of a smaller and smaller part of the ever-growing world wide web (see also Chapter 7).

Finding and using lists and databases

Some organizations keep track of lists of links to relevant cartographic material. An interesting example is *Oddens' Bookmarks* (**http://oddens.geog.uu.nl/index. html**). Currently Roelof Oddens, map librarian at Utrecht University, keeps a searchable database comprising, early in 2001, over 12,500 links to 'cartographic' websites. Maintaining such a list immediately reveals the horror of the web. Web links change continuously: web pages appear and disappear, while web servers are upgraded and change their URLs. However, so-called web agents or robots exist that automatically detect the availability of particular web links or a change in the

web page itself. Adding new sites to lists like these is done more or less random-
ly, using the above search engines, via web links available on sites already found,
or by the request of website managers.

Finding and using online map libraries

Online digital map libraries do exist, the prime example being the Alexandria Digital Library Project (Buttenfield and Goodchild, 1996; Buttenfield, 1997). This aims
'to deliver comprehensive library services to browse and retrieve georeferenced digital data distributed via the Internet'. Users can search the Alexandria Digital Library
via a dedicated graphical interface, as shown in Figure 8.3.

Following recent trends, the Alexandria Digital Library has now a follow-up in
the Alexandria Digital Earth Prototype (ADEPT) (**http://alexandria.sdc.
ucsb.edu/adept/adept.html**). Its current aim is 'to use the digital earth metaphor
for organizing, using, and presenting information at all levels of spatial and temporal resolution'.

Finding and using dedicated sites

To find a map showing particular locations or a map that explains a specific geospatial pattern, one would try to access an atlas. Depending on the nature of the question, there are available reference atlases, school atlases, topographic atlases, national
atlases and thematic atlases, as well as many atlases available online. An example of
the latter is the online *Encyclopedia Britannica* (**http://www.britannica.com**). Its clickable maps function as an entry to the encyclopedia articles, when available, of the
geographical elements on the maps. Some web atlases are derived from CD-ROM
editions such as *Encarta* (**http://encarta.msn.com/maps/mapview.asp**). Others
offer details down to street level (eg *MapQuest* **http://www.mapquest.com/**). The
national atlas displaying a nation's physical and socio-economic geography has an
interesting role to play on the web. Such atlases can be part of the national geospatial data infrastructure, for example those from Canada (**http://www.atlas. gc.ca/
english/index.html**) and the USA (**http://www.nationalatlas.gov/**) (see also Chapter 5). As such they can even be part of a geospatial world wide web search engine,
offering another entrance to geospatial data organized via a clearing-house.

Finding and using geospatial data infrastructures

More oriented towards geospatial data sets are the websites that belong to a

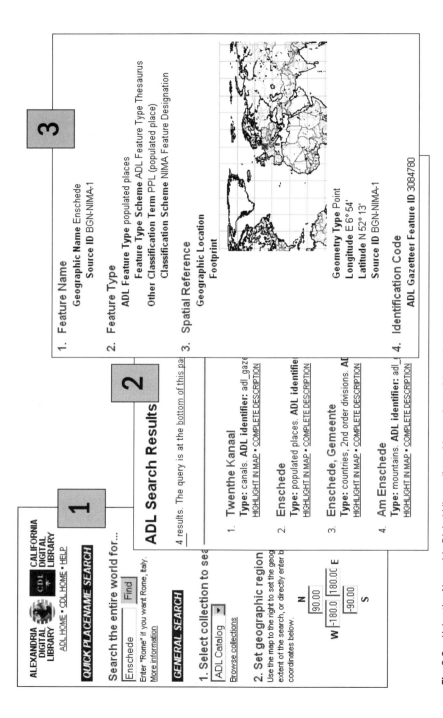

1

ALEXANDRIA
DIGITAL
LIBRARY   CDL   CALIFORNIA
DIGITAL
LIBRARY

ADL HOME • CDL HOME • HELP

QUICK PLACENAME SEARCH

Search the entire world for...

Enschede   [Find]

Enter "Rome" if you want Rome, Italy.
More information

GENERAL SEARCH

1. Select collection to se

ADL Catalog ▼
Browse collections

2. Set geographic region

Use the map to the right to set the geog
extent of the search, or directly enter b
coordinates below.

N
90.00
W -180.0 | 180.0 E
-90.00
S

2

ADL Search Results

4 results. The query is at the <u>bottom of this pa</u>

1. **Twenthe Kanaal**
    Type: canals. **ADL identifier:** adl_gaze
    HIGHLIGHT IN MAP • COMPLETE DESCRIPTION

2. **Enschede**
    Type: populated places. **ADL identifier**
    HIGHLIGHT IN MAP • COMPLETE DESCRIPTION

3. **Enschede, Gemeente**
    Type: countries, 2nd order divisions. **Al**
    HIGHLIGHT IN MAP • COMPLETE DESCRIPTION

4. **Am Enschede**
    Type: mountains. **ADL identifier:** adl_
    HIGHLIGHT IN MAP • COMPLETE DESCRIPTION

3

1. **Feature Name**
    Geographic Name Enschede
    Source ID BGN-NIMA-1

2. **Feature Type**
    ADL Feature Type populated places
    Feature Type Scheme ADL Feature Type Thesaurus
    Other Classification Term PPL (populated place)
    Classification Scheme NIMA Feature Designation

3. **Spatial Reference**
    Geographic Location
    Footprint

    Geometry Type Point
    Longitude E 6° 54'
    Latitude N 52° 13'
    Source ID BGN-NIMA-1

4. **Identification Code**
    ADL Gazetteer Feature ID 3084780

Fig. 8.3 *Using the Alexandria Digital Library (http://www.alexandria.ucsb.edu/adl.html)*

country's national geospatial data infrastructure (NGDI, **http://fgdc.er. usgs.gov/index.html**). As stated by the US Federal Geographic Data Committee, an NGDI is not just about the physical infrastructure. It 'encompasses policies, standards, and procedures for organizations to cooperatively produce and share geographic data'. This brings together cooperation between governments, the academic community and the private sector. Instrumental in the NGDI is the clearing-house. This aims to become a 'Geoplaza', a sort of shopping mall for all available spatial data. In other words it functions as a portal to the geospatial data of participating data providers. Currently however, most clearinghouses do not provide service to this level and only serve as useful shop fronts. Their web pages should allow the user to select a location and a theme, be given an overview of the data on offer, and give links to the providers (**http://www.fgdc.gov/clearinghouse/clearinghouse. html**). Maps can play any of the roles indicated in Figure 8.1. While the geospatial data retrieved may come to the user in map form, maps can also be part of the searching mechanism or offer a preview of the geospatial data to be downloaded.

Trends

Several trends in web mapping can be distinguished. Some of them are purely technological while others are more related to the organization of information flows. The first drive the future, the second bring the new opportunities to the masses. Many recent and future developments can be followed at the site of the World Wide Web Consortium (WC3, **http://www.w3.org/Graphics/SVG**). In relation to maps for instance, the developments related to the Scalable Vector Graphics are worth keeping an eye on.

One of the current technological revolutions brings the power of the Internet to Personal Digital Assistants (PDA), which increasingly include mobile phone capabilities (see also Chapter 7). Wireless Application Protocols (WAP) are used to realize the data transfer. The use of this application will really take off when the new Universal Mobile Telecommunications Systems (UTMS) frequencies can be used, since they overcome much of the narrow bandwidth problem that currently limits sending maps and other multimedia elements such as pictures and videos from one device to another. It will certainly increase the demand for web maps and at the same time force providers to present all Internet data, including maps, much more efficiently than is done at present.

Let us consider an example based on one of the typical web map user questions: 'How do I get from A to B?'. It demonstrates how map data providers can play the role of content providers to Internet infrastructure (Figure 8.4). With the above

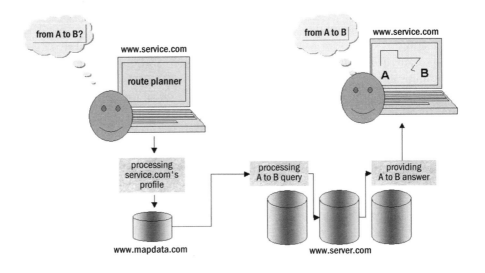

Fig. 8.4 *Organizing geospatial data flow: processing a query*

question a user visits a website that offers a route planner. There are many such sites that add route planners as an additional service to their core business. It could be an insurance company, the yellow pages, or even a map library. After the question is entered it is passed to the site of the map data provider. Here the query will be processed based on the profile of the website from which the request was sent. This profile holds specifics that could influence the map layout. For instance, the yellow pages might require a yellow map background. The profile can also hold information on the type of questions to be answered: some sites might only need answers to queries like 'Where is . . .?'. In processing the query it is sent to a set of servers that hold the geospatial data used to calculate the optimal path between A and B. Yet another specialized Internet company that offers server space could maintain these servers. The answer is converted into a table with route descriptions and a bitmap showing the route on a map. The layout of both is done on the website profile, and the result, coded in HTML, is sent to the website where the query originated. In the mobile world the results are sent to a mobile device using the WAP protocol. The user will not have noticed that many different service providers were involved in solving the question.

The website of a map library could function as an entry point to many of these services, or it could offer an organized access to 'Where is?' type questions. Results of the queries might be used to inform the user of library items that hold information related to the geographic object found in the gazetteer. These could be pointers to paper maps (catalogue numbers) or hyperlinks to geospatial data sets or online maps. Some issues that will require addressing in this new map library environment include payment for the downloading of maps and geographic data, copyright, privacy and security.

Another important initiative that will certainly have implications for map libraries is related to the OpenGIS Consortium (**http://www.opengis.org/ wmt/index.htm**) which is working towards a more open and flexible use of different GIS software and data, and therefore maps. Recognizing the importance of the web, the consortium started the Special Interest Group Web Mapping Testbed to create open geoprocessing web technology and to offer specifications as well. Since today's map libraries also hold all kinds of digital geospatial data sets, the website of the map library could offer access to the software that allows open use of particular geospatial data sets.

Conclusion

The above discussions, as well as those in the other chapters, show that change is at hand for map libraries. However, it also becomes clear that there is a definite role to play for map libraries in the days of cyberspace. Map libraries could function as map portals to the world wide web, and serve as guides to online maps and geospatial data sets. In this way they would become part of national or even global geospatial data infrastructures. Just as with traditional map libraries, the new map libraries have to specialize and cooperate, since to cover all of cyberspace is virtually impossible.

All these opportunities will actually increase the demands on map libraries. They will also have a future role to play in collaborative information visualization. People at different locations (such as map libraries) might access the same geospatial data or maps to discuss community projects, for instance (Krygier, 1999). The world wide web will also definitely be the medium through which map library services are distributed, especially when the resource of the traditional map library can be linked to web-based digital data.

References

Buttenfield, B P (1997) Delivering maps to the information society: a digital library for cartographic data, *Proceedings, 17th Conference of the International Cartographic Association*, Stockholm, 1409–16.

Buttenfield, B P and Goodchild, M F (1996) The Alexandria Digital Library Project: distributed library services for spatially referenced data, *Proceedings of GIS/LIS '96*, Denver, 76–84.

Elzakker, C P J M (2000) Use of maps on the web. In Kraak, M J and Brown, A (eds) *Web cartography: developments and prospects*, Taylor & Francis, 21–36.

Köbben, B (2000) Publishing maps on the web. In Kraak, M J and Brown, A (eds) *Web cartography: developments and prospects*, Taylor & Francis, 73–86.

Kraak, M J and Brown, A (eds.) (2000) *Web cartography: developments and prospects*, Taylor & Francis, available at **http://kartoweb.itc.nl/webcartography/webbook/**.

Kraak, M J and MacEachren, A M (1999) Visualization for exploration of spatial data, *International Journal of Geographical Information Sciences*, **13** (4), 285–7.

Krygier, J (1999) World wide web mapping and GIS: an application for public participation, *Cartographic Perspectives*, **33**, 66–7.

MacEachren, A M and Kraak, M J (1997) Exploratory cartographic visualization: advancing the agenda, *Computers & Geosciences*, **23** (4), 335–44.

Morrison, J L (1997) Topographic mapping for the twenty first century. In Rhind, D (ed) *Framework for the world*, Geoinformation International, 14—27.

9

Metadata and standards: confusion or convergence?

Jan Smits

 This chapter considers the changing nature and uses of metadata employed by the map library and spatial data community to describe the attributes of maps and spatial data. It defines metadata and classifies them according to different 'quality bands'. The relationships between standards are explored and possibilities of interoperability are discussed.

Introduction

In the last quarter of the 20th century two major developments have influenced the practices of map curators: the digital transition in cartography and developments in metadata standards and formats. The digital transition started out as a means of automating manual processes of cartographic production, but slowly the emphasis shifted towards creating more sophisticated tools for handling data, leading to the publication of digital mapping, instead of digitally produced paper maps. These changes have encouraged more homogeneous approaches to managing map collections. Standards help professionals to understand technological change, especially when curators act to integrate them into everyday practices, and help to upgrade them into practical tools. With the profusion of standards there lurks, however, the possibility that practitioners will be confused about their use. The question arises not only whether we use existing and emerging standards in an optimum way, but also whether we are able to make them interoperable (Nerbert, 2000). Perhaps we will reach the point where as many library processes as possible will become part of a single meta information system, with the catalogue no longer a separate tool, but rather serving as one amongst a host of interoperating devices.

The standards that are the focus of this chapter are based upon the following definition of spatial data, encompassing analogue and digital mapping: '[Geo]spatial data are data describing phenomena directly or indirectly associated with a location and time relative to the surface of the earth' (McKee, 1996). These data consist not only of Document Like Objects (DLOs). Some of them 'are of a dynamic nature, not at all corresponding to any physical entity, but created dynamically by some server programme, e.g. based on a database lookup' (Husby, 1997). Though for some time DLOs will be in the majority, we can expect that in time they will become more and more an expression or manifestation of dynamic data. Chapters 4–8 discuss the implication of spatial data themselves for the map library; this chapter focuses upon their description and upon metadata.

What are metadata?

In essence metadata are data about data, and whether in the traditional or Internet context, the key purpose of metadata is to facilitate and improve the retrieval of information. Metadata, in the first instance, help us to locate and select sources of information, but in the electronic age location and selection are not sufficient. Other information about data is needed, to help evaluate fitness to purpose.

Metadata are, however, hard to define. The term is so ambiguous that the Task Force on Archiving of Digital Information avoids using it altogether (Task Force on Archiving of Digital Information, 1996). Smits (1999) discusses some of the many different definitions, but for the purpose of this chapter the International Cartographic Association definition is used: '[geo-spatial] metadata are data that describe the content, data definition and structural representation, extent (both geographic and temporal), spatial reference, quality, availability, status and administration of a geographic data set.' (ICA Commission on Standards for the Transfer of Spatial Data, 1996).

This definition is all encompassing and relevant for describing sophisticated data sets. The extent to which it is relevant for describing traditional analogue material depends on local practice.

Metadata come in many shapes

In the 1990s the documentation community realized that electronic data or data sets needed a different approach from that which was appropriate for the documentation of traditional analogue materials. Since the early 1990s producers and users of elaborate digital data sets such as Digital Elevation Models, TIGER-files, and remote-sensing images, have started to develop sophisticated standards to document these. With the developing significance of the Internet further metadata standards emerged, such as RFC 1807 (Jacobsen, 1995), the Internet Anonymous FTP Archive (IAFA) (IAFA, 2000), the Summary of Object Interchange Formats (SOIF) (Hardy, 1995), and from 1995 onwards the Dublin Core (Dublin Core Metadata Initiative, 1999a, 1999b). Since 1997 IFLA has been evaluating whether the Paris Principles of 1961, on which their standards are built, are still a valid basis for bibliographic processes (IFLA Committee on Cataloguing, 1971). All these initiatives also evaluate the cost-effectiveness of processing metadata. Whilst these initiatives influence each other, they are aimed at different user communities and data formats. Though interoperability may be in the mind of the standard writers, practical, working, interoperable systems have so far only rarely been developed.

In libraries bibliographic processes have been aimed at the user tasks: 'finding', 'identifying', 'selecting' and 'obtaining'. Other metadata initiatives have catered for needs such as 'qualifying', 'managing' and 'housekeeping'. Information retrieval may be measured in terms of recall and precision: if a lot of relevant information is missing, there is poor recall and if a lot of irrelevant information is retrieved, there is poor precision.

The more detailed description and classification of metadata systems given in Table 9.1 should be judged in the light of retrieval performance. It classifies metadata types according to their 'quality level', which varies from very simple Band I systems concerned in the main with location, through to more complex and specialist Band IV types of metadata, designed for more focused and analytical retrieval. Data formats are explored in greater detail in Dempsey and Heery (1997a–e) and operate as coding systems for input, storage and processing of data by means of a computer.

Table 9.1 *Classification of metadata qualities*

Quality	Simple	⇒	⇒	Rich
Quality Level	Band I	Band II	Band III	Band IV
Diffusion	⇒	⇒	⇐ ⇒	⇐
Availability	Internet	Internet	Internet/Intranet	Internet/Intranet
Purpose	Location	Selection	Evaluation	Analysis
Unit of information	Individual digital information object	Logical set of digital objects; no links between documents	Publication; links between whole and parts	Databases with links between whole and parts on all levels
Standards	Proprietary	Emerging standards	Generic standards used in information world	Standards used in specialist subject domains
Form of record	Proprietary simple records	Dublin Core	AACR2, ISBD	FGDC, CEN, ISO, ANZLIC
Format	Unstructured	Attribute value pairs	MARC USMARC UKMARC UNIMARC MARC21	Highly structured mark up, eg FGDC DTD ANZMETA
Input	Robot-generated	Robot plus manual input	Manually input	High level of manual input
Conversion		DC/MARC/GILS	MARC2DC MARC2FGDC	FGDC2MARC
Protocol	http with CGI form interface	Directory service protocols (whois++) with query routing (Common Indexing Protocol)	Z39.50	Z39.50 (in future with collection navigation)
User Community	Internet surfers	Producers/Libraries	Libraries/Cartographic Information Centres	Producers/ Documentation Centres/Clearing-houses

Band I

These are simple records, created by full-text Internet indexing and by general search-and-auto-describe missions carried out mainly by robot search engines like NetFirst, AltaVista, or Infoseek. As these tools do not discriminate between the functions of the words they harvest, the resulting indexes show a lack of precision for those seeking qualified information. They return many inappropriate answers, and there is no notion of 'correctness' in such searches. The search engines tend to be associated with directory service protocols and are mainly used by web surfers who start out to explore available information in a random way. Fortunately these indexes have been used to generate more focused listings, such as *Oddens' Bookmarks*, which early in 2001 indexed more than 12,500 sites related to cartography (*Oddens' Bookmarks*, 2000).

Band II

At the instigation of OCLC and NCSA, workshops have been held since 1995 to try to find a modus in which metadata can be formulated. The first workshop held in Dublin, Ohio (USA) found consensus on a set of elements subsequently called the Dublin Core (Dublin Core Metadata Initiative, 1999a, 1999b). This is intended to be sufficiently rich to support useful field-based retrieval but simple enough not to require specialist expertise or extensive manual effort to create.

The participants agreed on:

- a concrete syntax for the Dublin Core expressed as a Document Type Definition (DTD) in Standard Generalized Markup Language (SGML),
- a mapping of this syntax to existing HyperText Markup Language (HTML) tags to enable a consistent means for embedding author-generated descriptive metadata in web documents (Weibel, 1996).

Table 9.2 describes the scope and elements of different Dublin Core fields.

Table 9.2 *The Dublin Core elements (derived from Dublin Core Metadata Initiative, 1999b)*

Scope	Element	Description
Content	Title	The name of the resource
Content	Subject	The topic addressed by the resource
Content	Description	A textual description of the content of the resource
Content	Source	Objects, either print or electronic, from which this object is derived, if applicable
Content	Language	Language of the intellectual content
Content	Relation	Relationship to other resources
Content	Coverage	The spatial location and/or temporal duration characteristics of the resource
Intellectual property	Creator	The person(s) or organization primarily responsible for creating the intellectual content of the resource
Intellectual property	Publisher	The agent or agency responsible for making the object available in its current form
Intellectual property	Contributor	The person(s), such as editors, transcribers and illustrators, who have made other significant intellectual contributions to the work
Intellectual property	Rights	A rights management statement
Instantiation	Date	The date associated with the creation availability of the resource
Instantiation	Type	The genre of the object, such as novel, poem, dictionary, etc
Instantiation	Format	The physical manifestation of the object, such as PostScript file or Windows executable file
Instantiation	Identifier	String or number used to uniquely identify the object

Dublin Core records are specifically created for resource discovery and as such generally require less precise description than traditional bibliographic records. Soon the user community (including amongst others the library field) found, however, that more precision was often needed to be better able to query DC databases. Precision is sought in qualifiers, which can be added to metadata tags and when possible using controlled systems. A problem to be solved is that most controlled systems or vocabularies (like Dewey Decimal Classification 21, Universal Decimal Classification, Library of Congress Subject Headings) are not freely available on the Internet. Use of these controlled systems would make it easier to operate Dublin-Core-based systems in conjunction with Band III- and IV-based metadata.

During the fifth Dublin Core meeting in Helsinki, Finland, 1997, there was a growing consensus for the use of the 'Coverage' element to support search for spatially referenced resources (Becker et al, 1997). For the map community it is, however, unfortunate that the Dublin Core Metadata Initiative advises that Coverage should use 'named places or time periods . . . in preference to numeric identifiers such as sets of co-ordinates or date ranges'. From experience we know that there are many problems with changes in the form or spelling of toponyms and exonyms, and with the transliteration of non-Western scripts. Similar difficulties relate to designations of time periods, especially those of more recent eras which are likely to change in the future. Also in a globalizing information world local language designations may be unacceptable in the face of internationally accepted names. If countries or organizations prefer to use local designations then it would be advisable to repeat the field, using the DCMI interpretation in one place, with numeric identifiers for the same information repeated in a second field. Should one wish metadata harvesters to produce clickable maps from these numeric data, then the harvester should include an algorithm to convert these geographical to vector coordinates (van de Waal, 1974).

Libraries use Dublin Core metadata to explore data but should also embed them in the electronic resources that they create and make available through the Internet. To create more uniform Dublin Core records some organizations provide templates to enhance the value of the metadata (Koch and Borell, 1998). Useful tools for this process are available in the Dublin Core Metadata Initiative (2000a).

An important issue that is emerging amongst Dublin Core users is whether the 15 Dublin Core elements might become more multilingual. The Dublin Core is still Anglo-American centred but translations are emerging (Dublin Core Metadata Initiative, 2000b). Another strand of research is to relate the Core to an underlying model, which treats information resources as having logical states with relationships to each other and to other resources (Weibel, 1999).

The inherent simplicity of DC cataloguing poses problems for map librarians. There is no consensus yet as to what is 'best practice' or 'minimal adequate' DC cataloguing. Though the syntax of DC is developing, semantic rules are lacking. Only intensive communication amongst DC user communities will resolve these issues and this may take a long time.

Band III

In 1961 IFLA adopted the Paris Principles (IFLA Committee on Cataloguing, 1971) as a basis for an international approach to 'headings' and 'entry words'. They were, however, solely meant for catalogues of printed books. In 1967 the Anglo-American Cataloguing Rules (AACR) were simultaneously published in London and Chicago and revised editions appeared in 1978 and 1988, followed by an inter-

pretation manual for map curators in 1982 (Stibbe, 1982). Convergence of cataloguing codes started in 1971, when IFLA published the first of the ISBDs for monographs and serials, soon to be followed in 1977 by the ISBD(CM) for cartographic
materials. Almost all ISBDs were revised in the 1980s and 1990s, the ISBD(CM)
appearing in 1987 (IFLA Universal Bibliographic Control and International MARC
Programme, 1987). The last ISBD, covering electronic resources, appeared in 1997,
but has caused some disquiet because its recommendations mean that most ISBDs
will have to be revised, to align them with the electronic materials guidelines.

As a result of changes in the expression of documents and their transport
media, IFLA started to evaluate the whole configuration of the Paris Principles and
ISBDs, which resulted in the report *Functional requirements for bibliographic records*
(IFLA Study Group on the Functional Requirements for Bibliographic Records,
1998). This study evaluated fields and elements, using a user-oriented conceptual
model, where elements are described as entities, with attributes and relations. The
attributes serve as the means by which users formulate queries and interpret
responses when seeking information. When these metadata are related to user services, their function is still restricted to finding, identifying, selecting and obtaining.

One of the implications of changing ideas concerning the principles on which
AACR and ISBD are founded, however, might be that it will be recommended for
national bibliographic agencies to create a *single* bibliographic record for items that
appear in *different* manifestations (eg a printed map and its digitized electronic file).
Another might be that a core bibliographic description could be defined to lower
cataloguing costs.

In many countries adaptations of AACR2 are used as local cataloguing rules or
are about to supplant existing standards, eg Switzerland (IDS, 1998). Studies are
underway to align the German cataloguing rules, RAK, and harmonize the Russian cataloguing rules to AACR (Universität Göttingen, 1999). Late in 2000 both AACR
and the ISBDs were under review. A revised third draft of the ISBD(CM) was circulated in May 2000 (Bäärnhielm, 2000), and this tries to amalgamate alterations
to the ISBD(CM) with changes to the ISBD(ER) where appropriate. The draft is largely adapted to the recent issue of *Cataloging & Classification Quarterly* (Andrews and
Larsgaard, 1999). It offers the choice to extend the material-specific area with:

- a statement of accuracy (for scale) (optional)
- a designation and structure of electronic resource
- the structure of resource (optional)
- the number of files, records, bytes (optional)
- a digital graphic representation method (optional)

- an object type (optional)
- a file format (optional)
- an object count (optional)
- geospatial reference data (optional)
- a designation of electronic resource (when applicable)
- the characteristics (ie structure) of electronic resource (optional)
- digital graphic representation data (optional).

There are also significant changes to the 'edition statement', to the 'physical and technical description area', and to 'notes on system requirements'. Whether the changes survive depends on IFLA's ISBD Review Committee, which may have other insights than those of the Geography and Map Library Section, which revised the map rules.

AACR and the ISBD are cataloguing codes, but before the user can search bibliographic databases and read descriptions they have to be electronically processed. For this purpose MARC (MAchine Readable Catalogue) formats were developed. More detailed descriptions of these are available in a series of web-based descriptions by Dempsey and Heery (1997a–e). MARC is an implementation of the international standard *Information and documentation – format for information exchange* (ISO 2709-1996) (British Library, 1999). The format involves record structure, content designation and data content of the record. In the 1960s the Library of Congress started automating the cataloguing process by introducing MARC, and later USMARC. In the 1970s this was followed by Intermarc, UKMARC, etc. Unfortunately this diversity showed a lack of standardized content designators assigned to the data content. To counter this lack IFLA developed an exchange format called UNIMARC (Universal MARC format). This did not stop the development of more MARC formats and by the mid 1990s there were some 50 different versions. In 1997 the European Commission sponsored a project called UseMARCON to alleviate the problems of exchanging data. The UseMARCON project (Noordermeer, 1997) aimed at developing a generic toolkit for ISO2709-compatible MARC formats to enable libraries to create rule-based systems to convert records between national MARC formats. On the website, applications are available for the conversion of records between UKMARC, USMARC and UNIMARC.

To alleviate problems with existing MARCs the Library of Congress, in consultation with various user communities, developed MARC21. This 'is an integrated format defined for the identification and description of different forms of bibliographic material. MARC21 specifications are defined for books, serials, computer files, maps, music, visual materials, and mixed material. With the full integration of the previously discrete bibliographic formats, consistent definition and usage are maintained for different forms of material' (MARBI, 1996). The format attempts to be compatible with UKMARC and UNIMARC.

In 1995, with the upsurge of Internet applications, the Library of Congress began the 'MARC DTD' project (Network Development and MARC Standards Office, 1999b) to enable the conversion of MARC data to an SGML environment and vice versa. MARC DTD data can be converted to the Internet, but organizations can also create MARC-like metadata on the Internet and convert these to MARC databases. Conversion is also possible between MARC standards and more complex metadata described in Band IV type systems. For example the Alexandria Project home pages include examples of the crosswalks necessary to convert to FGDC standards (Alexandria Web Team, 1997a, 1997b).

When an OPAC is configured in an appropriate manner it becomes possible to activate Internet hyperlinks embedded in MARC metadata, which connect the user directly to the resource described.

Band IV

Digital spatial databases have been created from the late 1970s onwards and nowadays offer country-wide coverage (at municipal, provincial and state level) for most developed countries. Through GIS they can be integrated with other databases. Initially these digital data were a continuation of existing analogue products, but the data are often available in vector format and include feature-coded attributes that can be manipulated independently from each other or in concert. To extend operability many producers are also digitizing existing analogue data in raster format. Producers have responded to market conditions and have started to think of ways to make these data more accessible. As the economic stakes are higher then before they have sought to create a descriptive system, which incorporates not only data usually associated with ISBDs, but also data that could help users to evaluate and analyse the fitness of use and quality of the available digital spatial data.

Examples of these standards are ANZLIC, covering Australia and New Zealand (ANZLIC, 1998), FGDC for the United States (FGDC, 1998), CEN for Europe (CEN, 2000) and ISO at the global level (ISO, 2000). The ICA Commission on Standards for the Transfer of Spatial Data was planning to publish a book that would compare all available national and international metadata standards and systems, as a companion volume to their book on transfer standards (Moellering, 1997).

Since large amounts of data are needed for evaluation and analysis, Band IV records can comprise hundreds of elements and require anywhere between a few thousand and tens of thousands of bytes of storage. As such they can be also used as tools to administer the databases they describe. Better programming of metadata modules within spatial databases will help automated processing of numerical values and other automatically generated data and will reduce manual data input times. These rich metadata rely upon more complex protocols for exchange between systems, notably the Z39.50 protocol (Nerbert, 2000).

Hybrid developments

Working with (re)new(ed) standards shows up deficiencies in the processing of metadata records and their retrieval, and has led to an integration of standards into hybrid systems. The two projects described below may be early examples of an important trend.

In July 2000 OCLC launched its CORC (Co-operative Online Resource Catalog) version 1.0. It focuses 'on optimized metadata creation services for electronic web resources and on providing an integrated view of those resources with other bibliographic records in WorldCat (the OCLC Online Union Catalog)' (OCLC, 2000). One of the features is the integration of DC and MARC21 records into a single system. It needs a current generation browser, eg Explorer 5.x or Netscape Communicator 4.7 or higher and will be freely accessible to participating institutions.

A CORC map record may be simple or complex, depending on the intentions of the participating institution and the professionalism of the cataloguer (Allen, 2001). There are, however, 'fundamental problems with CORC as a retrieval tool for historical maps, although most of them are shared with other software used for retrieving maps. Researchers looking for cartographic materials are likely to be concerned with two things: retrieving maps of a specific geographic area, and being able to retrieve materials by date of coverage. CORC has significant weaknesses in both of these areas' (Allen, 2001). Another CORC feature is the creation of 'pathfinders' (in this case for the State of New York) (Allen, 1999), which are HTML pages of narrative and links serving as bibliographies of web resources. When necessary they can be imported from the CORC database to local databases.

The other project concerns essential FGDC metadata within the National Biological Information Infrastructure (NBII) (Chandler et al, 2000). More than 50% of queries directed at the NBII node of the FGDC Clearing-house in a given period retrieved zero hits for the user, because the interface didn't work well or the clearing-house was not functioning. Another drawback of the present clearing-house system is that when it is re-indexed, the address for a record is changed. To make resources better retrievable, a crosswalk was created for 34 CSDGM elements to

MARC21, which may further be converted to DC elements for use in CORC. The crosswalk has 'similarities as well as differences with the "Metadata Entry System" for minimally compliant metadata that has been proposed recently by the FGDC' (FGDC, 1999b).

Interoperability

There are several ways to make standards interoperable. Crosswalks can be created, metadata databases can be enhanced to function in a broader environment like Z39.50 and the Resource Description Framework, or standards families can be created to enable consistent implementation across multiple applications and systems.

Crosswalks function like bridges between the standards, but are independent tools and by their nature rigid. Soon there might be more crosswalks than there are standards. Also when an organization that makes itself responsible for maintaining a crosswalk fails in its duty, the tool deteriorates quickly and rapidly stops functioning altogether.

The Resource Description Framework (RDF) will be an infrastructure that enables the encoding, exchange and reuse of structured metadata. RDF is an application of XML that imposes structural constraints to provide unambiguous methods of expressing semantics. RDF also provides a means for publishing vocabularies that may be read by people and processed by machines, and is designed to encourage the reuse and extension of metadata semantics among disparate information communities. RDF supports the consistent encoding and exchange of standardized metadata, so that separate packages of metadata defined by different resource description communities may be interchanged (Miller, 1998). For example RDF provides an infrastructure to support metadata across many web-based activities and offers a robust and flexible architecture. One obvious application for RDF is in the description of web pages, one of the basic functions of the Dublin Core initiative. An important consideration in the development of the Dublin Core was to allow simple description, but also to provide the ability to qualify, in order to provide domain-specific elaboration and descriptive precision. The RDF mechanism is a system for defining 'schemas' for descriptive vocabularies like the Dublin Core, that are understood by machines. It allows designers to specify classes of resource types, property types to convey descriptions of those classes, and constraints on the permitted combinations of classes, property types and values (W3C, 2000a). The same is true for other Document Type Definitions, such as schema for FGDC metadata and maybe also for Internet- and web-compatible MARC records.

To be able to read the descriptions a syntax is needed. The World Wide Web

Consortium (W3C) is developing eXtensible Markup Language (XML) for this purpose. XML syntax is a subset of the international text-processing standard SGML (Standard Generalized Markup Language) specifically intended for use on the web (W3C, 2000b). It promises to make the web smarter by including machine-readable information about the structure and content of web pages. As a basic rule of XML, content and presentation are separated and XML tags contain no information about how they should be displayed. Before a web browser can display an XML page it will have to get the corresponding 'style sheet' and format the page accordingly (van der Werf, 1998).

Another way of creating multiple access to databases is to develop a common protocol, like the TCP/IP used for communication between computers on the Internet. The Z39.50 protocol is a messaging standard between an 'origin' (Z client) and 'target' (Z server) (Z39.50, 2000) and was first used in the 1970s for cross-database searching of host organizations like the Library of Congress, OCLC and RLIN (Z39.50 International Standard Maintenance Agency, 2000). It became more widely used with its 1995 version, as this could be adapted to the needs of more divergent user communities, including spatial collections (Lynch, 1997). It does not determine how systems will be built, how they will present information to the user and so on. Over the next few years, services will become 'Z39.50 enabled' in much the same way that library OPACs have become 'web enabled'. The Library of Congress maintains a Z39.50 gateway which lists organizations that have implemented the protocol (Library of Congress, 2000), including some that specifically focus upon spatial data, eg FGDC clearing-houses.

The third approach is exemplified by ISO standardization. Developments within CEN/TC 287 and ISO/TC 211 have led to the development of integrated and consistently structured families of standards for geospatial information, including metadata. The projects under development with ISO [International Organization for Standardization]/TC 211 Geographic information/Geomatics are listed in Figure 9.3.

These families of standards also promote international interoperability. Paepcke (1998) recognizes that 'strong standards' are an important prerequisite for interoperability, but also sees the 'modular, integrated process column' implicit in ISO standards as a critical influence. All their different parts are based on the same conceptual model, which should greatly facilitate shared practice.

Conclusion: confusion or convergence?

The diversity of metadata is itself an important influence bringing together dif-

19101: Geographic information – Reference model
19102: Geographic information – Overview
19103: Geographic information – Conceptual schema language
19104: Geographic information – Terminology
19105: Geographic information – Conformance and testing
19106: Geographic information – Profiles
19107: Geographic information – Spatial schema
19108: Geographic information – Temporal schema
19109: Geographic information – Rules for application schema
19110: Geographic information – Feature cataloguing methodology
19111: Geographic information – Spatial referencing by coordinates
19112: Geographic information – Spatial referencing by geographic identifiers
19113: Geographic information – Quality principles
19114: Geographic information – Quality evaluation procedures
19115: Geographic information – Metadata
19116: Geographic information – Positioning services
19117: Geographic information – Portrayal
19118: Geographic information – Encoding
19119: Geographic information – Services
19120: Geographic information – Functional standards
19121: Geographic information – Imagery and gridded data
19122: Geographic information/Geomatics – Qualifications and certification of personnel
19123: Geographic information – Schema for coverage geometry and functions
19124: Geographic information – Imagery and gridded data components
19125: Geographic information – Simple feature access – SQL option

Fig. 9.3   *ISO standards projects in geographic information/geomatics (source
http://www.statkart.no/isotc211/pow.htm [Accessed: 25 April 2000])*

ferent organizations involved in their creation, perhaps more important even than progress in the processes creating the geospatial data that they describe. There will probably always be poorer and richer geospatial collections, unless the data are made freely available on the web. The role of libraries will be to create access to these data and when possible create low-cost gateways for non-commercial usage. Should a library itself own geospatial data, then its biggest challenge will be to integrate these and the resulting metadata, with other data held by the library, into a single integrated data system.

A global community may wish for convergence of standards but there are major obstacles to progress in this direction. Most of the standards, protocols and systems are created in such a way that they may be extended to incorporate future developments, or to cater for special user communities. MARC21 may well predominate for some time as a descriptive format for libraries, especially if the largest union-catalogue-like library databases such as OCLC and PICA are integrated in future (PICA, 1999). As the ability to answer Z39.50 calls and adapt to the RDF schema are not inherent properties of data systems themselves, we have to be proactive in promoting the use of these tools. It would be helpful for the geospatial data community if the ISO TC211 family of standards were to be seen as an integral set of concepts underlying database systems. It would be even better were metadata systems to be integrated into a single conceptual model. Libraries should question whether all their metadata, which encompass processes from acquisition to preservation, should be integrated into a single meta information system.

Only when we embrace the idea that a larger audience than our own uses our metadata, will convergence of systems take place. When reading the DCMI's advice on the use of geographical coordinates, it is obvious that we still have a long way to go, before we can claim optimal user satisfaction. The Internet is young compared to the era of mass printing, and our Internet tools are no more than 25 years old. Speculation about the future can only be conceptual, the nature of tools and systems resulting from ideas is hard to predict. As the amount of geospatial data grows at an exponential rate, so we need meta geographies to understand them. Geospatial collections should urge software developers to create user interfaces based on geographical coordinates, which act like visual search tools for the geospatial data.

The amount of metadata should also grow to help us find what is required. As production costs rise with the amount of metadata created, so attention will increasingly focus upon intelligent metadata generation. Meanwhile translators will probably replace crosswalks and converters, to enable meta information systems to be queried at different levels of complexity of inquiry and across different data sets. The user should be able to access all metadata systems in a single query, but also should be able to determine the form (eg DC, MARC or FGDC) in which results are presented.

References

Alexandria Web Team (1997a) *Crosswalk: USMARC to FGDC content standards for digital geospatial metadata*, ADL, available at
http://alexandria.sdc.ucsb.edu/public-documents/metadata/marc2fgdc.html.

Alexandria Web Team (1997b) *Crosswalk: FGDC content standards for digital geospatial metadata to USMARC*, ADL, available at **http://alexandria.sdc.ucsb.edu/public-documents/metadata/fgdc2marc.html**.

Allen, D Y (1999) *New York State map pathfinder*, SUNY Stony Brook, available at **http://www.sunysb.edu/libmap/nypath1.htm**.

Allen, D Y (2001) Using the Dublin Core with CORC to catalog digital images of maps, *Journal of Internet Cataloging* (Forthcoming).

Andrews, P G and Larsgaard, M L (eds) (1999) *Cataloging & Classification Quarterly*, **27**.

ANZLIC (1998) *Core metadata elements for land and geographic directories in Australia and New Zealand*, ANZLIC, available at **http://www.anzlic.org.au/metaelem.htm**.

ANZLIC Working Group on Metadata (1998) *ANZMETA DTD Version 1.1*, ANZLIC, available at **http://www.environment.gov.au/database/metadata/anzmeta/anzmeta-1.1.dtd**.

Bäärnhielm, G (ed) (2000) *ISBD(CM): international standard bibliographic description for cartographic materials. Revision including electronic resources, second draft.* (Not published).

Becker, H et al (1997) *Dublin core element: coverage*, available at **http://alexandria.sdc.ucsb.edu/public-documents/metadata/dc_coverage.html**.

Berners-Lee, T (1999) *Web architecture from 50,000 feet*, W3C, available at **http://www.w3.org/DesignIssues/Architecture.html**.

British Library (1999) *MARC home page*, BL, available at **http://www.bl.uk/information/marc.html**.

CEN (2000) *CEN/TC287 The Geographic information European prestandards and CEN reports*, AFNOR, available at **http://forum.afnor.fr/afnor/WORK/AFNOR/GPN2/Z13C/PUBLIC/WEB/ENGLISH/pren.htm**.

Chandler, A et al (2000) Mapping and converting essential Federal Geographic Data Committee (FGDC) metadata into MARC21 and Dublin Core: towards an alternative to the FGDC Clearinghouse, *D-Lib Magazine* (January), **6** (1), available at **http://www.dlib.org/dlib/january00/chandler/01chandler.html**.

Committee on Cataloging: Description and Access. Task Force on Metadata (1999) *Summary report, June 1999*, ALA, available at **http://www.ala.org/alcts/organization/ccs/ccda/tf-meta3.html**.

Committee on Cataloging: Description and Access (1999) *Final report (penultimate draft) of the Task Force on the Harmonization of ISBD(ER) and AACR2*, ALA, available at http://www.library.yale.edu/cataloging/aacrer/tf-harm21.htm.

Dempsey, L and Heery, R (1997a) *MARC (general overview)*, W3C, available at http://www.ukoln.ac.uk/metadata/DESIRE/overview/rev_14.htm.

Dempsey, L and Heery, R (1997b) *A review of metadata: a survey of current resource description formats*, UKOLN, available at http://www.ukoln.ac.uk/metadata/DESIRE/overview/rev_ti.htm.

Dempsey, L and Heery, R (1997c) *UKMARC*, W3C, available at http://www.ukoln.ac.uk/metadata/DESIRE/overview/rev_16.htm.

Dempsey, L and Heery, R (1997d) *UNIMARC*, W3C, available at http://www.ukoln.ac.uk/metadata/DESIRE/overview/rev_17.htm.

Dempsey, L and Heery, R (1997e) *USMARC*, W3C, available at http://www.ukoln.ac.uk/metadata/DESIRE/overview/rev_15.htm.

Dublin Core Metadata Initiative (1999a) *Description of Dublin Core elements*, DCMI, available at http://purl.org/dc/documents/rec-dces-19990702.htm.

Dublin Core Metadata Initiative (1999b) *Dublin Core metadata element set, Version 1.1: reference description*, DCMI, available at http://purl.org/dc/documents/rec-dces-19990702.htm.

Dublin Core Metadata Initiative (2000a) *Metadata related tools*, DCMI, available at http://purl.org/dc/tools/index.htm.

Dublin Core Metadata Initiative (2000b) *Web-accessible versions of Dublin Core in multiple languages*, DCMI, available at http://purl.org/dc/groups/languages.htm#multilingual.

FGDC (1998) *Content standard for digital geospatial metadata*, FGDC-STD-001-1998, FGDC, available at http://www.fgdc.gov/metadata/csdgm/.

FGDC (1999a) *FGDC Metadata DTD 3.0.1 19990611*, FGDC, available at http://www.fgdc.gov/metadata/fgdc-std-001-1998.dtd.

FGDC (1999b) *Metadata elements included in the metadata entry system*, FGDC available at http://www.fgdc.gov/clearinghouse/metadataesystem/mes_description.html.

Hardy, D (1995) *The summary object interchange format (SOIF)*, Internet Research Task Force Research Group on Resource Discovery, available at http://www.cube.net/harvest-docs/user-manual/node141.html.

Husby, O (1997) *Metadata, ELAG'97, Gdansk, June 18th 1997*, BIBSYS, available at http://www.bibsys.no/elag97/metadata.html.

IAFA (2000) Field descriptions for document, software, image, sound, video, mailarchive, usenet and FAQ IAFA Template Types, available at http://www.man.ac.uk/MVC//SIMA/MMFFDB/IAFA-help/document.html.

ICA Commission on Standards for the Transfer of Spatial Data (1996) *Working definition of metadata definition*, The Commission.

IDS (1998) *Warum AACR2 als Regelwerk für den KDH-Verbund?*, IDS, available at http://www.ub.unibas.ch/ids/aacr_arg.htm.

IFLA Committee on Cataloguing (1971) *Statement of principles, adopted at the International Conference on Cataloguing Principles, Paris, October, 1961*, annotated edition with commentary and examples by Eva Verona, IFLA.

IFLA Study Group on the Functional Requirements for Bibliographic Records (1998) *Functional requirements for bibliographic records*, UBCIM publications, new series, 19, IFLA, available at http://www.ifla.org/VII/s13/frbr/frbr.pdf.

IFLA Universal Bibliographic Control and International MARC Programme (1987) *ISBD(CM): international standard bibliographic description for cartographic materials*, rev edn, IFLA.

ISO (2000) *ISO/TC 211 Programme of work*, ISO, available at http://www.statkart.no/isotc211/pow.htm.

Jacobsen, D (1995) *RFC 1807: A format for bibliographic records*, W3C, available at http://www.ecst.csuchico.edu/~jacobsd/bib/formats/rfc1807.html.

Koch, T and Borell, M (1998) *Dublin Core metadata template*, available at http://www.lub.lu.se/cgi-bin/nmdc.pl.

Library of Congress (2000) *Z39.50 gateway to other libraries*, LC, available at http://lcweb.loc.gov/z3950/.

Lynch, C A (1997) The Z39.50 information retrieval standard, part i: a strategic view of its past, present and future, *D-Lib Magazine* (April), available at http://www.dlib.org/dlib/april97/04lynch.html.

McKee, L (1996) Building the GSDI: discussion paper for the September 1996 *Emerging Global Spatial Data Infrastrucure Conference*, Open GIS Consortium, available at http://www.opengis.org/techno/articles/gsdi.htm.

MARBI (1996) *The MARC 21 formats: background and principles*, LC, available at http://www.loc.gov/marc/96principl.html.

Miller, E (1998) An introduction to the Resource Description Framework, *D-Lib Magazine* (May), available at http://www.dlib.org/dlib/may98/miller/05miller.html.

Moellering, H (ed) (1997) *Spatial database transfer standard 2: characteristics for assessing standards and full descriptions of the national and international standards in the world*, Pergamon.

Nerbert, D D (2000) *Z39.50 application profile for geospatial metadata or "GEO"*, available at
http://www.blueangeltech.com/Standards/GeoProfile/geo22.htm.
Network Development and MARC Standards Office (1999a) *Dublin Core/MARC/GILS Crosswalk*, LC, available at
http://www.loc.gov/marc/dccross.html.
Network Development and MARC Standards Office (1999b) *MARC DTDs, document type definitions, background and development*, LC, available at
http://lcweb.loc.gov/marc/marcdtd/marcdtdback.html.
Noordermeer, T (1997) *User controlled Generic MARC converter*, KB, available at
http://www.konbib.nl/kb/sbo/bibinfra/usema-en.html.
OCLC (2000) *OCLC CORC Frequently Asked Questions*, OCLC, available at
http://www.oclc.org/oclc/corc/faq/index.htm.
Oddens' Bookmarks (2000) **http://oddens.geog.uu.nl/index.html**.
Paepcke, A et al (1998) Interoperability for digital libraries worldwide, *Communications of the ACM*, **41** (4), 33–43.
PICA (1999) *OCLC Inc. and Pica Foundation reach agreement about cooperation*, PICA, available at
http://www.pica.nl/en/news/press19991228.shtml.
Smits, J (1999) Metadata, an introduction, *Cataloging and Classification Quarterly*, **27** (3–4), 303–19.
Stibbe, H P (1982) *Cartographic materials: a manual of interpretation for AACR2*, ALA, 1982.
Task Force on Archiving of Digital Information (1996) *Preserving digital information*, CPA & RLG, available at
http://lyra.rlg.org/ArchTF/tfadi.index.htm.
Universität Göttingen (1999) *Project REUSE: aligning international cataloging standards*, OCLC, available at
http://www.oclc.org/oclc/cataloging/reuse_project/index.htm.
W3C (2000a) *Resource Description Framework (RDF) schema specification 1.0*, W3C Candidate Recommendation 27 March 2000, W3C, available at
http://www.w3.org/TR/WD-rdf-schema/.
W3C (2000b) *Extensible markup language (XML™)*, W3C, available at
http://www.w3.org/XML/.
Waal, H van de (1974) The application of geographical co-ordinates for the retrieval of maps in a computerized map-catalogue, *International Yearbook of Cartography*, **14**, 166–72.
Weibel, S (1996) *A proposed convention for embedding metadata in HTML*, W3C,

available at
http://www.oclc.org:5046/~weibel/html-meta.html.

Weibel, S (1999) The state of the Dublin Core Metadata Initiative April 1999, *D-Lib Magazine*, **5** (4), available at
http://www.dlib.org/dlib/april99/04weibel.html.

Werf, T van der (1998) *Metadata and libraries: background and introduction*, KB, available at
http://www.konbib.nl/persons/titia/publ/index.html.

Z39.50 (2000) *Z39.50, Biblio Tech, review, information technology for libraries*, available at
http://www.biblio-tech.com/html/z39_50.html.

Z39.50 International Standard Maintenance Agency (2000) *The Z39.50 document*, LoC, available at
http://lcweb.loc.gov/z3950/agency/document.html.

10
Old maps in a modern world

Christopher Baruth

▶ *Any non-current map is a record of a past landscape and deserves retention as an historical document for a variety of reasons. Retaining old maps can be a difficult and expensive undertaking, but with the aid of technology, preservation copies of maps can be made, which, with proper care, can last indefinitely. It is also possible to infuse many of these copies with a 'geographical essence' through georeferencing. To preserve our immense cartographic heritage, much thought must be given to developing methodologies and creating new institutions that will allow us to combine forces to accomplish this formidable task.*

Value of old maps to modern society

In the annals of the history of maps in libraries, one item is reasonably well known and has relevance to the topic at hand, namely, that the majority of map collections in today's research libraries were created in or after the mid-20th century. Thus, at least in the USA, these map collections are well supplied with maps produced by the US Geological Survey and what was then called the Army Map Service, through a large-scale government-administered depository system. The subsequent growth of these collections came to rely on several factors, including, naturally, the requirements of the user community, the level of commitment on the part of the library administration and the dedication and skill of the map librarian.

Old is of course a relative term. Compared with maps found in the Vatican or Chicago's Newberry Library, the ink on the maps in these modern collections is hardly dry, and they are unlikely to be referred to as 'historical'. Yet they are historical – they record a landscape often a half-century old – a landscape, in many cases ravaged by war and divided by ideology that has largely faded away under pressure from the economic and political realities of our rapidly changing world.

Maps are constantly being revised or reissued in completely new editions. Features no longer on the landscape are no longer on the map: a stretch of railroad, once a vital linkage, when removed from the ground, is removed from the map. A wetland, once drained, is no longer a wetland, and a paved or built-up orange grove now has the familiar pink or grey overlay of urbanization. The ubiquitous road map, updated yearly, can clearly illustrate, when compared to its predecessors, road network additions, subtractions or modifications that, while aiding the motorist, can spell either boom or doom for neighbourhoods, cities or economic enterprises dependent on the highway.

Thus, when we talk of 'old maps' we, in effect, need to be talking about any map that is no longer current, and the very reason that the map is no longer current is what gives it value as a historical document – it records a past geographical reality in the most concise and descriptive manner possible.

There are essentially five reasons why we preserve or ought to preserve cartographic materials that are no longer current: old maps provide a record of past landscapes; they record changes through time; they provide a record of geographical knowledge or perceptions from a given period of time; they constitute a record of cartographic and printing technology; and they provide insights into the values, beliefs and social structures surrounding the creation of the map (Skelton, 1972; Harley and Woodward, 1987–).

Record of past landscapes

If we wish to find, for example, a Polish village that was destroyed in World War 2, we normally would need to consult a map produced prior to 1939. Our village will be shown, and shown in relationship to its neighbours, which may or may not have shared its fate. A good map will not only show the location of the village, but may give clues to its economy and culture. Is it on a navigable river or stream capable of producing energy? Are there farms, factories or mines nearby? How well connected was our village to the outside world? Did it contain churches, synagogues? And, of course, just how big was it? Likewise, in the New World, large numbers of places have vanished, not victims of warfare, but as the result of econo-geographical restructuring which has rendered such small places obsolete. Locating these is not simply an exercise in the application of Central Place Theory, but can be a vital link in family or social history.

Changes through time

An important outcome of preserving a past landscape in cartographic rendering is the ability to compare various states of that landscape and observe its changes through time. In this way, we can observe the growth of cities and transportation facilities and networks, the draining of wetlands, the clearing of forests, and geomorphological changes such as stream migration, delta building, spit formation and, of course, volcanic and tectonic events.

Geographical knowledge and perceptions

Whether one is a serious historian or just a casual map reader, one of the pleasures of looking at old maps – maps which recorded the impressions, faithfully or not, of those who explored the ever-expanding fringes of geographical knowledge, or before that, theorized on the nature of creation – is observing the misconceptions, ranging from subtle to gross, which were recorded. Who can help but be amused by the medieval tripartite concept of the earth with Jerusalem at the centre, or Gastaldi's 16th century maps of Africa brimming over with fanciful detail, or Munster's map of America prominently displaying the Verazzano Sea, a product of wishful geographical thinking, or the many maps portraying California as an island or perhaps the Bellin image of Lake Superior complete with its fictional islands named for officials in the French Hydrographic Service. Historians and historical geographers can also study the more subtle errors and misconceptions that may have led to disastrous consequences, or at least futile results, in exploration and warfare through the cartographer's omissions, commissions or confusions.

Technology

When we look at a 17th-century map of Switzerland, we are immediately struck by the fascinating, and one might say quaint, yet artistic, depiction of that country's most obvious physical attributes. Depiction of mountains was long a problem for mapmakers, for not only did they lack the graphic techniques to portray heights accurately, but the recording of the heights and the shapes of these large volumetric entities perennially occupied some of the world's foremost scientific minds. By the mid-19th century, with the publication of the Dufour map, the long tradition of artistic representation was at last merged with effective cartographic techniques and a precise data-gathering technology. But far from being satisfied, the Swiss continue in a variety of ways to improve upon that which was already very good. Thus, cartography can be studied from the perspectives of the history of science and the history of technology – we can view over the long term how mapmakers have evolved their techniques, surveyors have perfected their quest for data, and printers have managed the often contradictory goals of increased quantity and improved quality, with colour introduced for good measure.

Values, beliefs and social structure

A factor left unstated in our discussion of the Dufour map, above, is that the whole enterprise was made possible through a complex social, political, economic, technological and scientific synergy that manifested itself in various ways in the course of the 19th century. The maps, what is displayed on them or what remains concealed, can reveal much information about a society and its leadership.

Problems of conserving old maps

The problems of conserving old maps have been widely discussed and agonized over, but no magic bullet solution has been developed or is likely to be developed in the near future. With the exception of the few libraries that limit their collecting to old maps, even the richest of libraries have but a small portion of their collections in maps from before, say, 1850. It was from that time onward that the great national topographic and hydrographic surveys, prodigiously generating maps and charts, were in the process of documenting in detail the contour of the lands and the depths of the seas. It is also true that this output of printed data worked hand in hand with developments in the paper industry that provided a product that everyone could afford. Unfortunately, this affordable product contained the seeds of its own destruction. And as we continue to contemplate the problem, our stocks of maps become ever more brittle and yellowed. This, unfortunately is a problem that is not going to go away (Allen, 1996).

The maps found in our collections can for convenience be divided into three categories. There are the old maps, ranging from the earliest printed maps produced in the 1470s to roughly the mid-19th century; the modern period, consisting of maps produced from the period of World War 2, or a decade or two earlier; and finally, a period of transition consisting of maps produced from around 1850 into the first decades of the 20th century. The bounds of these periods are certainly not hard and fast, and representation will vary substantially from collection to collection.

The early period

The characteristics of this first category include the use of woodcut and copper-plate printing technologies, durable hand-made papers and custom hand colour-ing done by artisans. The typical size of these sheets of paper was also conducive to their being bound in volumes which protected them from the usual wear and tear normally accorded a large sheet of paper, but also from the deleterious effects of exposure to light and dust and, to some extent, even fire. Hence, the survival rate among these maps is relatively good, and their condition is typical-ly also good – it is not uncommon to see even 15th-century material in stunningly fresh and crisp condition. This, however, is not to minimize the preservation needs of this category. These maps are of the most interest to collectors and, hence, have the highest monetary value. They have also the highest artifactual value due to their antiquity and the materials and processes employed in their creation. In this group, preservation of the actual maps is given the highest priority, and large sums of money are expended by libraries and individuals in keeping them viable. The money is willingly spent because the number of maps in this group is relatively small and the preservation results are considered to be long term. The maps in this group are generally well preserved and likely to remain so, but must be han-dled with care and with as little physical contact as possible.

It is these maps that have long provoked the most interest in producing copies: to make rare works more widely known in the scholarly community; to provide prints suitable for framing; and to provide surrogates for study and research, while keep-ing the originals from excessive handling. As scanning increasingly becomes the stan-dard for preservation copying, maps in this group will be accorded disproportionate interest, again because of their high monetary and artifactual value, but also because of the fascination these items hold for a large number of people.

Modern period

This is a grouping of convenience consisting mostly of modern, lithographically printed colour maps. These are the maps that predominate in the modern uni-versity or large public library map collection. Although they are printed on acid paper for the most part, they have not yet reached the age where preservation has become a serious problem. They include, however, some of the most heavily used items in a collection, and encapsulation is frequently employed to keep them from deteriorating.

Even though libraries have generally shown little interest thus far in the preser-vation imaging of these maps, a number of map producers, such as the US Geological Survey (USGS) and Ordnance Survey of Great Britain, have issued digital versions of their current editions. The USGS, for example, has produced geoindexed scans, called Digital Raster Graphics (DRGs), of their current topographical quadrangles. While these will preserve the informational content of the maps, the preservation purist will object to the projection manipulation employed to give uniformity and connectivity to the quadrangles and to the consequent distortion of the marginal text blocks.

Transition period

This period is characterized by the use of machine-made papers and the growing use of lithography to print the maps. Here we find the initial products of the great national surveys; the large, detailed (and brittle) charts of the world's oceans; fire insurance and county atlases; maps of canals, railroads and highways; and pioneering efforts at mapping the earth's crust and its natural and human resources. This group of maps will present the greatest challenge to the map curator of the early 21st century. It will be here where the nasty aspect of triage will first be met. These maps, unlike those of the earlier period, do not hold much fascination for the collector: they are not finely engraved works of art on fine hand-made papers coloured by artisans, but products of the burgeoning industrial age of which they are representative. They are often large, plain, monochromatic lithographs with little to recommend them except for their vital importance in documenting our world as it was transformed, for better or worse, from a traditional agrarian society into an industrialized one. Among these are maps that in all likelihood cannot be saved – deterioration has progressed to the point where merely attempting to unfold them in some cases causes tearing.

It is here that map curators must concentrate their efforts, and where, in fact, some effort is being expended. The Library of Congress has been actively scanning panoramic city views, Civil War maps and railroad maps, but this is only the tip of the iceberg.

Methods of transferring and archiving old maps in digital format

When we speak of digitizing maps in this context, we are not referring to the manual capture of points and vectors using a digitizing table, a technique of encoding data for automated mapping or Geographic Information Systems, but rather the overall imaging, or scanning, of the map. This is done either directly, through the intermediary of a photographic print or transparency, or with a digital camera, or scanner. A 'scan', or digital copy, represents a sampling of points drawn from a continuous analogue image. It breaks the image of the map into a matrix of rows and columns of tiny picture elements, referred to as 'pixels'. The density of these pixels, which is expressed in lines or dots per inch (dpi), is what gives the scan its clarity – the greater the density (or resolution) of the scan, the sharper the image. There is a considerable literature on the scanning of text and graphic materials (for example Kenney and Chapman, 1996; Besser and Trant, 1995; Reilly and Frey, 1996; Corsmeier, 1998; Allen, 1998; see also articles in Issue 12 of *Meridian*, 1997).

Dynamic range

When an image is scanned, the scanner records a colour value for each pixel. The number of colours available for each pixel is referred to as the dynamic range. In the simplest case, that of the *bitonal* scan, the scanner makes a black–white determination for each pixel. Relative to the size of the file generated by the scan, this is by far the most efficient system as each pixel is represented by only one bit. Bitonal scanning, while acceptable for text, is not well suited to map scanning, at least for archival purposes, even if the map is monochrome. The fine curved and angled lines so characteristic of maps, tend to look broken and jagged, and areas of half-tones or other patterns appear mottled. Also, the black–white character of the scan is not subtle enough to capture any texture in the paper. These shortcomings, of course, are not inherent in bitonal scanning, but rather in the resolution that is typically employed; after all, monochrome maps consist only of black ink on white paper. To ameliorate this situation, scanners of much greater resolution than currently feasible would have to be employed.

A practical solution to this problem is to introduce shades of grey into the palette. In this way, when the scanner encounters pixels neither wholly black nor white, along the edge of a line, for example, a number of different shades of grey may be selected. Also, areas of half-tone may be represented as the shade of grey originally intended by the printer. While the product of such a scan is not a perfect replica of the original, the results can be virtually indistinguishable from the original when scanned at a suitable resolution. Grey-scale scanning is typically eight bits (or one byte) in depth which yields a total of 256 shades inclusive of black and white. Although 256 shades is the norm, fewer have been employed with reasonably good effect. The USGS Digital Raster Graphics, mentioned above, actually utilize only one shade of grey interposed between black and white, and the appearance is quite acceptable for the use intended.

For colour maps, and even antique monochrome maps, scanners are employed that are able to evaluate each pixel in terms of the intensity of each of the three primary colours (normally red, green and blue) on a 256-point scale, where zero is black and 255 (the highest value) is the primary colour in its full intensity. Thus, each pixel is represented by 24 bits, or three bytes (some scanners actually evaluate the intensity of the primary colours on a 12-bit or 4096-shade scale, but generally reduce to the standard eight bits for recording the results). In this way, white is represented as the value 255,255,255, and black as 0,0,0. (A source of confusion here is that in computer graphics, both additive and subtractive primary colours are employed: printing uses the subtractive primaries of cyan, magenta and yellow, but in screen display, the red, green and blue additive primaries are used. With the additive primaries, the value 0,0,0 is black, while with subtractive primaries it is white). This system permits a possible total of 16,777,216 (256^3) colours including black and white, a palette more than ample to handle the needs of cartographic representation. In some instances the agency scanning the maps may actually wish to limit the number of colours represented in the palette. This could especially be the case with charts and topographic maps where only a few actual standard colours were originally employed. A good example of this is, again, the US Geological Survey's Digital Raster Graphics which employ a palette of only 13 colours. The use of such a limited, predefined palette allows for a uniformity that is especially important when map sheets are to be combined. It can also have the effect of greatly reducing the size of the data file.

Resolution

As mentioned above, the clarity of the scan is dependent upon the density of the pixels in the digital image. This density, or resolution, is expressed in lines, or dots, per inch (dpi). A considerable amount of experimentation has been conducted to determine the optimal resolution for the preservation scanning of maps. It can generally be said that the higher the resolution the better the image. The current maximum physical limitation of coupled CCDs is 600 dpi (higher stated resolutions result from interpolation and optical magnification (Bone, 1997)). However, various institutions have found that using this current maximum resolution has certain disadvantages: the file sizes for large maps become extremely large, they are difficult and slow to work with and, even when compressed, transferring them over the Internet can be a formidable undertaking. Furthermore, it has been found that as resolution increases, improvements in overall image quality tend to level off. In light of these difficulties, lesser resolutions have been selected for scanning projects by several major institutions. The Scanning Committee of the Center for Geographic Information of the Library of Congress Geography and Map Division has recommended that the Division's standard be 300 dpi (Mangan, 1997). The same standard has been adopted by such institutions as the National Library of Australia (National Library of Australia, 2000), and the Colorado Digitization Project (1999). Lesser resolutions (200–300 dpi) have been employed by Columbia University Library (Image Quality Working Group of ArchivesCom, 1997), and by the USGS for the Digital Raster Graphics (250 dpi) (US Geological Survey, nd). Following the recommendation of Cornell University (Kenney and Chapman, 1996) the Bibliothèque National of France has adopted the general resolution of 200 dpi for coloured maps, but recommends resolutions as high as 600 dpi for very detailed maps (Bibliothèque National, 2000). Values of even less than 200 dpi were ultimately selected for maps scanned by the Texas State Archives, with legibility being the main criterion (Velgos, nd).

Scanning methods

The scanning of a map can be done either directly or through a photographic intermediary, such as a print or negative, with a variety of different kinds of scanning devices. Scanners include drum scanners, sheetfeed scanners, flatbed scanners and digital cameras. There are also smaller high-density scanners suitable for film negatives and diapositives.

The original type of scanner was the *drum scanner*. It consists of a rotating Plexiglas cylinder to which the map to be scanned is attached. A sensor and light source move from one end of the cylinder to the other as the cylinder rotates, scanning the entire surface of the map. Although drum scanners have long set the standard for accuracy, they are expensive and the process is slow and not recommended for items of significant value as they can cause a great deal of stress to the original which must actually be taped in place.

Sheetfeed scanners are faster, capable of high-quality scans, less expensive and have no document length limitation. The problem with the sheetfeed scanner is that the cartographic document must be capable of being fed through the machine (somewhat like feeding a document through a fax machine); in addition, and this is somewhat more limiting, the curator must be *willing* to feed the map through the machine. The result is that few such scanners are being used in major library map preservation scanning projects at present.

Flatbed scanners are most commonly used at the present time, with smaller, inexpensive units becoming standard equipment for home and office computer installations. Although desktop scanners are presently very inexpensive, machines large enough to be practical for map preservation are still well beyond the means of all but the wealthiest institutions. For example, the Tangent scanner in use at the Library of Congress Geography and Map Division had a price of $65,000 quoted in 2000 (**http://www.colorscan.com/products/flat.html**). This scanner is a large format flatbed apparatus with a bed of 24 x 36 inches. While, perhaps, a majority of the maps in the average map collection will be of a size small enough to fit on the bed of such a device, a very sizeable number will not be, and these maps will require scanning in two or more sections. This ultimately requires a large outlay of staff time to put the images back together again. Another obvious disadvantage is that the item to be scanned must be inverted and placed down on the glass. This is not problematic for smaller maps, but large maps, maps attached in books and large atlases are difficult to manoeuvre and can be easily damaged by the slightest slip.

High end (as opposed to consumer) *digital cameras* possess certain obvious advantages over other types of scanners. The document need not be taped, fed through or inverted, but is simply placed face up under the camera. This is not only the technique least physically stressful to the document, but it permits the scanning of any format likely to be found in a map collection including atlases, fold-out maps in books and even globes, if desired. The National Library of Australia conducted a successful trial project in 1998 utilizing a digital camera capable of capturing an area of 20 x 28 inches at the selected resolution of 300 dpi. The report on this project indicated that a new camera by the same manufacturer, not ready in time to be utilized for the project, would be capable of capturing an area of 35 x 42 inches, and that this would probably be the instrument utilized by them in future projects. The disadvantages cited were the size limitation (to be somewhat ameliorated with the new camera), the length of time needed for scanning (25 minutes per map) and the resultant exposure of the maps to large amounts of light over the duration of the scanning process. The difficulty of ensuring a uniform light over the entire map was also cited. A digital camera of French manufacture, Jumboscan by Lumière Technology (see **http://www.jumboscan.com**), promises to resolve the few difficulties posed by other digital-camera-type scanners. It is capable of capturing an area of 40 x 50 inches at 300 dpi at the rate of only 90 seconds per scan. Jumboscan has also developed its own lighting system which has been declared safe by art museums (including the Louvre) utilizing the system. The main drawback is the price for this system, which would be more than double the cost of the large flatbed scanner cited above. It can be assumed, however, that prices for such systems will fall over the next few years as the technology matures and the competition increases.

Making old maps compatible with modern digital mapping

Thus far in our discussion of the scanning of maps, we could as well substitute the term 'art print' in each instance we have used the term 'map'. The main difference is the use of textual data in the map, but this is still of limited consequence – a good imaging of an art print would also be a good imaging of a map and vice versa. A large number of the maps in our collections that we would eventually want to scan could also be georeferenced, which is really what separates them from art prints. The object of georeferencing is to be able to display a scanned map in a Geographic Information System, not only as a simple image, but also in terms of the geographical location it represents. As the cursor is moved around the image of the map on the computer screen, the software is able to determine the coordinates of any point. Furthermore, we would be able to combine our map with other digital maps, other layers of spatial data, including digital aerial photographs, and even textual, tabular and pictorial data. In this manner, we would be better able to realize the full potential of scanned maps as historical documents.

Not all maps are candidates for successful georeferencing. The map must be constructed on some known projection and its graticule must be consistently scaled over the entire map. Furthermore, the positions of the geographical features shown on the map should conform reasonably well to those on current maps. If positional displacement between the old map and the modern digital map is systematic, it is likely due to the use of different datums, which can be rectified through the software. If, however, positional displacement is erratic, georeferencing is probably not especially useful, unless you are attempting to show how the location of a particular geographical feature, such as a lake, an island or even a continent, has been placed on maps through time. A motivation for georeferencing is the supposed ability to combine the scans of series sheet maps and present a virtual large-scale topographic map of a state or country. It should be considered, however, that individual sheets in map series are often projected individually and were not intended for combining with other sheets. Rasterized maps can be re-projected, as were the Digital Raster Graphics, but then, some of the original character of the map is violated, and one might question whether the map was actually *preserved*.

To georeference a map successfully, it must be scanned with a high degree of planimetric accuracy and the central meridian of the map must align precisely with a column of pixels. If the image of the map is spatially irregular due to shrinking, wrinkling, dissection, or imperfect contact with the plane of the scanner because the map is in a binding, or, if the graticule of the map is not aligned precisely with the scan matrix, GIS software will not be able to determine positions on the map with any degree of accuracy and overlays will not line up. Furthermore, the map's scale, projection and datum must be known. A good Geographic Information System will support literally hundreds of projections and datums, but it may well be that the projection that is required is not supported, especially when dealing with old or locally produced map series. In many cases, all that may be necessary is to adjust the projection and datum configurations. All too often, however, a map may not indicate the projection used, and even if it does, the specifics of the datum are rarely made explicit. Yet these elements must be known in order successfully to georeference the map, so further research may be necessary. As for scale, it must be borne in mind that when the map is scanned, the scale of the map can become quite elusive, and the real scale becomes the size of the pixel on the ground along the central meridian, for example. The map's scale factor can be adjusted fairly easily, however, to make the GIS graticule line up with that of the scanned map. If the map is on a known projection and the scan is aligned and regular, georeferencing can be easily achieved with the appropriate software, but the additional processing time for each sheet may be substantial.

Preserving the digital map

Of the various aspects related to the preservation of digital maps, some of which are analogous to traditional map production and some of which are common to all digital libraries (Task Force on Archiving of Digital Information, 1996), those of file format and preserving the unpublished are of particular interest to cartographic collections.

While file format is of general interest in the digital library community, the prevalence of vector map formats, in addition to the wide range of exotic raster formats in spatial data collections, poses special problems. It is not unusual for a map library to possess digital data files, but lack the software to view them. However, over the past several years, the convenience of the end-user has become more of a concern to data producers with the result that data sets are now usually offered in a limited number of standard file formats that are likely to remain viable for some time to come.

Preserving the unpublished is also a matter of growing concern. There have long been maps of an official nature existing in a state of continual compilation and revision. Such maps as Spain's *Padrón Real* or a town's municipal tax map have remained unpublished for such diverse reasons as national security or low demand. Collecting and preserving these fugitive materials has often not been possible because of state secrecy, unknown availability, or because they are too voluminous to maintain.

Digital cartographic technology is presenting both challenges and opportunities to the map library in this regard. The challenge is that most large-scale mapping is being computerized, and the maps, if previously published, are often now being made available only as prints on demand. The opportunity is that, given the cooperation of the mapping authority, whole sets of maps can be deposited in map libraries, at regular intervals, in space-saving digital formats.

An excellent example of this is the recently implemented plan in the UK whereby Ordnance Survey will henceforth distribute its large-scale digital data (originally captured at scales of 1:2500 or 1:1250) to the nation's six legal deposit libraries, as an annual 'snapshot', on CD-ROM. These maps are now only available as vector data or as maps printed on demand from an evolving national topographic database, and not as litho print runs. This has raised concerns about how a consistent time series of these data could be preserved (Board and Lawrence, 1994). The data are to be imported into a customized version of the MapInfo software package for viewing by readers in the copyright libraries, but will be archived in both NTF and MIF format (Fleet, 1998).

What will/should map librarians be doing to archive old maps appropriately now and in the future?

The Geography and Map Division of the Library of Congress holds around five million sheet maps and a collection of some 60,000 atlases which is estimated to yield an additional eight to ten million maps. This is the largest collection in the world, but even at this size, it is far from containing a copy of every extant map in the world today. There are, no doubt, millions of additional titles of printed maps found in libraries around the world plus unknown millions of manuscript maps held by libraries and archives. Few people would disagree that it is our collective responsibility to preserve this body of information for posterity, but it is indeed sobering to view the vastness of the task before us, especially in light of the primitiveness of the tools in hand and the lack of a social structure to accomplish our aims.

By primitive, I don't wish to suggest that our present tools are not capable of producing a lasting result. On the contrary, today's finest equipment is capable of excellent results that should satisfy most research and reproduction requirements indefinitely. On the other hand, the cost is very high, and the necessary equipment is available only to a select few libraries with large budgets or the wherewithal to acquire suitable scanners free of charge, such as the Library of Congress. Furthermore, the rate of scanning is very slow. Assuming, unrealistically, that the 13 to 15 million maps in the Library of Congress were all of a size capable of single-shot capture on the Library's present large flatbed scanner, the time required to scan the collection, assuming ten minutes per scan, and an eight-hour day, would be almost a thousand years!

Aside from technology, which will certainly change dramatically over the next few decades, the real issue involved here is the social and political structure needed to accomplish such a task at an appropriate scale of activity. Map curators work in an environment in which map cataloguing has traditionally been considered a frill, staffing levels kept minimal, acquisitions budgets low or non-existent, and where expansion is usually not an option. How then can we ever assume that there will suddenly be the resources needed to preserve this cartographic heritage?

There are, however, several factors working in our favour here. Firstly, the really old material is generally not disintegrating very rapidly, if at all. Furthermore, the amount of this material is not overwhelming, and it seems to attract most interest when preservation projects are planned. Producing digital copies of our oldest and rarest cartographic treasures also makes sense because providing good copies to researchers will eliminate much of the need to handle the actual items. This principle has actually been applied for years as many libraries have routinely photographed their rarest maps and made these photographic products available to researchers. On the other hand, provided that they are not carelessly used, these maps will likely be around for centuries more whether or not we take an active role in their preservation.

Secondly, the great mass of material dating from roughly World War 2, or even somewhat before, to the present is still in generally serviceable condition. Although the oldest sheets in this grouping may be yellowing and are less supple than they used to be, the preservation of these items can still safely be put off to a later time. An exception would naturally be heavily used materials to which scanning could provide greater access without the inevitable degradation of the originals. The maps in this category are also the ones most likely to be still under copyright, and being able to delay action will tend to make matters much easier later on.

The material of greatest concern, as mentioned earlier, consists of printed maps and atlases produced from roughly 1850 into the first decades of the 20th century. Although saving them as artifacts will soon cease being an option, it is, of course, possible – and necessary – to preserve the contents of these maps. This is at present not an easy mandate.

When encountering a map or series of maps that has deteriorated beyond the point where it may generally be used, we currently have few options at our disposal. If we're dealing with only a few items, they well may be mended and encapsulated. A larger set could be taken out of the general collection and placed in protective storage. In either case, we're only postponing the inevitable. The paper is disintegrating and the map will eventually have to be discarded or sent out for very expensive conservation work. Deacidifying a map will not miraculously restore it. A map of great artifactual value can be deacidified, reinforced and encapsulated. This will hold the map for a while, but at considerable expense. There are many maps that certainly deserve such treatment, but as much as we would like to save everything, this will not be possible.

Beyond attempts at preservation, there is currently little that we can do. Most libraries do not yet have the facilities to scan and archive cartographic materials, but even if they did, they would find it difficult to determine what to do. There is, for example, no clearing-house of scanned cartographic materials where one could go to find out if someone else has scanned the map in question, and if someone had, what standards were applied and whether a particular library could have access to the data file.

The need for cooperation

The whole idea of shared responsibility for the digital preservation of cartographic materials assumes a level of communication and cooperation not currently present in the map library community. Because of the great expense involved in archival scanning, redundancy is a waste of valuable resources. Unfortunately, with the absence of a central registry of work already done, it may at this point be virtually impossible to avoid duplication. While a number of scanned maps are available via the Internet, there is no utility which provides consistent, easy, unambiguous or even reliable access to these documents. To use an analogy to cataloguing, the present situation is not unlike what existed in the library world prior to the introduction of the *Anglo-American Cataloguing Rules* and online cataloguing utilities: while there were standards set by the major national libraries, individual libraries were free to adopt their own standards, and while libraries in the USA, for example, came to rely on printed card sets from the Library of Congress, there was nothing else in place to prevent a massive duplication of cataloguing effort. It would seem that what is now needed are developments similar to AACR with respect to map scanning.

Although at least preliminary standards have been set by various national libraries and individual university library scanning projects, a generally accepted set of international scanning standards will need to be adopted as a first step. Such standards will not only refer to the physical quality of the scanning process, but must address such issues as documentation and availability. The issue of documentation is crucial – a scanned map must be carefully identified and the specifications of the scan itself must be fully recorded as metadata. In an ideal world, the scan would be loaded on a server and made generally available via the Internet at something resembling the resolution specified in the standard. In addition, there must be a simple, reliable way of finding both the scanned map and its documentation. To return to the example of the Library of Congress, an active scanning programme was established in the Geography and Map Division in 1995. The programme was well conceived and could serve as a model in most respects. Technically, the scans are of excellent quality and are delivered to users via the Internet through the medium of the MrSID compression system. To the user, MrSID has several advantages: it allows convenient and rapid panning and zooming both over the Internet and (with free downloaded software) on your own machine; it permits a lossless compression ratio of 22:1 enabling rapid downloads of map data files; and, it permits, with the downloaded software, regeneration of the original TIFF image files on your own machine.

Beyond this, however, all of LC's scans are well documented and can be accessed not only through the *American Memory* web page – the Internet 'front door' for all of LC's scanning efforts – but also through their online library catalogue (which provides hot links to the scanned maps), and through the corresponding MARC records loaded in major online cataloguing utilities such as OCLC. Thus the scans, the record of their existence, and other pertinent data are available through established, reliable means.

The idea of OCLC serving as a clearing-house for map scanning is an intriguing one, and deserves some consideration. OCLC serves a very large number of libraries and has become international in scope; it has also become institutionalized within the library world and is unlikely to go away in the near future. The use of such a utility would tie the scanning process to the bibliographic record, which is, of course, highly desirable. Also, the MARC format is flexible enough to contain notes on the availability of the scan and Internet URLs.

There are, however, certain difficulties. The Library of Congress is in the position where, when it modifies its MARC record, the utilities, like OCLC, simply load the updated version. A member library, upon producing a scan, could not simply update the applicable record in OCLC. If the original record were theirs (not altogether likely), it could be modified, but otherwise, a new and essentially duplicate record must be produced which, of course, makes locating the scan more difficult and adds to congestion in the database. Furthermore, since there are no established standards, we have no way of ensuring that a cited scan would adhere to generally acceptable standards. OCLC, although officially 'international', is essentially an

American utility: few great libraries beyond the borders of the United States contribute their holdings to it, and even in the USA, most major research libraries don't use OCLC at all. Furthermore, a large amount of scanning is done outside of the library world by institutions and even individuals who would have no reason to join OCLC, and to whom the MARC format is alien. Finally, MARC's difficulty in dealing with map series would make the recording of scans of the individual sheet in a series a difficult matter. If, for instance, a library wished to scan the historical topographic maps covering its immediate geographical region, there is no way bibliographically to attach these under the entry for the series as a whole.

Therefore it would appear that the existing bibliographic infrastructure is not suited to handle the clearing-house function that will be required over the next decades as increasing numbers of libraries, archives, agencies and individuals begin to scan substantial numbers of their at-risk cartographic documents. There needs to be a centralized online utility where libraries and other agencies could report their scanning activity and refer to when selecting materials for scanning so as to avoid costly duplication of effort. This utility would also enable those actively engaged in scanning to report in advance items scheduled for processing. The features of this utility would include: 1) a sufficiently detailed bibliographic record that could distinguish between editions, states and variants of individual map titles; 2) a bibliographic structure that would enable individual parts of a larger work or series (an atlas or map series) to be recorded subsidiary to the title of the work as a whole; 3) the technical standards and details of the scanning process; and 4) the availability of the scan.

This utility, or clearing-house, will need to be run by a national or major research library or by a consortium of libraries. It will need to be institutionalized to help ensure its perpetuity; it cannot, for example, rely solely on the enthusiasm (and good health) of some ambitious map curator. And it should be established with the cooperation and involvement of the principal libraries and archives to ensure their participation.

Bearing the costs

The final, and perhaps most difficult, issues are how the digital map library of the future will be built and then administered. As we have already established, the cost of building this digital library will be enormous, and the assumption, perhaps, is that this cost will be borne by the libraries or their parent institutions with inputs from various granting agencies. It may also be an assumption, reasonable enough, that this virtual library will exist over the Internet, and, based on ample precedent, that access will be free and unlimited world wide.

It might be asked here why libraries, which have built their collections, sometimes over hundreds of years, should go to unprecedented lengths and great expense to preserve their collections through scanning and then be expected to distribute their products free to all. This would of course be very egalitarian: the most humble community college would at once have the same information resources as Harvard and Oxford. This may be viewed as a laudable goal, but one, perhaps, best left to politicians, not librarians, to achieve. It is the librarian's responsibility to build, preserve and administer collections for the benefit of his or her clientele. It is also the librarian's responsibility to understand the magnitude of the task at hand and to work to develop a preservation model that recognizes both this magnitude and the library world's economic realities. Simply put, if someone wishes to utilize our resources, they must also be willing to help shoulder the cost of making these resources available and to agree to abide by specific limited-use principles.

Helping to shoulder the cost can take various forms. It can, for instance, take the form of a simple fee payment by a library or individual to gain access to data files, or it can take the form of elaborate consortial arrangements in which contributing libraries and archives essentially barter their data. These options can certainly exist side by side.

One possibility for the virtual map library of the future is for map collections actually to form this consortium, and through it, to run the clearing-house, divide the responsibility for preservation scanning, monitor the bibliographic and technical standards of its members, maintain the data files and administer the digital library's 'circulation', ie the distribution of data to members and non-members alike. In this way, the virtual map library would be a creature of our own making and under our own control.

And finally, as we enter the new millennium and the outlines of the digital library come into view, it is essential that we as map librarians do not succumb to the temptation of short-term gain offered by vendors proposing to scan collections free of charge, even throwing in a digital copy for good measure, in exchange for the future rights to control the data. The digital copy of a Mercator map must remain our property as much as the highly valued original in our vault. If not, the digital library of the future will be an increasingly expensive one to our users, and one over which we will have no control. We must bear in mind that, as map curators, librarians or archivists, we have been entrusted by society's cultural institutions to preserve and make available our cartographic heritage now and in the future. And, in that future, as digital resources become ever more prominent features on the scholarly landscape, it would be unfortunate if we found ourselves eclipsed by enterprises motivated not by the precepts of good library stewardship, but rather by ordinary business considerations.

References

Allen, D Y (1998) Creating and distributing high resolution cartographic images, *RLG DigiNews*, **2** (4), available at
http://www.rlg.org/preserv/diginews/diginews2-4.html.

Allen, R S (1996) Map collection physical condition assessment survey methodology and results, *Special Libraries Association Geography and Map Division Bulletin*, **184**, 11–27.

Besser, H and Trant, J (1995) *Introduction to imaging: issues in constructing an image database*, available at
http://www.getty.edu/gri/standard/introimages/01-Intro.html.

Bibliothèque National (2000) **http://www.culture.fr/culture/mrt/numerisation/fr/dll/ resoluti.html**.

Board, C and Lawrence, P (eds) (1994) *Recording our changing landscape: the proceedings of the Seminar on the Future History of our Landscape held at the Royal Society on 16th October, 1992*, The Royal Society.

Bone, J (1997) *Do you really need all that resolution?*, available at
http://www.infomedia.net/scan/TSF-Resolution.html.

Colorado Digitization Project (1999) *General guidelines for scanning*, available at
http://coloradodigital.coalliance.org/scanning.html.

Corsmeier, T (1998) The microreproduction and digitization of maps: a comparative analysis, *Western Association of Map Libraries Information Bulletin*, **30** (1), 10–34, available at
http://gort.ucsd.edu/mw/waml/corsmeier.htm.

Fleet, C (1998) Ordnance Survey digital data, its access, usage and archiving, *The British Cartographic Society 35th Annual Symposium, Proceedings*, 20–5.

Harley, J B and Woodward, D (eds) (1987–) *The history of cartography*, University of Chicago Press.

Image Quality Working Group of ArchivesCom (1997) *Technical recommendations for digital imaging projects*, available at
http://www.columbia.edu/acis/dl/imagespec.html

Kenney, A R and Chapman, S (1996) *Digital imaging for libraries and archives*, Cornell University Library.

Mangan, E (1997) LC/G&M's scanning program: where we are and how we got here, *Meridian*, **12**, 37–43.

National Library of Australia (2000) *Rare map digitisation project report, March 2000* , available at
http://www.nla.gov.au/rmaps/rmap_report.html.

Reilly, J M and Frey, F S (1996) *Recommendations for the evaluation of digital images produced from photographic, microphotographic and various paper formats*, American Memory Project, available at
http://lcweb2.loc.gov/ammem/opirpt.html.

Skelton, R A (1972) *Maps: a history of their study and collecting*, University of Chicago Press.

Task Force on Archiving of Digital Information (1996) *Preserving digital information: report of the task force on archiving of digital information*, Commission on Preservation and Access.

US Geological Survey (nd) *Overview of the USGS Digital Raster Graphic (DRG) program*, available at
http://mcmcweb.er.usgs.gov/drg/drg_overview.html.

Velgos, J (nd) *One bit at a time: bringing the State Archives to the Internet*, available at
http://www.txla.org/pubs/tlj75_1/archives.html.

11
Access to maps and spatial data

Chris Perkins

▶ *This chapter considers the nature and patterns of availability and access to maps and spatial data that have arisen as a result of technological change. It reviews spatial variation in coverage and availability of national framework data and explores the quality of mapping variation across the globe. Changes in data availability that flow from digital mapping are explored and thematic variation is discussed. Explanations for these patterns include organizational, economic and political factors. Library responses to these variations and to technological change are considered, with particular emphasis upon data format and the role of the web. It is concluded that there is a powerful trend towards access and away from acquisition of maps and data.*

Introduction

In the 1970s Ken Winch was able to document the availability of in-print published paper mapping – the significant national variations charted in his global survey reflected what could be acquired by any well resourced map library (Winch, 1976). Most maps were fixed in format and mass-produced as lithographic prints, largely on to a paper medium. By 2000 the impact of the technological transitions described throughout the present book had profoundly changed the nature and patterns of this availability and new forms of access to maps and spatial data were increasingly competing with the local provision of paper mapping (Parry and Perkins, 2000). It is these variations and the implications they pose for library practice that form the special focus of this chapter.

Changing patterns of availability

There is a Western technological view that we have the capability to map the world in hitherto undreamed-of detail, a view reflected in the upbeat proposals for the creation of a 'digital earth', at a resolution of one metre and held in a three-dimensional database (Goodchild, 1999). Technologies already exist to deliver such a project. High-resolution commercially available Russian and American satellite imagery is now available on global markets, and data from the IKONOS satellite launched in 1999 provide one-metre-resolution panchromatic images (Petrie, 1999). Orthorectified 1:10,000-scale orthophoto coverage has been commissioned in several European countries to provide seamless digital aerial mapping. New spatial data sources are increasingly being released and derived from independently collected data, a significant shift from the practice of the 1980s and early 1990s when data were captured and converted from previously published printed maps (see Chapter 12). Geodetic control has migrated to GPS-based systems and offers more cost-effective and precise underpinning to national framework surveys. These changes mean that it has become possible to capture digital map data in a much more economic manner than was possible using analogue photogrammetry or ground survey.

Meanwhile GIS has matured with at least a decade of developing implementation by many organizations across a very wide spectrum of the economy, and now supports the manipulation of spatial data across many different platforms and application areas. Storage and display technologies have evolved in parallel to the development of software and systems, and a significant new demand for data has grown with mapping agencies changing their practices to cater for these new market possibilities. The fixed format, multi-layered published and printed map that predominated until the 1990s has increasingly been disassembled into different products, delivered in digital form and targeted at specific markets.

Changes in data collection and geodetic control, and the release of digital spatial data sets for use in GIS applications have become all the more significant with the development of the web as a means of disseminating and distributing products to the market. One of the major implications of the rise of networked data lies in the distribution and decentralization that the web encourages, but revolutions in communications technology have also encouraged a more global approach to mapping, with moves towards standardization of data and metadata at continental scales (see Chapter 9).

Small wonder then that calls are made for new global mapping initiatives, which might apply these technologies and establish overarching global monitoring and mapping systems. However, upbeat aspirations such as those of Goodchild (1999) or Morrison (1999) are not yet reflected in available or accessible global data sets and the best complete global mapping remains at the relatively coarse scale of

1:1,000,000, albeit now as digital data. Indeed as Rhind (1999) has argued the future potential of technologically led global mapping initiatives depends upon the political and economic context.

We should acknowledge that the last decade of the 20th century witnessed substantial progress, but recognize that coverage of mapping remains uneven in its spatial extent, varying in thematic depth, and that access to maps and spatial data is still problematic for many areas of the globe. The following sections of this chapter describe these complex patterns, explain their variation and discuss the implications for access.

Variations in national framework data

The availability of topographic coverage and national framework data (Rhind, 1997) reflects a mixture of international mapping efforts and a much more patchy local practice varying from nation state to nation state.

Amongst the most significant recent global initiatives to yield larger scale topographic maps were the major programmes initiated by the US and Russian military during the years of the Cold War. Chapter 16 discusses the profound impact in the 1990s of the release of ex-Soviet mapping on to global markets – topographic coverage is now available for most nations, compiled to a single Russian specification and published at scales of 1:50,000, 1:100,000 and 1:200,000 for most of the land masses of the world. These maps have also been converted into digital formats by Western commercial agencies, but their currency declines year on year. US military products have also been deposited in North American map libraries and have filtered into the global civilian marketplace. Published US medium-scale military map series form the core of many collections. They do not offer the same resolution of data as the Russian mapping but printed world series such as the 1:1,000,000 scale *Operational navigational chart* have been captured as digital data and global coverage of the latter is available in the *Vmap* range.

Meanwhile significant advances have been achieved in topographic mapping programmes carried out by indigenous national mapping agencies. The framework data collected by these official agencies usually still provide a unique source of spatial information for a nation, and official bodies responsible for their collection and dissemination usually still remain as the monopoly supplier. However the specification, resolution and attributes of national maps and data sets vary greatly, as does the extent of spatial coverage.

Global attempts to evaluate national progress in mapping have emphasized topographic programmes, and have sought to quantify progress in coverage, rather than evaluating quality or investigating the diversity of framework data offered by different nation states. The regular surveys sponsored by the United Nations and published for the period from 1968 until the end of the 1980s (Brandenberger and Ghosh, 1990; 1991) exemplify this practice. Böhme (1989–93) also only addressed topographic programmes and his data also predate the shift to digital mapping.

From these surveys it is possible to generate simple maps charting variations in spatial coverage of particular scale bands of data. Some of the earliest attempts to chart the status of mapping were published in the first edition of *Bartholomew's citizen's atlas of the world* and reproduced in the millennium edition of *The Times comprehensive atlas of the world* (Times Books, 1999). More recent mapping of coverage showed how much of the world had been mapped at scales of 1:100,000 or larger in the mid-1980s (Parry and Perkins, 1987). Current patterns have also recently been generalized into a simple world map, presenting information towards the close of the 1990s and charting coverage of 1:100,000 scale or larger mapping (Parry and Perkins, 2000). Figure 11.1 reproduces these data and shows that at the millennium Eurasia and North America were the best covered. A more detailed explanation of contemporary patterns is provided in the country sections of *World mapping today* (Parry and Perkins, 2000).

These quantitative indices simplify the significant national variation in mapping progress. The spatial patterns that they depict depend upon the chosen scale band (Parry and Perkins, 1991) and a more complex appreciation of variation is needed by the map librarian. One approach has been to substitute a multi-factorial index of cartographic progress encompassing coverage, temporal depth of production, scale variation, availability and thematic depth (Baudouin, Inkel and Lapointe, 1999). In 2000 this index was used to construct continental mapping of indices of cartographic development, eg for Africa (Baudouin, Inkel and Lapointe, 2000). These maps, however, largely reflect the weighting placed upon factors used to derive the index and also fail to reflect any diversity of social and political context.

When considering acquisition the map librarian really needs a more complex appreciation of global variation and in particular needs to understand influences upon the *health* of mapping in different nations, which underpin issues such as data availability (Perkins and Parry, 1997). Health might include other factors such as the number of mapping agencies, the historical depth of data coverages, the survey quality, the existence or frequency of revision programmes and the diversity of mapped themes. It might encompass the existence and nature of digital programmes, or include pricing policies and legal contexts.

Health is closely related to availability of mapping. If access to resources is the concern then availability is a much more useful index for a map library than cov-

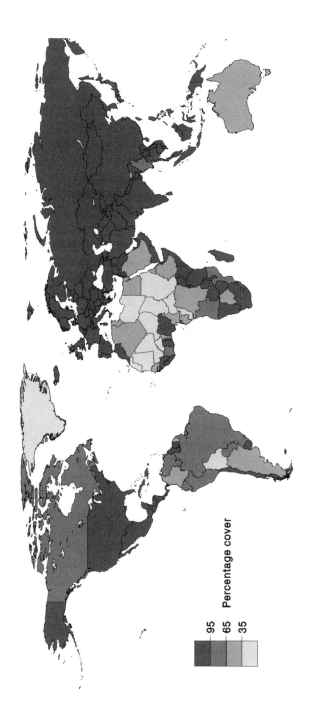

Fig. 11.1 *Topographic map cover at scales 1:100,000 or larger, 1999*

erage, reflecting as it does the areas from which maps and spatial data might be acquired. Figure 11.2 was also compiled from data collected during the compilation of the second edition of *World mapping today* and shows three classes of topographic map availability (Parry and Perkins, 2000).

Drawing attention to the contrasts between our two figures allows disparities in access to framework data to be revealed. For example the wealth of Chinese maps and spatial data is not available on global markets and many restrictions apply to locally published south-east Asian mapping. In contrast European mapping may be relatively straightforward to acquire on international markets, or increasingly to access on the world wide web. Some of the reasons for these disparities in availability are explored in greater detail below and in Chapter 12.

Digital developments

Perhaps the most significant trend affecting the generation of framework maps and spatial data has been the continuing impact of the digital revolution. Data from national mapping agencies are increasingly available in digital form, and remote sensing, GPS, GIS and web development are now central to the mission of many mapping agencies (Calvert, Murray and Smith, 1997). In the developed world production systems have migrated to a digital environment in almost all organizations, and digital revision is commonplace. No longer is digital development seen as merely a way of producing paper mapping in a more cost-effective manner. Instead digital conversion offers new possibilities.

Data themselves may be served as raster versions of published mapping, or increasingly as structured vector data, made available in coverages that differ significantly from their parent map-related sources. Thus the topographic survey might be broken down into land parcel data for a cadastral market, digital terrain data captured from contours, land cover data sets, street centre line data, building outlines or many other themes, perhaps also available as spatially referenced data separate from digital mapping. At the start of the millennium technology allows thematic data sets to be integrated with planimetric detail, digital elevation data or raster data from air photographs or satellite imagery in GIS systems. There is a large spatial variation in the availability of such data. Progress in Africa is very patchy: only nine African nations operated digital mapping programmes in 1999 (Parry and Perkins, 2000). In contrast Western European and North American organizations are likely to market maps and data in a number of digital formats and resolutions.

In the developed world spatial data sets are increasingly released from new agen-

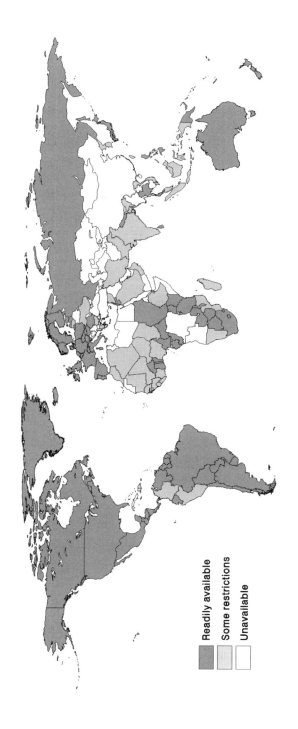

Readily available

Some restrictions

Unavailable

Fig. 11.2 *Availability of topgraphic mapping at 1:100,000 scale or larger, 1999*

cies, and derived from sources other than hard-copy mapping. In the past national mapping agencies enjoyed monopoly control over spatial data, but the digital revolution is coming to threaten this hegemony. Competition in the market for digital framework data is likely to increase, with offshore and image-based databases increasingly becoming available and more local competition becoming possible from purely commercial agencies, in markets that were formerly the remit of the national mapping agency alone.

Gazetteers and toponymic information

Names appearing on maps may now be acquired separately from the digital map data with which they may have been associated. Of course gazetteers have for many years been published and incorporated lists of different kinds of names, sometimes with associated geographical information, but their prime use was always to facilitate a search for specific places. Such a function transfers particularly well to a digital environment and it is hardly surprising to discover a wide variety of digital lists of place and other names packaged with search software. These listings appear on the web and as data on CD-ROM. Pre-eminent in digital data sources of place names is the *GEOnet names server*, which in 1999 replaced hard-copy published versions of US Board on Geographic Names' gazetteers and offers global coverage. The availability of street-level name data reflects the amount of investment in digital data programmes and local demand. Coverage is richest in urban areas, where street and property gazetteers form a significant new sector, and is also richest for the developed world.

Bathymetry and charting

Hydrographic and aeronautical charting reflect a greater degree of standardization than has yet been possible in the world of topographic mapping. International coordination of charting has led to the development of standardized symbologies and internationally agreed standards for electronic chart display systems. As with national framework survey data there has been a migration to an increasingly digital production environment, with raster scans of charts increasingly available, and with vector data incorporated into navigational systems. The availability of chart data reflects use: higher resolution charting is available where navigation requires it, as in port or airport charts (Perkins and Parry, 1996). In contrast en route charts of airspace between airports, and bathymetric charting of the world's oceanic depths far from port, remain at a low resolution.

Thematic mapping

International coordination of resource mapping has also been significant in the last decade and witnessed by continuing programmes at global scale (GRID) and at a continental scale in Europe (CORINE) and Africa (AFRICOVER). Meanwhile paper-based national resource mapping inventories have tended to move to a digital environment, and many series have been replaced in the 1990s by more user-oriented database systems, with customer payment. Geological mapping has also increasingly become more focused in the developed world on to applied fields (Cook, 1994), whilst mineral exploration has continued to drive mapping in sparsely populated mineral-rich countries such as Australia, Canada and Namibia.

Socio-economic data sets are a rich source for new thematic mapping. Official statistical agencies such as the US Census Bureau, or the Office for National Statistics in Great Britain increasingly disseminate in a digital form the results of regular national data collection surveys, and users may generate their own mapping of these data. In some cases the digital transition has led to a decline in the publication of paper census maps, but it has also led to an increased output of innovative digital products, distributed on CD-ROM or over the web. Other geographically referenced data sets relating to aspects of our social or cultural environment are also increasingly captured in a digital form, and independent of agencies charged with data provision: these too may increasingly be mapped (Chapter 13).

National atlases

A similar digital transition is taking place in the publication of national atlases, but paper as a medium of publication remains popular. Whereas socio-economic data are released to be used in GIS systems, atlases as a genre also serve the interests of their publishing agency and reflect cultural values, well suited to the fixed medium of publication on paper. Long the apogee of cartographic quality these flagship multi-thematic overviews continue to represent a nation and serve as cultural ambassadors, sponsored and underwritten by official scientific and mapping bodies. Almost every Western nation now has its own national atlas, and a continuing trend in publication has been the popularity of the genre amongst developing countries and newly independent nations (Parry and Perkins, 2000). The transition has allowed web and CD-based publication, and a more frequent update of thematic information. Similar data are now quite often released in media targeted at different market sectors. Germany and Spain, for example, are releasing hard copy and CD-based versions of their new national atlases, whilst Sweden and the USA are releasing national atlas data on the web, with commercially published CD-ROM spin-offs.

Commercial mapping

The technological transition has allowed many smaller cartographic houses to exploit specialist niche markets. A decline in the domination of the nation state, and in the monopoly control of national mapping agencies, has led to increased commercial activity across a very wide range of themes. The fields of tourist mapping, urban cartography and route finding continue to offer most possibilities for mass-market creation of conventionally published mapping. Digital data available in the public domain underpin the thriving US commercial mapping sector. In countries of the former Eastern European bloc new agencies have been formed, often by staff formerly employed in monolithic state mapping agencies, to cater for increasing demand for mapping in their liberalizing economies. Some of these new companies are selling conventional hard-copy maps, but of course the digital products described in Chapter 6 are also well represented. The precise role played by agencies in this sector varies (see Perkins and Parry (1996) for a pen portrait of the diversity of organizations in the surveying and mapping business in the UK). To their list may be added new kinds of specialization offered by the upsurge in web-based cartography described below.

Explaining the patterns

Whilst there have been significant advances in mapping, the 'window of accessibility' continues to swing open and shut in response to changing local economic and social factors. In 1987 we commented on the variation in accessibility of mapping and concluded that

> there is a continuum which ranges from the optimum (a public sector centralized official mapping agency in the western developed world, with civilian mapping responsibilities including the compilation of general and topographic mapping of its own state, which sells direct to the customer), to the worst possible organization for map acquisition (a public sector decentralized official mapping agency in the third world in a pro-Eastern block country, with military responsibilities including a very wide range of mapping tasks, whose maps are compiled through overseas aid programmes and which either operates only a very indirect sales service or does not sell maps).
>
> (Perkins, 1987, 16)

Is this organizational emphasis still relevant and what factors explain the patterns in 2000?

Organizational change

One of the most profound influences on the nature of map availability still lies with the nature of organizations disseminating mapping and spatial data. In 1987 1173 agencies were recorded in the first edition of *World mapping today* (Parry and Perkins, 1987). In 2000 the same authors recorded the existence of 2253 map publishers (Parry and Perkins, 2000). A very dynamic period has been framed between these two survey dates, in which there has been a significant turnover in the number and names of agencies. This period has also seen profound changes in the responsibilities held by mapping agencies. Many new agencies have been formed, and regional mapping responsibilities have expanded to reflect moves to devolve power, at the same time as pan-continental programmes have expanded. Mapping agencies have responded to technological change by shifting their emphasis away from making maps, towards the dissemination of spatial information. Many official Western agencies have invested significantly in new technologies, employ fewer staff, outsource increasing amounts of work, and are more likely to act as regulators of data quality, instead of being producers of mapping.

Economic context

The most important influence on map and data availability lies with national economic well-being. There is a clear association between economic development and mapping, and the worst mapped developing nations are invariably those with the lowest GDPs. African mapping often still reflects systems established in the colonial era, with any subsequent developments dependent on aid programmes often charged with very specific and local ends, rather than with the provision of a modern mapping infrastructure. Meanwhile in the West many official mapping agencies have been increasingly commercialized, and have responded to government pressure to recover more revenue by a radical shift in the nature of their publication programmes.

Legal and political background

Many of the constraints limiting availability of mapping stem from particular local legal or political contexts, often associated with an official view of the status of information (see Chapter 12). For example the restrictive Indian policy towards official map data stems in part from the historical context and military significance of the mapping of the sub-continent. The policy severely limits access to Survey of India mapping. Despite its absurdity in an era of readily available satellite data the local cultural background continues to be of greater significance than technological change (Shrikantia, 1999). The legacy of tight central control continues to regulate the availability of official Chinese topographic mapping, despite burgeoning Chinese economic growth. Elsewhere politically powerful military interests may limit access to data, as in Turkey. Instability severely limits availability of data, wars greatly encourage mapping activity, but during conflict civilian access to mapping is often restricted, eg in the Falklands or Bosnia. Nations marginalized from the global economic order remain notoriously difficult places to procure mapping, eg North Korea and Libya.

Acquisition or access?

The nature of map acquisition has also been changed in profound ways by the digital transition and libraries now have to decide whether to acquire, or to access data held elsewhere. Whether they choose to acquire, or to rely upon accessing someone else's data holdings, the format of the data plays a newly significant role in the process.

Acquisition of fixed-format material

In the era of fixed-format maps printed on paper and published in series or as monographs the processes of map acquisition were relatively straightforward. The map librarian faced similar choices to those confronting the acquisitions specialist concerned with 'grey' literature that was only poorly bibliographically controlled. Granted there were certain other spatial problems, but at least the format was fixed. The difficulties should not however be underplayed, and many remain relevant today.

A decision had to be taken over whether to anticipate user need, or whether to acquire in response to new demands. Did the demand fit with the library collection development policy? Should money be spent on acquiring the item, or might it be possible to acquire it through one of the extensive gift or exchange programmes that have underpinned the operation of map library services (Larsgaard, 1998)? If money were available, how should the inquiry be satisfied? How should the item be identified, what sources were there for its acquisition and how should an order be generated? Should money be risked on pre-payment, and a direct order placed with a supplier, or should a dealer be employed to procure the item, thus increasing the price, but perhaps avoiding the risk of financial loss? If so, which dealer should be employed, who held the best stocks, or could be relied upon to acquire the difficult material? If a new series of maps was about to be instigated should the map library place a standing order for items, or wait until its progress became more certain?

Identifying the mapping illustrates some of the problems that still plague the acquisition of printed mapping. Even if the librarian knows who publishes a map it might be very hard to trace where it can be acquired. Until the publication of *World mapping today* in the mid-1980s no single authoritative listing of map publishers existed (Parry and Perkins, 1987). Even their listing remained very partial for some nations and listed only address details. The turnover in mapping agencies described above illustrates this problem, and the latest listings (Parry and Perkins, 2000) are unlikely to remain current for long. No in-print listings of maps exist at a global scale, national sources are also still partial and inconsistent. Publishers' bibliographic standards vary very greatly, and map dealer listings are often partial. It is often very hard to discover who publishes a listed map or whether a commercially published map is a new edition, or an existing map, issued in a new cover. To discover whether a new edition of an officially published map has been released often poses a major problem.

Perkins (1987) urged map librarians to try to acquire material by direct contact with publishers, but it is small wonder that most major overseas map procurement by libraries in the years since the publication of *World mapping today* has relied upon the services of an international map dealer such as GeoCenter and Omni Resources.

The difference the format makes . . .

From the beginning of the 1990s additional factors were becoming significant. Probably the most important was the rise of a wide diversity of formats in which maps and spatial data could be acquired or accessed. No longer was the printed map the only acquisition option for a map library. Instead the range of output defined in Figure 11.3 became increasingly available.

Hard copy continues to be used by publishers, but some mapping is now printed on demand, rather than published to a fixed format and on standard sheet lines. New markets may be targeted in an on-demand service and printing costs reduced. More focused products emerge from this process. For example the constraints of a fixed sheet line system might disappear following a move to site-centred output from a digital database, or unnecessary detail might be stripped out from a map. On the other hand a map library may be unable to acquire consistent spatial coverages. Even greater flexibility is offered when the specification is under the control of a user who can decide what to include and how it should be mapped. Here the role of the library becomes very problematic. How should retrieval systems deal with user-defined and created hard-copy mapping? Every printed map output from a database becomes a unique library item and the con-

Hard copy	Electronic package: by thematic function
lithographic print	general reference atlas
fixed specification printed on demand	route planner
user-defined specification, printed on	census atlas
demand	urban atlas
	earth science atlas
	national/regional atlas
Electronic package: by medium of delivery	gazetteer
floppy	
CD-ROM	**Digital data**
web	raster
	vector
	boundaries
	attribute
	digital terrain
	gazetteer

Fig. 11.3 *Diversity of possible map output*

cept of a series is rendered redundant.

The *new electronic products* described in Chapter 6 also significantly alter the acquisition process. These electronic atlases may be tied to particular platforms or operating systems, and certainly in the past have been much more ephemeral creatures than their printed cousins. With the passing of an operating system so might the functions and data offered by an atlas also become redundant. Should something be acquired if it will only be capable of being used for a very few years? The other most significant problem that this new medium poses for acquisition is that publishers' descriptive information is often especially lacking. A good description needs to document function, data sources and quality. Only rarely does the librarian have access to enough critical material to know exactly what is being acquired.

Digital map data themselves are also increasingly marketed from almost every kind of cartographic agency. The format in which these data are available affects use and influences acquisition and access, and it is the diversity of format that creates some of the most significant acquisition problems. Quite simply there are too many different formats and a supplier is unlikely to provide data in the format most convenient for use. Conversion is likely to be needed (Larsgaard, 1998). The activities of conversion and serving data bring with them very significant cost overheads, but if data are to be served then interfaces may be required, software made available and support offered. Many users are unlikely to be able to 'do it themselves' or to have the background in GIS to be able to exploit full data value. There remain significant barriers to widespread public use of raw digital data, and even in 2000 it was concluded that 'it is in the professional and business applications that such data are visualized' (Parry and Perkins, 2000, 19).

Access via the web

Perhaps the *world wide web* offers the solution for the delivery of raw digital map data to users in a map library. The advantages of a common interface, hyperlinked structure, multimedia data and distributed data sets offer great potential for the map library to enhance the quality of access which it offers to users (see Chapters 7 and 8). No longer is it necessary for a map library to acquire mapping or spatial data, instead users can access remotely held data, which can be served to many locations from a single central source, in response to a database search. Data no longer needs to be distinguished from metadata, the catalogue can also link to the source it describes. Data delivered from password-protected sites such as that pioneered in the Ordnance Survey Digimap service are seen by many as a way forward for the map library. Carefully designed front-ends to data warehouses can guide users through download options, and reduce demands on a librarian's time. Material may be accessed that would never be acquired in standalone map libraries.

There are also significant advantages in such a model for data holders and producers. A single master version of a data set may be maintained and updated, without the need to disseminate revisions to many users on CD-ROM or other offline media. Licensing of use may be controlled centrally and if necessary charges may be levied for access, without the need to police data use. The increasingly commercialized web is likely to become more and more popular as a source of data to download and many cartographic agencies are experimenting with increasingly complex home pages, designed not only for marketing, but also as serious revenue sources. Parry and Perkins (2000, 20) concluded that 'we can expect more serious and larger scale digital map data sets to become available over the internet from sites with a charging facility'.

Meanwhile the web also serves significant numbers of finished maps to users. Many are user defined, the outcome of searches at routeing, tourist or weather-related sites, but appear on screen as GIF or JPEG format images for download, display or local printing. The increasingly commonplace use of interactive web mapping packages such as Autodesk Mapguide underpins this explosion of mapping (see Chapter 8). Other sites offer online digital libraries of images, such as the University of Texas Perry-Castañeda Library Map Collection (**http://www.lib. utexas.edu/PCL/Map_collection/Map_collection.html**).

Hyperlinks on a library website can form an overarching structure linking online public access catalogue records of material held in local collections to the wider world of the web. By constructing a sensible range of pointers on its home page, a map library may use the web as an increasingly viable alternative to the direct local acquisition of material (see Chapter 8). Inquirers may be pointed to records describing material held in the library in hard copy when these are most appropriate, or to other sites for material that could not be acquired locally. In 1998 the *Oddens' Bookmarks* list site was able to assist in up to 30% of inquiries in the University of Utrecht (Oddens, 1998). This site has nearly doubled its number of links in the three years since and its use has been enhanced through the construction of browsing and database search facilities. Other sites also bring together rich distributed resources made accessible through digital libraries such as the *Alexandria Digital Library Project* (Buttenfield, 1997). The reader is referred to Parry and Perkins (2000, 21–4) for a more detailed discussion of the kinds of access that are facilitated by the web.

Of course the increasing use of the web also has negative impacts. Users may no longer feel the need to visit the map library. They may rely upon web-based sources, when advice from an informed map librarian would have led to a richer set of answers to their needs. It must also be acknowledged that as yet the web is nowhere near to replacing the paper map for many types of inquiry. Download time and screen size severely limit the value of many web sources, and few expert systems yet offer the careful interpretation of source material provided in the map library. Many websites are ephemeral, URLs change more frequently than the physical address of a publisher. Advancing technology is also causing problems: software 'plug-ins' may be required to access newer mapping applications, frames-based interactive mapping sites may not be accessible to all users. Above all an infrastructure is needed to access the web, and networking, hardware and software may not be available, particularly in poorer nations, or less well resourced map libraries.

The changing context of map dissemination

The 1990s have seen the development of an increasingly global map market, in which dealers advertise their wares from websites and over the Internet using e-mail. Here we can only highlight the most significant changes.

The web has not only altered the nature of map use, it has also allowed different kinds of agency to deal in mapping (see Chapter 16). Map publishers are now able to market their wares direct to the customer, small map retailers are able to compete with larger wholesale operations, and the whole nature of map distribution and acquisition has been changed in a very profound way. Even map distributors with long and well regarded histories have had to change their practices in order to adapt to the new medium: witness the launch of a website by Edward Stanford in the autumn of 2000. Some have made a successful transition, but others have seen market share eroded. The most important change in this context has been the increasing significance of a number of North American dealers, notably Omni, Maplink and Eastview, and the rise of the International Map Trade Association (IMTA). Meanwhile the pre-eminent position held by GeoCenter ILH has progressively been eroded. The geo-scientific wing of GeoCenter was sold off in 1999 in a major corporate restructuring exercise, and the company no longer has the global significance that it enjoyed at the start of the 1990s.

Websites now offer detailed and regularly updated information about map products, together with samples of mapping. Dealers mail out targeted publicity over the Internet, and regularly use specialist listservers, such as MAPS-L to update potential customers about new products. Following up web addresses listed in the second edition of *World mapping today* gives the map librarian access to material beyond his or her dreams just a decade ago (Parry and Perkins, 2000). If money is available in acquisition budgets then a much more informed process of acquisition has become possible, and wider access provided to sources than was available in the past.

Conclusion

Changes in the availability of mapping have been associated with technological change, but also with the broader dynamic of socio-economic and political development. The technological shift towards more user-oriented mapping, in a wide diversity of data formats delivered increasingly over the web, has taken place in the context of a globalizing world economy. The paper map continues to be available, if declining in significance. Spatial patterns of publication and availability reflect the particular local contexts, which may be very ephemeral. In contrast the dynamic of change in the map library, stemming from the technological transition in mapping, leads relentlessly towards access, rather than acquisition. Collections that fail to make this shift may jeopardize their long-term chances of survival.

References

Baudouin, Y , Inkel, P and Lapointe, M (1999) Bilan cartographique mondial des pays en difficulté analysé à l'aide de l'indice de développement cartographique, *Proceedings of the 19th International Cartographic Association Conference, Ottawa 1999*, 121–4.

Baudouin, Y , Inkel, P and Lapointe, M (2000) *CDI: production years and cartographic details of Africa*, Université du Québec à Montréal, Department of Geography.

Böhme, R (1989–93) *Inventory of world mapping*, Elsevier, 3 volumes.

Brandenburger, A J and Ghosh, S K (1990) Status of world topographic and cadastral mapping, *World Cartography*, **20**, 1–102.

Brandenburger, A J and Ghosh, S K (1991) Status of the world's topographic mapping, official geodetic networks and cartographic services, *Surveying and Land Information Systems*, **51** (3), 178–84.

Buttenfield, B P (1997) Delivering maps to the information society: a digital library for cartographic data. In *Proceedings of the 18th Conference of the International Cartographic Association, Stockholm, Sweden, June 1997*, Swedish Cartographic Society, 1409–16.

Calvert, C , Murray, K and Smith, N (1997) New technology and its impact on the framework for the world. In Rhind, D (ed) *Framework for the world*, Geoinformation International, 133–59.

Cook, P (1994) The role of the geological surveys in the 21st century, *Episodes*, **17** (4).

Goodchild, M F (1999) Cartographic futures on a digital earth, *Proceedings of the 19th International Cartographic Association Conference, Ottawa 1999*, 5–14.

Larsgaard, M L (1998) *Map librarianship: an introduction*, 3rd edn, Libraries Unlimited.

Morrison, J L (1999) Important initiatives in geographic information science and spatial data collection with implications for cartography, *Proceedings of the 19th International Cartographic Association Conference, Ottawa 1999*, 43–9.

Oddens, R P (1998) Websurfing with "The Fascinating World of Maps and Mapping". In Fairbairn, D (ed), *Proceedings of the 35th Annual Symposium of the British Cartographic Society and Map Curators' Group Workshop*, British Cartographic Society, 2.

Parry, R B and Perkins, C R (1987) *World mapping today*, Butterworth Scientific.

Parry, R B and Perkins, C R (1991) Measuring the state of world mapping, *Mapping the Nations. Proceedings of the 15th Conference and 9th General Assembly of the International Cartographic Association, Bournemouth 1991*, 844–55.

Parry, R B and Perkins, C R (2000) *World mapping today*, 2nd edn, Bowker-Saur.

Perkins, C R (1987) Map acquisition. In Parry, R B and Perkins, C R *World mapping today*, Butterworth Scientific, 15–26.

Perkins, C R and Parry, R B (1996) *Mapping the UK: maps and spatial data for the 21st century*, Bowker-Saur.

Perkins, C R and Parry, R B (1997) Quality and quantity in world mapping, *Proceedings of the 18th International Cartographic Association Conference, Stockholm 1997*, Swedish Cartographic Association, 1167–74.

Petrie, G (1999) Characteristics and applications of high-resolution space imagery, *Mapping Awareness*, **13** (10), 33–7.

Rhind, D (ed) (1997) *Framework for the world*, GeoInformation International.

Rhind, D (1999) Business, governments and technology: inter-linked causal factors of change in cartography, *Proceedings of the 19th International Cartographic Association Conference, Ottawa 1999*, 29–35.

Shrikantia, S V (1999) Modern maps but outrageous regulation, *GIM International*, **13** (7), 68–71.

Times Books (1999) *The Times comprehensive atlas of the world*, 10th edn, Times Books.

Winch, K (1976) *International maps and atlases in print*, Bowker.

12

Spatial data and intellectual property rights

Robert Barr

This chapter introduces the changing implications for intellectual property rights that accompany the progressive digital transition from printed map to digital data set. It argues that there are profoundly changed economic relations arising from the dematerialization of information, and that the changing legal context of the digital world also poses significant challenges for the map library. Two models of data delivery are explored, and contrasts are drawn between arguments for restricted or free dissemination of digital spatial data. Security, data quality issues, organizational factors such as strategic advantage and profit, as well as data protection issues can be advanced to justify a restrictive policy, whereas notions of scientific knowledge and progress, the freedom of information and commercial gain can be used to justify a much less restrictive approach to digital data. The chapter concludes by arguing that map libraries need to adapt to short-term changes in their economic and legal contexts, but that a longer term and more proactive role may also be needed.

Introduction

When map sheets, or atlases, were the usual media for the delivery of spatial data, intellectual property issues were relatively straightforward. The material form of the data, and the limited scope for reproduction and abstraction, reduced the possibility of breaches of copyright. Librarians were in a position to advise on what constituted fair use of the materials and what required copyright clearance or the payment of a royalty.

Mapping software and Geographic Information Systems, popularized in the early 1980s by the release of commercial products by companies such as ESRI, led to a demand for data in digital form. However for much of the 1980s few such data were available. The main sources of data for automated mapping or analysis were the traditional paper maps that needed to be digitized. As the elements of these maps that were needed for particular projects varied, there was little exchange or sharing of data. Digital data were not widely available, with the exception of satellite or aerial photography or scanned reproductions of maps. Such raster images provided little scope for disguising the source of the data, and, as a result, were not much more challenging from a copyright point of view than paper products had been.

This situation changed when digital spatial data started to become available in larger quantities. There were two main kinds of such data. The first was boundary data to meet a demand for the thematic mapping of statistical and administrative data, mainly from censuses. Boundaries were typically digitized from a topographic paper map on which they had been drawn by following the appropriate features. In the USA a much more ambitious endeavour led to the digitization of both census boundaries and approximate street centre lines to facilitate both the taking of the 1980, 1990 and the 2000 censuses and the mapping of their results. This system, now known as TIGER (Topologically Integrated Geographical Encoding and Referencing), was very expensive to create, but under US Freedom of Information legislation, was re-sold by government at the marginal cost of reproduction and could then be re-distributed with no further charges.

Secondly national mapping agencies and cadastral agencies around the world started to capture their existing map base, as well as to update information, in digital form. Updates now need never be drafted on paper, they can be captured digitally in the field and incorporated into an agency's database directly. In the case of Britain's Ordnance Survey the primary purpose of the large-scale digital database (the capture of all large scale 1:1250 and 1:2500 maps was completed in the mid-1990s) has been to allow the plotting of a versatile series of maps using alternative symbolism where appropriate. However such digital maps need a substantial amount of post-processing to structure them into a form suitable for the attachment of attribute data to geographic objects identified on the map. This is a necessary step before the maps can be analysed in a GIS.

This conversion from paper maps, or digital maps derived from paper originals, to a fully digital product has not only dematerialized the map, it has also created a new form of information that is much more difficult to track. While the creation and ownership of a printing plate and the products produced from it are relatively straightforward so far as intellectual property is concerned, digital map data are much harder to track, control and own. This is particularly so when the laws that are applied to such data were often framed in an era of printed paper rather than weightless, invisible and easily transmuted binary digits.

What are spatial data?

In a material era it was clear that spatial data were made up of marks on a page, be they the notations in the original surveyor's notebook, or the finished symbology of the paper map. The provenance and the ownership of that material are relatively easy to establish.

In a digital era, however, spatial data, like many other informational resources, have dematerialized. This dematerialization of many informational goods has led to what has been called 'the weightless world' (Coyle, 1997). No adequate economic theory yet exists for informational goods, because they defy most of the conventional laws of economics. As with any other resource, an informational good costs money to produce. However, once produced it can be duplicated and distributed at a marginal cost that approaches zero. This leads to a fundamental mismatch between the aspirations of consumers and producers. Producers wish to recoup the original cost of production and expect to make a 'normal' profit. This, in the economic sense, is the amount of profit required to give a producer the incentive to produce the good in the first place. By contrast many consumers expect a good that can be reproduced at no cost to cost nothing. Most users of traditional map libraries clearly fall into this category of consumers, and the whole ethos of the library as a storehouse of knowledge is in part predicated on assumptions of free access to publicly available knowledge.

To complicate the issue further, digital spatial data can be transformed in many ways that make it difficult to trace its lineage. For example, a simple shift of a digital line will change every coordinate that makes up the line, while keeping its shape perfectly intact. Is the 'new' line a new spatial object? The law's 'reasonable man' would almost certainly say that it is not. However if one were to compare the coordinate pairs that make up each vertex of the line, each would be different from the original. There are many processes that will change spatial data but preserve intact its relationship to the original surveyed objects. Logically any such process that is reversible, or that is the result of the application of an algorithmic process to the original data, cannot create a 'new' item of spatial data. Not surprisingly there is again a conflict between users (in our context map library users) and producers. For example a producer of a set of digital boundaries would feel that when a user applies a generalization routine to the data, the resulting data are a 'derived product' of the original data and intellectual property rights in the new data set still belong to the original supplier. By contrast the user who has applied the transformation on a machine in a map library may feel that this new derived product is their invention and that a new intellectual property right has been established. The legal view of who is right has generally not been tested in law and is likely to vary between courts, and certainly between countries. The map library administration is placed in an uneasy position between user and producer, perhaps liable, and certainly forced into a role of policing or controlling the use of spatial data.

Boundary maps and other selective maps of cultural objects can be argued to be the result of an act of creation or of invention. However the recording of the location of topographic objects could be argued to be the discovery of a scientific fact. The distinction between an artistic creation, a useful invention and a scientific discovery is important in intellectual property law. Creations and inventions can be protected using copyright law or patents, while the discovery of a fact cannot. This issue has been central in the race between academic scientists and those working for commercial enterprises, where a fierce debate is raging over the patenting of human gene sequences together with potential applications. This has blurred the line between discovery and invention.

In the case of spatial information, cartographers are generally protected because the map and spatial data derived from it are interpreted versions of the true locations of objects on the earth's surface rather than a scientific discovery. Known errors in mapping agencies' files have been used in the past to prove copyright infringements where another party has claimed to have recaptured locational data from an independent source. Inaccuracies are often left in digital data sets where it is known that users, such as gas, electric, water or telephone utility companies have superimposed other information on the digital base (see Barr 1998a, 1998b). Such companies are interested in the relative positions of pipes and ducts to buildings rather than their absolute location in a scientifically established geodetic framework. In such cases mapping agencies may choose not to 'correct' the base data (Murray, 1997).

Laws in many countries do not allow copyright or patent protection for scientific facts, or 'sweat of the brow' compilations of facts such as gazetteers (Cho, 1998). This may cause a difficulty as improved locational tools such as GPS and differential GPS receivers, or better techniques for building gazetteers using database technology, remove the creative element, or the element of judgment, in the production of geographic information. It seems ironic that, as the techniques for the production of spatial data improve (though production costs may continue to act as a limit on spatial data quality), the protection of the law to allow the recovery of those costs may be reduced. Once again the map library as a holder of data may be placed in a difficult dilemma.

Behind the legal framework

Branscomb (1994) contends that a new legal framework must be devised to cope with the issues raised by digital information. However such a legal framework will take some time to develop and will not necessarily develop consistently between countries. Data protection laws have been formulated, particularly in Europe, to protect the privacy of the individual in an increasingly computerized environment. These laws caused a commercial rift between Europe and the USA when the export of personal information for processing was banned by the European Union if the recipient country did not have an equally strong data protection law. The respective laws were finely balanced, the European perspective gave primacy to the privacy of the individual while the US laws were designed not to impede the commercial processing of personal data. The issue that this example raises is that the legal framework, or the interpretation of the current, not necessarily relevant, laws will be influenced by the values of the state, organization or individuals who wish to have the information they are interested in treated in a particular way. There are few, if any, absolute legal principles concerning spatial information that will be uniformly interpreted by the courts.

This would suggest that a detailed analysis of how existing laws have been used to argue a range of intellectual property principles for spatial data may not be helpful in predicting how such principles may be applied in the future. The law, and national policies, can be adjusted in order to meet the needs of particular interest groups. These adjustments are then often used to justify a position on intellectual property rights. However, in the longer term, it is likely to be more useful to investigate the motivations that drive the various actors concerned with spatial data than to get bogged down in interpretations of the often-inconsistent verdicts that make up case law.

Taking stances

There is a schism between those who believe that spatial data should be free and those that feel that access to it should be restricted. It is interesting that this divide is not a straightforward one between the commercial sector, which may be considered most in favour of treating such data as a commodity that is sold, and the academic and public sectors that might be expected to be most in favour of free dissemination. The arguments and stances are far more complicated and are almost always based on the special interests of their proponents.

Attitudes and policies that affect spatial data are driven by a number of primary motivations. These motivations usually lead to one of two positions:

- A policy of restricted dissemination, which applies restrictions either to give a non-financial advantage to those holding or having access to data, or, to create artificial scarcity (given that data can be reproduced in a digital environment at a near-zero cost) in order to justify charging a particular amount for the data.
- A policy of 'free' dissemination of information, where the maximum charge is the cost of dissemination, not the cost of original production, nor any recompense for the ownership of the intellectual property. The implicit objective of 'free' dissemination is to maximize availability and, or, the use of data.

Arguments in favour of restricted dissemination

Security

Many states still restrict access to mapping and to digital spatial data for reasons of national military security. The armed forces are still the largest users of mapping data around the world and many mapping organizations were founded specifically to meet military needs. For example the British Ordnance Survey was founded over 200 years ago in order to ensure that Britain's army had accurate and up-to-date maps of the parts of the country that were under threat of invasion. Through much of the Far East even relatively small-scale maps are restricted by law and may not be exported (see Chapter 11). Such security considerations may override a wish to have up-to-date mapping funded out of revenue from data sales. Data are made available only to the military and to other organizations that are considered secure and unlikely to leak the data to a potential enemy. Libraries are unlikely to be able to acquire or access such data sets.

However such considerations are subject to rapid change of policy. The US Department of Defense had ensured that civilian use of the satellite Global Positioning System was degraded in accuracy in order to prevent enemy use of the technology for accurate targeting. But, on 1 May 2000, in anticipation of an international conference at which radio frequencies for positioning satellites were due to be allocated, the President announced that the 'selective availability' encryption was to be turned off with immediate effect. The intention to take this step had been previously announced, but the date was brought forward by many years as a matter of political expediency.

Data integrity

Certain data sets are controlled in order to ensure that the quality of the data is not undermined. Crown Copyright, copyright protection for government works, was introduced in the UK during the 19th century (Chancellor of the Duchy of Lancaster, 1998) in order to ensure that the market was not flooded with poor copies of Ordnance Survey maps and legal statutes. While Crown Copyright did guarantee an income to the Crown for government publications, preserving the integrity of those publications appears to have been the primary motive for the legal protection of government publications. This principle has continued to an era where cost recovery through the exploitation of tradeable information has become the primary motive, rather than the integrity of the data (Rhind, 1992). The implication for map libraries has often been that data have been priced well beyond local acquisition budgets.

Organizational strategic advantage

Access to, and the control of, particular spatial data sets can provide an organization with the ability to carry out certain functions that its competitors cannot match. For example customer lists provide an organization with a detailed picture of their own market penetration and the gaps in the market that they may still exploit. This is particularly so with utility companies, such as the former state monopolies, once they have to face the full force of competition. Typically such records are geo-referenced by address and collectively they make up a valuable geographical resource; however, they tend not to be available.

Telephone books are a good example of this. Telecommunications companies need, on the one hand, to publish the numbers of subscribers who have agreed to be listed, in order to maximize the number of calls made through their network. However for competitive advantage, and sometimes to make an additional income through directory inquiries, it is important that the data are not freely available, particularly in an electronic format, to competitors. A landmark legal judgment (*Feist Publications v Rural Telephone Service*), in the US Supreme Court, ruled that telephone numbers cannot be protected in the USA by the copyright laws.

In the UK it has been realized that, by allowing the former state monopoly supplier of telephone services to own and control the numbering system, new entrants into the telephone market would be at a disadvantage as switching supplier would involve the loss of one's number, an important personal identifier. The regulatory body, OFTEL, has now ruled that telephone numbers belong to subscribers and that impediments should not be placed in the way of subscribers wishing to switch companies while retaining their number.

The liberalization of the numbering system coincided with the advent of offshore companies that re-captured the UK phone directories and added geo-graphical search and mapping capabilities, as well as reverse look-up facilities to their digital and online directory (*192.com*, **http://www.192.com**). The ability to locate the owner of a number from the number alone was previously treated as an invasion of privacy and banned by the telephone networks. However once in digital form and referenced by address and location, the telephone directory has become a much more powerful tool – but one which raises issues of privacy. Whilst Chapter 13 argues for map libraries to take on board the provision of all such geo-graphically referenced data sets, it must be recognized that the legal implications of such access may pose severe difficulties for map libraries.

Financial advantage

The profit motive would appear to be the most obvious reason for protecting the intellectual property rights in spatial data. However it is a characteristic of most spatial data that they are both expensive and cumbersome to capture. As a result, most spatial data sets are unique with no direct equivalent. This means that the owner of the data has a monopoly and a fair market price for the data cannot be arrived at through a competitive process. Spatial data seldom, if ever, find an equi-librium price based on the interplay between large numbers of suppliers and con-sumers. The absence of a market-based mechanism for establishing price, complicated by the near-zero marginal cost of duplicating data, places suppliers in a difficult position with regard to price. Frequently restricting the distribution of data to a small number of tied customers, with a high capacity to pay, can opti-mize income. While it is possible that reducing prices and increasing demand may lead to an increase in income in the longer term, many state agencies, as well as private suppliers, opt for the certainty of a local optimum price, with a small and manageable number of consumers, rather than seeking to maximize income by maximizing the size of a market that may have severe limits to its growth. Libraries are only rarely well enough resourced to contribute to the profits of producers if a high-price low-volume policy predominates.

Data protection

In a digital environment spatial data can, and do, become personal data once they refer to a small and identifiable set of individuals. Access to data that would allow a user to breach the data protection principles has to be restricted by many agen-cies. Yet, here again, practice varies substantially between countries. In the USA some police departments publish regular maps showing the locations of individual crimes. The maps are usually at a small enough scale, and the geo-coding of the locations is sufficiently coarse, to make the identification of individuals unlikely. However the use of similar techniques in the UK is impossible, despite accurate geo-coding (using products such as Address-Point (Ordnance Survey, **http://www.ordsvy.gov.uk**)) and the existence of large-scale mapping. Data protection legislation is strong, and such data may not be published or distributed. Instead aggregated data covering areas large enough to guarantee anonymity are used.

The ability of the GI industry to deliver products that will retrieve the names of occupants of a house (based on the electoral register entries) by pointing to the house on a map, and the attractiveness to organizations such as the police of such systems, makes it important to protect geographical references that may be indirect references to individuals. It should be noted that in the UK the unit postcode, which covers an average of 14 households, has been regarded by some agencies as adequate to ensure spatial privacy. However the modal number of properties in a postcode is one, so this is clearly not the case, and data geocoded by postcode must be considered insecure from a data protection standpoint.

The emergence of third-generation mobile telephones that will have the capacity to report the carrier's location to within a metre, using a combination of GPS and radio mast triangulation techniques, is going to lead to a massive explosion of personal spatial data and may be a considerable threat to privacy unless the consequences of the technology are carefully considered. Once again the legal and ethical implications are profound for any map library making such data available.

Arguments in favour of the free dissemination of data

Science

The Jeffersonian ideal of enlightenment encouraged through public access to libraries, together with the ethos of publication that has characterized the scientific academic community, would imply that maps and other digital data should be published for the use of society as a whole. Spatial data should be treated as scientific publications that add to the common wealth of human knowledge and can be improved by the repetition of 'experiments' to measure and re-measure the locations shown.

However, the need to fund exploration and survey has led to the assertion of intellectual property rights over the 'facts' that make up digital data. Rhind (1992) and Larner (1998) argue that this is necessary to ensure the continuing flow of data and the maintenance (usually involving improvements in quality) of the existing stock.

The parallels between the mapping of the human genome and the collection of spatial data have been discussed above. Mapping, even more so than the apparently patentable human blueprint, has been deemed, by its creators, as lying outside the scientific domain. Weather data in particular have caused controversy with very different views of their status, marketability and value on the two sides of the Atlantic. The scientific ideal of shared data underlies much of the discussion of spatial data infrastructures, and underpins the very existence of many map library organizations, yet has so far had little impact on the actual availability of data.

Freedom of information

Those arguing for freedom of information believe that a social contract should exist between governments and citizens that ensures a right of access to information both as a limit on the power of the state over the individual and to maximize the use of resources created with taxpayers' money (Onsrud and Lopez, 1998).

The reactionary view is that the operations of government will be impeded by excessive public surveillance of government materials including data, and that the only economic test of the efficient production of the appropriate spatial data products by state and quasi state agencies, is the imposition of market mechanisms – however imperfect. Such a policy is driven by a wish to minimize public expenditure, and often simultaneously, limit the scrutiny of the executive by the public.

As with the defence and security arguments, changes of policy can come swiftly. It has been announced in the UK (Department of Trade and Industry, 2000) that, with the exception of those agencies that operate under a trading fund (including Ordnance Survey), and are dependent on trading for their income and survival, all other government departments, both national and local, should, in future, adopt marginal cost pricing to ensure the maximum dissemination of their data holdings, including spatial data. After many years of argument about the need for cost recovery, and the disadvantages of freedom of information, a simple ministerial announcement has been sufficient to overturn these policies that were thought to be deeply imbedded in the British political system. The volatility of such policies and their implications for data pricing are a significant influence on map library practice.

Commercial incentive

It is not only governments and scientists that have the urge to disseminate data free, or at the marginal costs of distribution. Many commercial organizations have strategies that involve the provision of free, or near free, information.

For example data are supplied with GIS software to provide an immediately useful system. Similarly, spatial information may be provided free as an incentive to purchase delivery systems (eg Traffic Master) or in order to generate traffic on websites that are then funded by advertising or sponsorship. Often information may be provided on a 'try before you buy' basis and then charged for on a metered basis (eg 192.com).

In much the same way as the paper map has been seen as a potent advertising vehicle, digital information, particularly on the world wide web, will increasingly be distributed freely in return for the attention of consumers to carefully, spatially, targeted advertising content. While the consumers may feel that such data are the proverbial 'free lunch', the point at which they pay is soon likely to become apparent.

Conclusion

Neither the behaviour of digital spatial information as an economic good, nor its legal status, are fully understood or defined. It appears unlikely that these issues will be clarified in the near future. Map libraries will have to operate access and acquisition policies in an uncertain environment.

However it is clear that a wide variety of different views exist about the nature of geographic information (see Barr and Masser, 1997) and its function in society. Recent political decisions around the world that have reversed previous policies (for example: GPS encryption in the USA, tradable information in the UK and cost recovery from mapping in New Zealand) suggest that the detailed analysis of how previous legal frameworks apply to spatial data may be unproductive.

It appears likely that in the near future the status and the availability of geographical information will be influenced by public opinion, lobbying and political debate as much as by any technical evaluation of the mechanisms available for the protection of intellectual property.

It is also clear that both the commercial sector and governments are becoming increasingly aware about the indirect benefits, that are eventually reflected on the financial bottom line, that the wider availability of geographical information may bring.

In the short term potential library users of spatial data will need to be aware of the current rules under which they must work to avoid potential penalties under either the criminal or civil codes. However they must also be prepared to lobby and argue for change by demonstrating how society may best be served by changing the regimes under which such information is produced, transformed and used.

References

192.com **http://www.192.com/**

Barr, R (1998a) The price of privacy, *GIS Europe*, (July), 12–13.

Barr, R (1998b) Artistic licence, *GIS Europe*, (August), 12–13.

Barr, R and Masser I (1997) Geographic information: a resource, a commodity, an asset or an infrastructure? In Kemp, Z (ed) *Innovations in GIS 4*, Taylor & Francis, 234–48.

Branscomb, A W (1994) *Who owns information?*, Basic Books.

Chancellor of the Duchy of Lancaster (1998) *Crown copyright in the information age – a consultation document on access to public sector information*, Cm 3819, HMSO.

Cho, G (1998) *Geographic information systems and the law*, Wiley.

Coyle, D (1997) *The weightless world – strategies for managing the digital economy*, Capstone.

Department of Trade and Industry (2000) *Click-use-Pay*, DTI Press Release 2000/602, HMSO.

Eechoud, M M M van (1998) Legal protection of geographic information in the EU. In Burrough, P and Masser, I (eds) *European geographic information infrastructures – opportunities and pitfalls*, Taylor & Francis.

Larner, A (1998) Legal and institutional issues to be resolved with respect to the integration of European data. In Burrough, P and Masser, I (eds) *European geographic information infrastructures – opportunities and pitfalls*, Taylor & Francis.

Murray, K (1997) Anticipating trends in geospatial data applications – research developments at Ordnance Survey, *AGI '97 Conference proceedings*, Association for Geographic Information.

Onsrud, H and Lopez, X (1998) Intellectual property rights in disseminating digital geographic data, products and services: conflicts and commonalities among EU and US approaches. In Burrough, P and Masser, I (eds) *European geographic information infrastructures – opportunities and pitfalls*, Taylor & Francis.

Ordnance Survey **http://www.ordsvy.gov.uk/**.

Rhind, D (1992) War and peace: GIS data as a commodity, *GIS World*, (November), 37–9.

13

Taking care of business : map libraries and the new 'mapping' industry

Pip Forer

▶ *The rise of digital spatial data and geographic information technologies has not only rewritten the nature of what a map collection might contain, but has revolutionized the industry that creates 'maps' and the intellectual property regime associated with spatial data. This chapter traces the evolution of a new landscape in which suppliers of major infrastructral data sets combine with smaller data providers focused on niche problems and services. It reaffirms the role of map libraries in providing an environmental memory, and argues for the need for a proactive stance by curators in forging new relationships with the new mapping industry.*

Introduction

This chapter has had an unusual history, for in its lengthy gestation it took on a life of its own and became a reflection on how map libraries relate to the commercial world rather than on their relationship to the mapping industry. It was only on re-reading a final draft that I realized, with horror, how far from my original brief and abstract I had strayed. But then the reason for this dissonance between intent and outcome became clearer: essentially there had been a slow and initially unconscious acceptance on my part that these days potentially everyone, or at least a great majority of organizations, is in the mapping industry. Web mapping means many more groups are map publishers. Geocoding means many more organizations create spatial data that are mappable. Control over specialist geographic data leads many more organizations into their own or collaborative analyses and mapping. A new mapmaking industry is out there, and the inevitable revision of the chapter has focused around both the evolution of traditional mapping shops, and this new, diffuse 'industry', the evolution of its structure, and its implications for map libraries.

The nature of the mapping industry and of map libraries

Firstly, we need to define just what the mapping industry is. The old certainty has certainly disappeared, since although the traditional printed map and its production processes survive, they have been augmented by new means of capturing, analysing and displaying data that redefine what running a map-oriented library might entail. This chapter takes the view that the mapping industry is in two sectors. One is the traditional mapping industry, as typified by national mapping organizations, and is still out there with a core focus on producing national map series of generalist themes, typified by the topographic mapping enterprise. The second sector is one that is based on more purpose-specific (sometimes incidental) spatial data capture for mapping and analysis. Address lists of customers provide one example of such a data set, but a whole range of organizations not traditionally involved in mapping are enabling the spatial potential of their data for analysis and mapping. This sector supports mapping and analysis, often without any direct traditional capture of XY coordinate data.

Next we need a definition of the scope of the map library in this new context, and perhaps contentiously, this chapter accepts that spatial data, in a map-displayable form, is as legitimate a component of a new millenium map library's holdings as a printed topographic sheet. One justification for this view is that the library should be based around spatial knowledge, not simply printed map sheets or their GIS equivalents (Jankowska and Jankowski, 2000).

For all their image as calm, reflective places, libraries are frequently places of tension. These tensions, too, need definition. A tension has always existed between a library's *functions* as a largely passive archive of information, as an active gatekeeper of knowledge, and as a conduit for the free distribution of facts and ideas. *Technologically induced tensions* have been significant at certain periods in library history, none more so than now as a result of the rise of digital media. The closest period to rival the tensions that the Internet and digital texts or maps currently generate is probably the period of transition of book production technology from the pen to the printing press. But this transition started and finished for maps with hard-copy cartographic representations based on paper, vellum, parchment or the current printing technology of choice. The digital shift brings in the ability to treat maps as entities that can be manipulated, and as specific representations of underlying spatial data. Consequently, a map library (on the digital side) can easily defend the view that it should, on top of its 'permanent' maps, hold or access collections of mappable data and mapviewing procedures (in the form of mapping software packages). If accepted in the full, this new domain widens the library's scope dramatically, as well as redefining the source and the nature of much of its mappable collection.

Equally, or more, important have been the *ideological tensions* surrounding the access to information. From the ultimate liberal, who argues for equal and free access to key public knowledge, to the arch member of the New Right who would place all access in the marketplace, different stands have generated a debate on access to and use of knowledge that has raged and swung for centuries. These 'user-pays' tensions are underpinned for map libraries by specific issues of intellectual property rights and the arrangements for access to cartographic data from government and other sources (Chapter 12). Policy and practice in the area of government data have evolved dramatically in the last decade in response to neo-liberalist policies, and so has the industry that collects 'map' data, whether in traditional or more radical form (Cho, 1998; Morrison, 1997; Calvert, Murray and Smith, 1997). Estimates of the size of the global spatial data industry are notoriously unreliable, but the sector is dynamic, aggressive and rapidly growing its share of the production of mappable data within a free market framework.

For national mapping organizations and similar non-profit enterprises the market has intruded ever more, with demands for users to pay, and with substantial changes in the legislation and interpretation regarding copyright and intellectual property rights. Interestingly, the situation in various countries in this regard does not automatically map on to the political map of New Right hegemony, and some countries have avoided or reversed moves in this direction (Rhind, 1997; LINZ, 2000). For the private sector the restatement of intellectual rights in spatial data has been essential in providing the protection necessary to underpin a functioning business that is harnessing new technologies such as high-resolution satellite imagery, position-aware devices and transaction processing.

Growth in the volume of spatial data derived from such diverse developments complicates the job of collecting mappable data into any form of coherent geographic and environmental library, but it is made even more problematic by the growing appreciation of the market value of geographic data. This has encouraged the collection of more (and more immediately useful) data, but usually such data come at a cost and come with restrictive use rights. The simplification of the technology of geospatial data collection, and the dynamism of the market for such data, are now such that more and more enterprises both capture and seek reward from geospatial data.

This chapter seeks to address the question of how map libraries relate to 'the mapping industry' in the broad, and how they might flourish in the new order of things. The key elements in this tale are essentially the two inter-related ones of how coherent map holdings get assembled, and how they are made available. The traditional model of acquisition for most of the latter half of the 20th century was that map libraries were advantaged by the heavily subsidized nature of most nations' major map series. For small or very marginal costs many national agencies provided ongoing updates to their key map series to bona fide map collections. They also operated a fairly relaxed environment for onward use of the maps, and specifically for the data contained therein, which allowed the libraries to offer a number of services to a relatively small number of users. For most map producers the map libraries represented an avenue for making their work more widely available, at a cost which to them was the marginal cost of producing the extra copies of each map sheet. A flow diagram of the key supply relationships for map libraries would have been a very simple one. The rest of the chapter identifies just how far this has changed.

Business, commerce, map libraries and cash flows

We could start by observing that the topic of this chapter sits right astride the line of one of the major and currently active tension faults in map libraries. Put baldly, the ethos of librarianship is at great variance with the ethos of rampant commerce. In Western culture, on the cusp of the new millennium, librarianship would still normally be seen as leaning on the doctrine of providing support for a public good, in order to provide the free distribution of data. It would also feature the creation of 'collections' that are consistent and comprehensive representations of a field of knowledge, often with a long-term temporal perspective in mind. The 'public good' in this context may exist for a limited public (as in research libraries within organizations), a virtual community (as in online research libraries) or for the population at large, but responsive service to that public constitutes the core of librarianship. A fundamental goal in that service is to create and maintain collections of value to the user community.

In map libraries these collections have historically derived from a mapping industry that has been predominantly based around the practitioners' guilds of survey and cartography, and predominantly located in the public sector. Their key acquisition has been the authoritative map, usually topographic or devoted to one of a limited number of systematic themes. Apart from sensitive military maps, these map data have often been subject to fairly lax intellectual property regimes and minimal associated cost-recovery structures. The quantity of data has been small, and the production of knowledge as represented in the map relatively uncontested. The pace of revision has been slow, the collections very stable and very dependent on physical visiting for use by clients. The map providers often supplied maps at subsidized or zero cost to map libraries, which in turn provided a significant opportunity for the exposure of their products. The pattern of re-use or re-combination of map data featured sparse usage and unsophisticated analysis. Most map libraries acquired data from a relatively small number of 'map agencies'. Over the latter part of the 20th century the art of map librarianship had become well honed in this environment, which is epitomized by the culture of North American map deposit.

In the new environment the relationship between map libraries and the spatial data industry, through their map acquisitions and the services they provide, remains important but is far more complicated as a result of the nature of the product (spatial data) and the number of actors in the industry. The supplier relationships may have to change to reflect the appreciated value of spatial data and the broader nature of the industry. For acquisition this probably means either using a direct market model by buying more data at cost, or less directly by negotiating preferred status arrangements that recognize the mutual benefit to library and the data owner. At the service end, downstream usage and the value of mapped data become issues of greater importance. Digital maps in particular lend themselves to combination, analysis and querying: the essence of geographic information services. In a map library there may be calls for revenue generation to fund acquisition fees, and consequently some provision of map-related services to users may be established. The fact that these services may be in direct competition with the reconstituted mapping industry itself then raises issues. It is accepted here that few mainstream library-based services for commercial returns would be competitive with commercial enterprises, so there will be limited opportunities to generate revenue. In general, acquisition and service become more problematic in the new environment, and active collaboration with the much wider group of spatial data creators, sponsors and custodians who comprise the new 'mapping' industry, will be a necessity. From the industry's side the provision of exposure to their products, the building of a corporate image or the realization of marginal long-term benefits or insurance through the archiving of their products may all be seen as useful benefits. For the librarian, the mix of levers that can be used to acquire map data will depend greatly on the national and disciplinary context of each library collection. Doubtless, though, the scent of commerce will be stronger in the air.

To examine this more complex relationship further we look firstly at the changing place of spatial data in human activities and social spatiality. In this section the emphasis is on how society uses and encodes geospatial data, and consequently what the process creates as our social representation of the environment (Curry, 1998). The next section identifies the dynamics of change of the provision of 'infrastructural' data, these being the data traditionally provided as the components of topographic and other national map series. This is followed by an exploration of the issues surrounding customized spatial data sources, and finally these developments are tied back into a reflection on how map librarianship can best liaise with the new sources of mappable data and map products.

Human spatiality: maps, data and business

Maps as cultural artifacts have stood the test of time, having proved useful over millennia (Hall, 1992). There is no reason to think that this utility will wane. But maps and their use are in dramatic flux, being internally reinvented through digital mapping systems, and more widely re-engineered and augmented by new visualization techniques and new arenas in which to work (the domains of the WAP phone and the Position Aware Device (PAD) for instance). These changes should not be seen in isolation for they are part of a shift in human spatiality: the way we perceive, navigate and utilize space (Curry, 1998; Forer et al, 2000; Golledge and Stimson, 1997). Chrisman (1999) sees geographic information, of which map representations are a crucial part, as socially embedded technology. We can only agree that as we embed map usage and spatial data services in new ways in our activities, so the perception of maps and spatial data and what they offer will change. Naturally our views on the role and function of map libraries will evolve to reflect this. A population used to working with digitally mediated mapped data will seek no less in its libraries' modus operandi.

In this new spatial order maps are increasingly viewports on to often dynamic data sets, and they are increasingly available (as the growing number of web-mapping sites testifies) to people anywhere and any time. They are also part of an environment in which geographic queries (such as how to get to B from A, or the age of a historic house one is just walking past) may be posed with the aid of systems that know one's location, and that reply in text terms. Maps are coming out, with a vengeance, from the position of the archival representation of certain chosen, and often dated, truths into a central role in the new spatial media, those aspects of Communications and Information Technology that are changing the way in which people and their organizations interact with space. Most maps produced (if not published) are now transient representations of the environment, and we will increasingly use such maps to position ourselves in, and inform ourselves about, that environment. Commercial interests will contest that medium as never before. In parallel there will be a growing need and demand for objective and authoritative representations in multimedia and transient web mapping as much as in printed maps. The use of spatial data, in both business and consumer services, will grow and many more specific map-mediated spatial queries will be formulated by society and individuals. People will continue to want easier access to consistent and integrated spatial information, however, and the very dynamism of the sector also creates a dislocation and a demand for ordered knowledge.

As we have noted, many data, and their visualizations, will be of transient value and existence. Much spatial knowledge that was once embodied in permanent maps, will now reside in the possible combinations of maps and various sets of mappable data, and their singular manifestations at particular points in time. But transience is not the essence of libraries, just as, traditionally, spatial data have not been the focus of map libraries. The new data environment poses new challenges in these areas that need recognition, and have underlying goals that are far from transient. The fact that a growing plethora of current mapping representations exist should not disguise the fact that little of the ongoing change of mapped areas is being captured, and little of it may be related to longer-term issues in a consistent way.

One challenge is to tame the transient data. From a temporal perspective many data have value for longitudinal study, but may not be consistently collected over time. An instance might be the number of cars in motion in a city at any moment, as detected by cell-phone monitoring and used for commercial real-time traffic advice services. The data can provide detailed long-term series for research and planning if archived, but the 'market' for these data is totally different and may be outside the original collector's short term interest, resulting in loss of the data for further use. So, particularly in the early stages of the digital mapping industry, a data preservation role may exist for map libraries.

A more obvious issue is that many transient services sit on an increasingly rich foundation of niche environmental data that documents substantial changes. And beyond that the number of data sets collected specifically for long-term monitoring has grown as new capture methods come into existence, and as traditional activities get 'spatially enabled'. Examples of each class might include the regular creation of land cover maps on the coat tails of more accessible and timely satellite images (Thompson and LCDB2 Project Development Team, 2000), and the movement of road accident statistics into GIS-enabled data banks. There is a second challenge here to assemble meaningful and substantial holdings of such themes.

A third and broader challenge is to find that modus operandi for working with digital spatial data and the new economic environment, moving from *mapped* data to *mappable* data as the basis for the collection, and from cartophiles to spatial thinkers as the basis of the clientele. Finally, an overarching challenge must be to work successfully with the data custodians for access to their holdings, whether by local mirroring or remote site access.

If one works from the status quo to address this new context of mappable data, the logical question to ask first is how libraries work to maintain their traditional areas of holdings, even if these are not now provided in printed form. The traditional backbone of many map libraries is composed of generic topographic map series such as the 1:50,000, inch-to-the-mile or 1:25,000-scale sheets of different countries. In the last few years the data embodied in such series have been subsumed within a larger term, that of the Spatial Data Infrastructure (SDI). This is generally taken to denote the fundamental data that other analyses, decision-making and mapping revolve around, and that the national interest requires to be consistently available for processes such as search and rescue or planning. In national contexts this is often originally seen as the national topographic data sets, but as jurisdictions have explored the wider needs for consistent data so the net has widened (Federal Geographic Data Committee, 1997; National Research Council, 1993). SDI initiatives in various countries have shown more or less depth of thought in their formulation, and have derived from a need not just for a guaranteed, comprehensive national spatial data coverage, and a consistent definition of cartographic objects (both otherwise likely to be market failures), but also for consistent coverage over time.

The SDIs have a further attractive feature, in that one purpose of infrastructural data is to provide a referential lingua franca for widespread use. An additional recognition, in some jurisdictions, is also that many spatial data products that create wealth rely on combining often quite small customized databases with basic information about an area. A business directory web-mapping site that shows the location of doctors against the wider city environment is such a case in point. Both benefits only work if such data are easily accessible to users and are of low cost, so most SDIs have that as their goal. This makes the new infrastructural data an important digital foot in the door for any forward-looking map collection. However, internationally the scope and effectiveness of SDI initiatives, and the availability of SDI data, vary greatly. The next section examines some SDI models currently in place, and their implications for libraries.

Spatial data infrastructure, topographic map series and national mapping agencies

The crucial issue for spatial data provision in an age of (often colonial) power exerted by conventional military means was to know what was needed to explore, garrison, exploit or wage effective warfare in an area. On such needs grew many national mapping series, such as those of the significantly if anachronistically named Ordnance Survey in Great Britain. With the growing complexity of the economy and the state in more recent times, spatial data have come to be seen to serve national interests more in the way they can expand and enhance economic power and effective planning. Their importance is underlined by the topic even making it on to the speech-making agenda of the former vice-president of the United States (Gore, 1998).

The SDI initiatives effectively create a two-tiered structure for mapping: an agreed mapping framework (1) to which additional custom data sets (2) can be related so that specific maps and applications can be developed. Such custom data sets might be the material on which specific local map library holdings and collections could be based.

The traditional 'mapping' industry fits into this model of the world in part by refocusing its activities towards creating the top-level infrastructure data bases, as well as the current versions of the 'definitive infrastructural maps', ie the national mapping series.

From the map library's perspective, infrastructure data have a key role, if, as they are generally intended to do, they provide a definitive, consistent structure of data collection at certain scales across an entire nation. The definition of what the key infrastructure data are varies greatly. In some jurisdictions, such as the USA, government bodies identify a range of data across a broad range of government and semi-public enterprises, with clear guidelines of expectations (Federal Geographic Data Committee, 1997). In others the existing topographic service is seen as the core item, and little informed policy emerges to debate the details of what would be the appropriate content of the ideal 'infrastructure'. What debate there is often takes place in committee and is focused on issues of direct revenue opportunity rather than overall economic gain or functional consistency. Spatial data that are widely used but embedded in chargeable transactional processes, such as cadastral data, are often hotly contested. Other data that are of great significance but collected by independent or corporate institutions may be left outside the definition of infrastructure because of minor cost considerations or differences in organizational culture. While 'purpose of use' is often taken as a basis for defining the data themes and their accuracy, this does not always yield consistent debate and decisions on the inclusion of material.

The international experience of available coverage varies, as do national positions on access to the data. The key issues for the state in defining infrastructural data availability are intellectual property rights and revenue options. For the librarian they are intellectual property restrictions and cost. At present these matters vary dramatically between countries. Within the more developed nations at least three models exist with profoundly different characteristics, while in a number of other countries data provision is hampered by military concerns or unresponsive or underfunded (or non-existent) mapping bodies. This section concentrates on three current Western models.

Public data and state mapping

The first model is represented by the USA. Here a clear philosophy has existed for many decades that data funded by the tax-payer should be freely accessible to the tax-payer. Also, infrastructural mapping and spatial database creation are embedded within the public service, notably within the US Geological Survey (USGS) and the Census Bureau. In this situation the state retains intellectual property, but arranges for distribution at marginal cost and free use of data. For much of the 1980s and 1990s the US model withstood ideological pressures and managed to stand in stark contrast to developments elsewhere that were driven by a narrowly focused user-pays agenda. Perhaps bolstered by arguments of the positive multiplier effect of having readily accessible data, the model has persisted, and the growing ambit of the spatial data infrastructure initiative in America additionally provides some local opportunities for assembling a wider range of infrastructural data. The longstanding availability of USGS maps, and the early engagement of the USGS with digital spatial data delivery (latterly over the web), have also fostered a strong client base, and a tradition of available map holdings, as well as a data environment that has spawned various commercial map products and services. The Census Bureau with its DIME and TIGER file structures for population data has similarly enriched this environment. Products such as *Business Analyst* using the ArcView GIS (ESRI, 1997), or travel support systems such as *Tripmaker* (Rand-McNally, 2000) are testament to the power of combining public and custom map sources for economic growth, and are also arguably important map library acquisitions.

User-pays data and state mapping

In spite of far-sighted investigations such as the Chorley Report (Department of the Environment, 1987) most European spatial data have found themselves caught in a context of user-pays, where the worst of both worlds exists. The scope of national mapping agencies ensures a market dominance and an ability to pursue revenue targets by a restrictive high-cost/low-volume pricing strategy. The limited competition gives little incentive for new developments. Consequently such organizations are in danger of being both low on innovation and high on cost. Restrictive licensing agreements limit the deployment of data into new areas or within new analyses and products. These lead organizations also frequently set the example by which secondary suppliers of spatial data (other government departments, for instance) make their own data available. Many national agencies have achieved strong cash flows by the aggressive pursuit of data usage rights, and the setting of high user charges. But to travel in Europe and talk with those who use spatial data, especially librarians, is to experience frustration and even anger. The appearance of new services lags notably behind the US market. The consistent appearance of barriers related to funding unavailability, or more commonly to usage rights, is a pervasive issue.

Public data definition and private-sector mapping

The turn of the century has seen a variant of the US model appear, one that has been increasingly implemented by New Zealand since 1998 and is attracting other adherents. At that time in New Zealand the (Right Wing) National Party government, influenced by national debate and by related Australian research on the economic multiplier generated by low-cost spatial data sets, moved to restructure the provision of state public data. The first step in this process had already occurred in 1997, and was the separation of the responsibility for ensuring the collection of adequate national data from the actual collection and mapping of the data. The national mapping organization, the Department of Survey and Land Information (DOSLI) was abolished. The task of defining the state's spatial data and mapping needs was devolved to a government department, LINZ (Land Information New Zealand), and the task of mapping and survey to a state-owned enterprise (Terralink), that was planned to be sold to the private sector.

For some time in New Zealand, spatial data had been subject to cost recovery, with many of the problems that such a process involves (Robertson and Gartner, 1997). The evolution of spatial data usage agreements in that period, from informal one-page letters to 14-page documents and back to five-page contracts, could form a chapter in its own right. The next step, implemented fully in 1999, was to enforce the Crown's intellectual property rights only through acknowledgment by the user, and to make all pertinent government data, as well as the topographic spatial data holdings, available on a 'transfer cost only' basis. The result in the first year of 'public' spatial data has been a significant freeing-up of this contractual context, and a major kick in new products from geographic information service providers, whether in the production of small planners for hiking trips or the development of major web-serving sites by land information firms (**http://www. emap.co.nz**). More widely, the policy direction has encouraged a range of government departments to provide web-enabled public access to data files such as census and traffic count data (**http://www.statsnz.govt.nz** and sites from **http://www.govt.nz**). In topographic data terms versions of the national 1:50,000 scale database declined in price from six-figure sums for an annual licence to NZ$400–500 (around US$ 175–225) for the CD-ROM set of the same data. The cost of the national census enumeration district boundaries (mesh blocks) fell from NZ$20,000–30,000 to the price of little more than download time.

These experiences have major implications for the development of a value-added mapping industry, but what are the implications for map libraries in these different domains? The main differentiation, of course, is in respect of digital data where 'publication' costs are trivial compared to the printed map or to any commercial licence costs, and where the potential for onward use and refinement is far higher. For all the concessionary deals from state mapping agencies, the ability to provide cheap data access with a limited concern over the policing of copyright lubricates the wider use of mappable data, and naturally also the deployment of spatial data in libraries. In domains with marginal cost infrastructural data, digital map librarianship would seem inevitably both simpler and faced by greater opportunities than in the 'European' model areas. On the printed map side, the issue of transfer cost (ie map printing and distribution cost) is far more neutral, and indeed may lead to higher costs in the more liberal domain. This is because there may be more indifference to outreach via the printed maps, when a number of offerings exist based on the 'free' digital data that could be argued to meet any public outreach responsibilities.

Easily available infrastructure data certainly means that, at least in New Zealand and the USA, a map library can hold substantial national, digital spatial data. Several examples of such an arrangement exist in the USA (Jankowska and Jankowski, 2000; Argentati, 1997; Yu, 1999; Adler and Larsgaard, 1999) and the University of Auckland has just started a one-year project to serve local infrastructure data to its members. At the same time, however, two related issues arise. One is whether holding data locally is redundant when there are websites serving the current versions of the data. The answer to this depends on the cost and time of downloading data versus storing it. The other is one of archiving and temporal consistency. Infrastructural data are usually defined to serve current needs, and may not be consistently archived. Where infrastructural data come from different suppliers, then it is certainly true that interoperable sets of current data on the web do not necessarily mean interoperable archiving policies. A serious collection in this context needs to work with various data providers in identifying the form that a data archive might take and what should be held locally (or in some academic web repository). Observation suggests this is not an issue that current data providers are looking closely at.

The side servings of data

It is certainly inaccurate to equate the traditional 'mapping industry' only with infrastructural data sets and the new 'spatial data product providers' with the area of customized and specific data. Indeed, various traditional mapping firms have formed alliances with other data publishers, such as business directories, to diversify and grow. Equally, the various agencies that have embraced mapping and map-related products from a non-cartographic background are arguably going to redefine for us what our infrastructural data are. Our various geocodable methods of recording human cash transactions or movements are capable of delivering dynamic geographies that can redefine our view of the geographies of cities. Mosaiced national coverages of detailed satellite imagery are a similar case. But certainly a great deal of the non-infrastructural mappable data that we would seek to deploy comes from specific problem domains, and is driven by data collection procedures related to real-world processes. One example might be school zoning and the determination of school grants on the basis of the needs of the community. Digital databases of student addresses combine with census data to identify the school's service area, and analysis establishes the typical incomes for the catchment. Another example might be a map-enabled directory of medical practitioners noted earlier. A more major and longstanding option might be meteorological data, or even web-cam data from the local ski field. Of course, major retailing chains maintain loyalty cards and various demand-monitoring schemes. Every club or business has a client address list that is potentially a point map of a social area of influence, once suitably masked to ensure confidentiality. The electoral list, at least in New Zealand, provides the key to a comprehensive geography of occupations if combined with an address-matching geocoding algorithm. The list, if fully compiled, is a long one.

The number and nature of mappable data sets have become almost unmanageable, and mappable data producers have become almost ubiquitous. In the short term most of these data have value and some are extremely valuable. Some are copyright restrictive, some liberal, ambiguous or relaxed in terms of rights. Some are confidential and closely guarded. All say something about the human or physical environment at a point in time. Most decay in value (and thus cost) quite quickly, and many are not archived with any sense of continuity in mind. In some cases a niche exists to develop consistent holdings of such data by working with data custodians who are willing to provide (possibly embargoed) data as a contribution towards a historical record that may benefit them as well as the society that supports them. It is hardly possible to write about the nature of these new data providers in respect of their responsiveness to providing access to their data: the experience is too recent. However, they hold the key to adding local value to the broader infrastructure data, and to providing a consistent knowledge base in areas of key interest in any institution.

Finally, we should acknowledge that many of the customized data sets are combined with infrastructure data to create domain-specific applications with mapping front ends, such as car route-finder packages. Such products are also legitimate holdings within a map library.

Maps, digital spatial data and the permeable map library

This brief review of issues has worked on the assumption that the core of any map library is the 'Collection', which itself is a manifestation of the need for a consistent 'memory' of things spatial, or to use a more emotive but justified term, an *environmental memory* for society.

The chapter has highlighted one factor above all others in creating the challenge for map libraries: the transformation of the supply of map data, in terms of its volume, its sources and its formats. The reformulation of the library's client needs has been largely unspoken, but acknowledged. It has tangentially touched upon the argument that in the end the map library will be virtually served by other sites. In closing we need to return to what the new data environment does in this regard and what it might mean for establishing effective map libraries or their ilk. In so doing we need to examine the concept of a virtual map library comprising remote links to the map data providers in the light of knowledge-based services.

The legacy holdings of printed maps are not irrelevant in this, for they are our current perspective back to past mapped environments and successful custodianship, as well as to our current status. In the process by which the value of the published can be enhanced, and information cycled to users in an added-value form, printed maps allow the cross-links between data sets or maps to add value (across themes or over time, for instance). Such referencing can happen only because the maps are in one place, the library. Added value can also appear because changed circumstances make a historic data set valuable. In Great Britain the value of detailed

Ordnance Survey maps from past series has been enhanced by the increased requirements to track potentially noxious activities over time on or near sites for development. Several English university map libraries offer a report and access service based on this example. In New Zealand the revised interest in finalizing Maori land claims has also revised the value of unvisited maps to government and lawyers (MacDowell, 1999). In the new map-keeping environment the two phenomena, combination of data and serendipitous added value, remain important ways by which knowledge is created and value is added. But the old maps can be scanned to digital form and the added value captured through a distributed service, so not all independent collections need remain.

From a different perspective Keller (2000) makes the point that separate map libraries traditionally existed because of the unusual storage requirements of large maps, and goes on to suggest that they may continue to exist in a digital age because of the hardware needed to view and plot the digital equivalents. Given progress in consumer digital electronics, and the availability of plotting bureaus and couriers, this may need examination. Indeed, much recent research focused on distributed and interoperable GIS points towards the metadata-mediated creation of very large distributed spatial databases (Wang et al, 2000). Such a system, given appropriate access rights, could theoretically provide users with a distributed access to enormous quantities of spatial data as well as the architecture for a distributed map library using other browsing and interface concepts (Goodchild, 1998; Rock, 1998).

But if we have a distributed map library the core librarianship issues remain, namely the definitions of what should be available in a collection, and of who has access and by what process. These issues need representation in any future where the commercial imperative will drive one particular range of databases, and governance may drive another. In this split environment some data of inherent long-term research value may disappear because of short-term commercial imperatives or simple myopia. Distributed library systems will not offer effective access solutions to clients unless they are governed by appropriate policies for establishing long-term data holdings. There is also a geography to data: local people need local data for local solutions and insights. Collections have various geographic scales within them, and need to reflect local issues. It is in this context that one can argue that map libraries need to be close to their spatial roots to develop the best relevant collections, and that the best Virtual Map Library will be a federation of localized knowledge custodians. The 'spatial roots' are, of course, defined by the local manifestations of the mapping industry. Then there is the issue of the 'navigable' collection – the collection that places the user in a situation where key information, from a local perspective, is easy to find and combine, without getting lost in the enormity of myriad web sources.

Good map libraries in this context will continue to be two-way nodes, the value of which will lie in three things:

- the quality of their links to sources of geospatial information (current and past)
- their local data holdings (legacy and digital)
- their ability to enable users to combine the data in meaningful ways.

Establishing a valuable collection is going to involve some deep thought on how to maximize access to infrastructure data, and how to generate representative and accessible holdings of more specific themes. This will perhaps mean map librarians taking a more active role in defining what their holdings should be (rather than it being defined by the gatekeepers of the traditional mapping industry), and pursuing their goals with guile. It is also going to involve a great deal of cooperation with data suppliers and with other map librarians who now have the tools to collaborate more easily on joint holdings.

In the current environment the case for a revitalized map library may be hard to make, and the often carto-centric profession may not be the best group to make it. However, the change in sources and nature of mappable data should make us restate the imperative virtues of good knowledge management, and the fact that spatial data are special just as mapped data are magic.

Conclusion

This chapter has argued that map libraries, in essence, are about developing and maintaining holdings of geospatial data rather than about spatial analysis or cartography alone. It has asserted that technological changes are changing the functional options for map libraries. It has also suggested that these changes should be mirrored in some of the services such libraries offer their users. To the author's surprise, it has not argued that map libraries are redundant or becoming totally virtual, but rather that they need to refocus their efforts and that this refocus needs to reconceptualize their concept of holdings management to relate to the new and more complex environment of the 'mapping industry'. The major opportunities out there are not the short-term ones of provision of services, but the long-term ones of working with business and government to restate and reposition the mission of map libraries in ensuring consistent and accessible *environmental memories* for society. This mission is much more exciting than in the past, and requires a whole new set of tools from map librarians (aka geospatial data custodians), both individually and collectively. It may frustrate the accountants looking for cash recovery from libraries, but essentially the mission is one that reinstates the concept of Public Good where it needs to be to perform the complex and vital function that libraries cover.

The chapter has ended up focusing on three very geographic phenomena: flows (of information), the value of aggregation and collaboration, and the nature of place (at least in the sense of the multi-dimensional aspects of a library collection). In the end, good map librarians must act to provide a continuity of (environmental) memory that transcends the limited wisdom and intellectual reflection of the marketplace and debating chamber. There is an unparalleled challenge to map libraries to ensure we may yet reap not just short-term partial insights into our changing world but also some longer-term and critical perspectives. But the placid river of traditional mapmaking that flowed by the door is now a much more tumultuous and substantial torrent of information that librarians must seek to harness. Proactive relationships with various members of the 'mapping industry', from traditional commercial survey and map shops down to research students, are the key to this. A sound national spatial data publication policy is a huge head start for some, but for all, the contact network will need to stretch far further and tap the mutual value in shared data with a new skill and flexibility that transcends status-quo map keeping.

Acknowledgments are due to Igor Drecki, Lynda Ferguson, Jan Kelly, Russell Kirkpatrick, Brian Marshall and Jonette Surridge for comments on earlier versions of this chapter, and/or for their sustaining enthusiasm and professional passion for maps and mapping.

References

Adler, P and Larsgaard, M (1999) Applying GIS in libraries. In Longley P et al (eds) *Geographical Information Systems: principles, techniques, applications and management*, 2nd edn, Wiley.

Argentati, C (1997) Expanding horizons for GIS services in academic libraries, *Journal of Academic Librarianship*, **23**, 463–86.

Calvert, C, Murray, K and Smith, N (1997) New technology and its impact on the framework for the world. In Rhind, D (ed) *Framework for the world*, Geoinformation International.

Carver S (ed) (1998) *Innovations in GIS 5: selected papers from the Fifth National Conference on GIS Research UK (GISRUK)*, Taylor & Francis.

Cho, G (1998) *Geographic Information Systems and the law: mapping the legal frontiers*, Wiley.

Chrisman, N (1999) What does GIS mean? *Transactions in GIS*, **3** (2), 175–86.

Curry, M (1998) *Digital places: living with geographic information technologies*, Routledge.

Department of the Environment (1987) *Handling geographic information*, HMSO.

ESRI (1997) *Business Analyst GIS software/data package*, ESRI.

Federal Geographic Data Committee (1997) *Framework: introduction and guide*, Federal Geographic Data Committee.

Forer P, He, Y and Yeh, A (2000) *Proceedings of the 9th Spatial Data Handling Symposium, Beijing*, IGU Commission on Geographic Information Science/ Beijing University.

Forer, P C (1999) Fabricating space. In Le Heron, et al (eds) *Explorations in human geography: encountering place*, Oxford University Press.

Golledge, R and Stimson, R J (1997) *Spatial behavior*, Guilford Press.

Goodchild, M (1998) The geolibrary. In Carver S (ed) *Innovations in GIS 5: selected papers from the Fifth National Conference on GIS Research UK (GISRUK)*, London: Taylor & Francis.

Gore, A (1998) *The digital earth: understanding our planet in the 21st century*, speech released by the Vice President's Office, Washington DC, 26 March, 1998.

Hall, S S (1992) *Mapping the next millennium*, Random House.

Jankowska, M A and Jankowski, P (2000) Is this a geolibrary? A case of the Idaho Geospatial Data Center, *Information Technology and Libraries*, (March), 4–10.

Keller P (2000) Thoughts on the future of the map library, *New Zealand Map Society Journal*, **13**, 1–12.

Le Heron, R, et al (1999) *Explorations in human geography: encountering place*, Oxford University Press.

LINZ (2000) **www.linz.govt.nz** (Land Information New Zealand website)

Longley P, et al (eds) (1999) *Geographical Information Systems: principles, techniques, applications and management*, 2nd edn, Wiley

MacDowell, C (1999) *Investigating the gap between intent and practice with the use of geographic information systems*, thesis submitted for the degree of Master of Arts, University of Auckland.

Morrison, J (1997) Topographic mapping in the twenty-first century. In Rhind, D (ed) *Framework for the world*, Geoinformation International.

National Research Council (1993) *Towards a coordinated data infrastructure for the nation*, National Academy Press.

Rand-McNally (2000) *Tripmaker car travel decision support system*, Rand-McNally.

Rhind, D (ed) (1997) *Framework for the world*, Geoinformation International.

Robertson, W and Gartner, C (1997) The reform of national mapping agencies: the case of New Zealand. In Rhind, D (ed) *Framework for the world*, Geoinformation International.

Rock, M (1998) *Monitoring user navigation through the Alexandria Digital Library*, thesis submitted for the degree of Master of Science, Colorado State University.

Thompson, S and LCDB2 Project Development Team (2000) *Land environmental performance indicators*, Technical papers 61, Wellington: Ministry of the Environment.

Wang Xiaolin et al (2000) A study on spatial metadata and an agent-based searching scheme for spatial data. In Forer, P et al (eds) *Proceedings of the 9th Spatial Data Handling Symposium, Beijing*, IGU Commission on Geographic Information Science/ Beijing University.

Yu Lixin (1999) Knowledge discovery in spatial cartographic data retrieval, *Library Trends*, **48**, 249–62.

14
A map user's perspective

Alan Godfrey

▶ *The author publishes reprints of old maps and is a frequent user of map libraries, from academic and national institutions to small local archives. Although accepting the value of computers and the Internet in making maps available, he is concerned that librarians are in danger of forgetting the prime importance of the paper map. In a personal and openly subjective chapter he raises points including censorship, the quality of digital mapping, and cooperation between academic and local libraries, which he feels deserve discussion, and he questions whether the needs of map users, from historians to ornithologists, are being considered.*

During the winter of 1999–2000 we moved office, an upheaval that threw the nature of paper maps, both their convenience and their bulk, into sharp relief. Day after day, for the better part of three months, I carried maps down a rickety staircase at one end of the move, and up a rather more salubrious (but still exhausting) staircase at the other. Of course, we could have employed a professional removal firm to help us, but in what order would they have arrived? I have too often heard the laments of map librarians on returning to their library after a move, to find maps torn, creased, sent in the wrong direction, or simply lost. And these maps were my livelihood, my pension, all 600,000 of them – not to mention positives, negatives, old archival maps, street maps, topographical maps, and all the clutter that goes with running a publishing firm, however small.

So Herculean was the task – and remember, we were continuing to run the business through all this and, like the Windmill Theatre of old, 'Never Closed' – that four of my neighbours volunteered to help, forever carrying maps, maps, maps, with no more recompense at the end of it than a pint or three of beer. Occasionally workers from other units stopped to help, perhaps carrying a box or two down the stairs – here our van collections had become a thrice daily ritual – or, in the age-old tradition of the British worker, giving uncalled-for advice.

And so it was one morning, after around a dozen trips down the stairs, two boxes (some 600 maps) at a time, that a stranger stopped me outside the van. He cast a beady eye over the contents, a beadier one over my sweating frame, and combined them into one glance of withering contempt. 'Why don't you put them all on CD-ROM?' he asked. 'Then you wouldn't have all these maps to carry.'

I was too exhausted to hit him, too confounded to answer with anything approaching intelligence. 'It's what we do,' I replied, 'publish maps.'

'Paper's a thing of the past', continued our Know-all. 'You should put them all on CD-ROM. Then you wouldn't have all this to do.'

Of course, I should have asked him when he last bought a CD-ROM – most people, in my experience, acquire most of them as freebies with their computer, and probably end up using the majority as coffee mats – but I made the mistake of trying to employ reason. 'What about the rambler out on a walk?' I asked, suspecting that our expert never walked further than the nearest cappuccino bar, 'or climbing in the hills?'

'Little palmtop computer', was the quick response. 'Just press a button and there's the map you want. Paper's a thing of the past.' And my mind went straight back to a lecture by David Rhind in the early 1980s, long before he became Director General of Ordnance Survey, in which he extolled a future of paperless maps 'You'd just need to put the computer on the back of the lorry', I recall him answering to one interlocutor – and several years later he was able to put his ideas into effect.

Since then those of us who use, produce and enjoy paper maps have gradually found ourselves marginalized, as conference after trade show after symposium has seen the digital map lionized, the computer idolized and the Internet continuously explained. Are we in danger of becoming dinosaurs? Are those of us who publish paper maps going to become the forgotten motel on the B-road while the traffic streams by on the highway? Can we expect, and are we entitled to expect, libraries to cater for our archaic habits? And if so, will libraries treat us as equals, or as secondary customers, shunted off with uninterested librarians, old and decaying stock, and yesterday's facilities? Will there, indeed, be the funds to buy both computers and plan chests?

I am not, I hope, espousing the cause of paper maps in a Luddite manner. Indeed, I run and construct a successful website, with several thousand hits a week; it makes money! Moreover I am a regular user of the Internet and, like most publishers, a devotee of the Apple Mac and QuarkXpress. Nevertheless, I do have serious misgivings about the growing dependency on computers for maps and before I go on to discuss the requirements of the paper map user it is appropriate to mention some of these. These reflections will inevitably be subjective, but they are, I believe, shared by many other map users.

Firstly, I am not convinced that we have yet arrived at a common formula for computer usage, and here I might list my own computer history. We first acquired a computer in 1984; this was a BBC computer (remember them?) and over the subsequent years we have moved on to an Amstrad PC with 5¼ in. disks, to an Amstrad PCW, and to the present Apple Macs and more standardized PCs. We have used several sizes of disks only to find that many modern computers no longer give a disk option at all. Just ten years ago we were meticulously saving our authors' historical notes on 5¼ in. disks, which are now, to all intents and purposes, unreadable. For the historian this begs the question as to the future compatibility of present-day computer systems. A paper map, with reasonable conservation, will still be of use in a hundred years; can we really be so certain of today's GIS systems? And are all professional or academic readers going to be comfortable with these systems? Certainly, if we as publishers demanded that all authors contribute their texts in a particular format we would deprive ourselves of some of the finest talents; many good writers have scarcely entered the world of the typewriter.

Secondly, a computer screen can only display a tiny area of map and although it is possible to move from one area to another with MrSID or other programs, this is a slow and laborious process compared with the natural reflexes of the human eye across a paper map. Because a map on the screen appears as if by magic, we are in danger of forgetting just how basic it is, and it is a useful exercise to scan a map in oneself on a home computer scanner. I scanned in an extract from an Ordnance Survey *Popular Edition* one-inch-to-the-mile map from the 1920s and it came up with a perfectly acceptable image; in fact, it came out so well that I have put it on to my website. But to have reasonable definition on the screen only an extract around 4 in. by 3 in. was feasible; a fraction of the map area; in fact, it would have taken 42 such images to cover the entire map. Indeed, on our website we regularly include a 'mystery map', where readers have to identify a small extract of a map and tell us where it is or who lived there: to do this we display a tiny extract from one of our map reprints, showing (for instance) a church, railway station, handful of houses but making sure that no clearly identifiable names are there – and yet this tiny extract fills the best part of the screen.

Thirdly, I believe the emphasis on digital mapping has brought about an alarming drop in cartographic standards, arguably accentuated by the worry about wasting memory – the small JPEG extract mentioned above comes to 134 Kb. My principal research is as a historian, often wanting to compare old maps with new, and yet some current digital mapping is so over-simplified as to be virtually worthless. The Ordnance Survey database, for instance, as made available on computers in some libraries, is impressive in that it delivers large-scale areas at the touch (well, a few touches) of a button, either at 1:1250, 1:2500 or 1:10,000 according to area. Yet the larger-scale displays, though doubtless accurate and reasonably up to date (although it is difficult to discover an actual survey date), give nothing of the character of place we should expect from a map; while the 1:10,000 scale displays for mountain and moorland, a few lines across the screen like a minimalist abstract sketch, are sad maps indeed. And though there are many fine maps to be found on the Internet – notably through the Library of Congress website (**http://lcweb.loc.gov/rr/ geogmap/gmpage.html**) – those you are most likely to want to use are often basic in the extreme. Look at the Best Western Hotels site (**http://www. bestwestern.com**), for instance, a good and efficient site with information about the rooms you are booking around the world; it is a pleasant surprise to find many of the hotels given a location map, yet surprise turns to frustration when the poor-quality maps lead even the experienced mapreader an unmerry waltz around the back streets of Vienna, luggage in hand.

So the requirement for paper maps is not nostalgic, not a longing for the paper of my youth, not a fetishist's wish to smell the freshly dried ink, but at least partly a result of the absolute shortcomings found on computerized maps. Of course I, like many others, have no wish to spend all my hours at a computer screen, but family historians have shown that that is a price well worth paying if the information becomes more readily available; the microfiche readers, with their census or registration details, have been one of the great successes of the library and (especially) record office movement over the last two decades but their robust, basic technology is not one the map world has readily adopted (and map images on microfiche are uniquely awful). Good maps may well become available on the Internet, but since the vast majority of professional users would prefer to surf the web at home or in the office, it is difficult to see what long-term relevance that can have to libraries except to close them down.

The requirements of the paper map user

What requirements, then, do I have of a map library, and what about readers in other disciplines? Let us start with my own uses, principally as a historian and specifically as a publisher of reprints. These can be summarized under three headings: collections, cataloguing and convenience. Let us look at them in order.

Collections

The map collection is, of course, the nub of it all, and its variety is the lifeblood of our trade. Users' demands may be simple – a landscape photographer told me all he expects is that his local library have a good collection of 1:50,000 *Landranger* maps to help plan his location shoots – or they may be specialized in the extreme. A specialist may well have to travel a thousand miles to find the map he or she seeks – and here the Internet must eventually prove of benefit – but it would be folly in the extreme to presume that the former, more standard reader is easily served. In my experience the maps most in demand are standard topographical maps, typically at 1:50,000 scale, with the reader then moving on to more detailed or specialist maps. In the UK I would expect the eclipse of the 1:10,000 scale maps, traditionally a popular scale with students, to lead to a much greater demand for the 1:25,000 scale maps, awareness of which will at last be awoken by the admirable new Ordnance Survey *Explorer* series.

These topographical maps should be the bedrock of any map collection. When I visit Birmingham University, which has the busiest map library that I know of in the UK, I see desks and counters awash with such maps – yet with scarcely a computer in sight – while a scattering of other maps shows that a fair percentage of readers then move on to something at a larger scale or more specialized. It is, perhaps, the ultimate in low-tech libraries and yet its fast-moving librarian and constant stream of readers leave one in little doubt that it is at the hub of the geography department.

Having established the basis of a map library – whether in a university or city reference library – we move on to the specialist collections which, by their nature, will vary from one library to another. At least, they should vary, or we must ask whether librarians are just grabbing the same handouts as each other! In a town or city reference (or local studies) library I expect a good collection of maps of the area, including large-scale Ordnance Survey or similar maps; in an academic library we would expect collections specific to the requirements of students and staff, and hopefully also a reasonable local collection, presuming that the university reflects its region. This will be made up of maps acquired (a) through donation, (b) through sensible scouring of discarded collections, such as town planners or the military, and (c) by thoughtful use of the (often limited) budget available. A good map library will also have some part of its collection reflecting the interests and enthusiasms of the librarians themselves, often items acquired at minimal cost – ephemera, foreign maps picked up at trade fairs, the maps of a local or friendly publisher are examples that come to mind – and over the years these can build up into the very jewels of the collection.

I do therefore expect a good map library to have some cartographic character of its own and an aspect of the digital revolution that alarms me is that every library might end up with the same maps or, perhaps worse, the maps that a government or establishment body chooses for them to have. In its mildest form this is caused by national map producers only allowing the map library a percentage of its output. Fairbairn (Chapter 15) has properly discussed the many virtues of EDINA Digimap but even this acclaimed project suffers from a '30% rule' for its large-scale Land-Line™ mapping. This means that not all tiles are instantly available to casual users entering a map library, as a demonstration to me highlighted. Not unnaturally, I chose Leadgate, in northwest Durham – a somewhat run-down former mining and steelworks area, but also home to our office – but alas! all Digimap could come up with, after several minutes of searching, was a tiny extract of a small-scale map which might as well have come from a road atlas. In fact, come to think of it, it probably had.

More seriously, is there not a danger of state censorship? More than half of Europe's current countries have had totalitarian regimes in my lifetime. Paper – whether used for maps or literature – has a remarkable resilience to attempts at suppression, but any future dictators will surely employ the best computer (and Internet) experts corruption can buy. The difficulties still faced by mapmakers in Romania have been highlighted in *The map report* (Metcalf and Florea, 1999), but anyone who thinks censorship does not happen to Western mapping should glance at *Sheetlines*, the organ of the UK-based Charles Close Society for the Study of Ordnance Survey Maps, whose somewhat esoteric pages often bear examples of features omitted by Ordnance Survey across the years. For instance, until the 1870s their large-scale maps showed prisons and military bases in great detail but subsequently, perhaps as a reaction to Fenian disturbances, blank areas were substituted.

Clearly one can see the potential for criminals and terrorists in the use of highly detailed large-scale mapping (it has been suggested that such maps were used for a major prison break-out in Britain a few years ago) yet sometimes such censorship can be more insidious. The Ordnance Survey of Northern Ireland has very high standards and yet their large-scale mapping is very scarce in British libraries. Various reasons – cost, space, methods of production – are given as to why such maps are not available in all our copyright libraries, yet for the historian such an omission is of concern. Areas such as west Belfast, the Bogside area in Derry or the Garvachy Road in Portadown are of prime interest to social commentators of today and tomorrow and it would be lamentable if detailed maps of these and other areas are not being acquired by map libraries in Britain. Doubtless there is very little positive censorship – the opening of my mail after a map launch in Crossmaglen may have been a coincidence, the confiscation of a map (one of my own!) at a Fermanagh checkpoint was not – but I remain uneasy that coverage of Northern Ireland is so poor in British map libraries.

This problem relates to paper as well as digital maps, of course, yet at least with paper maps the interested librarian can (given the funds, of course!) go out and acquire the maps on the open market. Here librarians must try to forget the notion – sometimes still prevalent – that they are privileged customers. Because we all meet together and, hopefully, enjoy one another's company, it can sometimes appear that publishers rely on map libraries for their trade. In fact, for most map series libraries are only a minority market. To give an example, when I started publishing map reprints in the early 1980s I was told that I would need to keep some of the maps unfolded because that was how libraries required them. We ended up having to take those flat sheets back to the folding machine as I realised what a small niche market the library really was. Even today I estimate that less than 1% of our sales go to academic libraries and even when local libraries' purchases are added in (though excluding maps bought by them for resale) the figure is still only between 1 and 2%. With so small a percentage, the special library edition (eg unfolded) of a commercial map is seldom sustainable. Librarians will increasingly need to go out and discover which paper maps are being published, yet it is disturbing how few librarians are currently going to the International Map Trade Association meetings, where so many interesting publishers, notably from Eastern Europe, display their wares.

Cataloguing

Above all, the professional or academic reader wants to be in control, and with this in mind my first requirement is for clear index maps, ready for my own perusal. Index maps – rather than index cards which are seldom of more than peripheral value, although sometimes I fancy many hours has been spent on them – need to be readily available, and although guidance is always welcome the reader will often want a few minutes just to peruse the index map, perhaps with a small-scale topographical map of the area to hand.

Beyond this, however, it is necessary for knowledge within the map library to go beyond its own four walls and take in other map libraries in the locale. These will typically include the university map library, county record office and central reference (or local studies) library. The collections should be complementary to one another and if there is no union catalogue, then there should be broad awareness among the three institutions as to their respective holdings. Sadly this is too often not the case. Until recent years the record office and local library would frequently act in near total isolation from one another, sometimes adopting weird sheet-numbering systems destined to confuse all but immediate staff. As an extreme example of this approach, I once met a local studies librarian who, despite several years in the post, had never visited the record office just across the car park. In the north of England the story circulated in the 1970s of an archivist who threw out a collection of maps, which had to be rescued by librarians from the lorry taking them to the incinerator.

Things have much improved since, and many record offices and local studies libraries have now either merged or moved into adjacent premises, something that can only benefit the flow of ideas for both readers and staff. Yet, within the UK at least, contact between academic map librarians and their counterparts in the public sector (normally local studies librarians and archivists) remains patchy and sometimes non-existent. For the professional researcher, however, reasonable contact between the various institutions can bring real benefits. In the mid 1980s, when we broadened our map range beyond our native North East, we regularly held informal meetings at Sheffield's Crucible Theatre after work, where I would be joined by librarians and archivists from Doncaster, Rotherham and Sheffield, and people from Sheffield University's map library and geography department. The resultant craic, in the bar of the theatre, helped ferment many of the ideas that have since stood my map series in such good stead.

Some libraries, such as the Guildhall Library in London, the National Library of Scotland, or New York Public Library have traditionally spanned this divide. However, within the UK at least, cutbacks and reorganization in public libraries, often with devastating impact on staff morale, have increasingly seen the loss of dedicated local studies librarians; though seldom bearing the title of map librarian, their interest in the use of maps has been beyond question – I am delighted that so many have won the Godfrey Award, which we host jointly with the British Cartographic Society – and it would be a disaster for the world of maps if they are not replaced.

Convenience

One of the curiosities of the map library is that the greater the institution, the easier it is to use. The novice entering the hallowed halls of some august library is almost invariably amazed at the relaxed atmosphere of the place. Go to the National Library of Wales, or the Library of Congress, or Bibliothèque Royale Albert I in Brussels and you will find a library as welcoming and easy going as if you had gone round the corner to borrow the latest Patrick O'Brian novel.

Elsewhere the picture is extremely varied, particularly within the public sector, as is the degree of welcome, where staff can be over-protective of their superiors (after many years of publishing there are still record offices where I have not been allowed to meet the archivist). But once encountered, the librarians and archivists concerned are almost always helpful, even enthusiastic.

Having talked my way into the library I then require the maps, lots of them, and here we encounter a problem. My experience is that it is unfair to ask for more than a dozen or so maps at one visit, and even that number is likely to put pressure on the staff. Unfortunately I may wish to look at many more; good index maps can facilitate the search, and computer-scanned maps clearly have a role here. There can be little more frustrating than to ask for three maps, wait 20 minutes for their entrance, and then find they are not quite what is wanted. How many times have I ended up idly gazing at the maps for ten or 20 minutes, when a quick glance tells me all I need to know, because I do not wish to offend the librarian who has probably faced an obstacle course to unearth them. Clearly, electronic retrieval systems are a potential boon here, in eliminating the irrelevant maps if nothing else, but the paper map remains essential, not just for looking at the broad expanse of the map, but – most essentially – for putting two or three maps down side by side, perhaps of adjacent areas or contrasting dates.

Even with the best-quality index map it can be difficult to know exactly which map you want or whether it is likely to be of real use and so we come to that most forbidden of subjects: access to the stack. We library readers are nervous beasts and know we are likely to get short shrift if we ask to find the maps ourselves; yet I have to say that I achieve infinitely more, and more quickly, and hopefully with less stress on the librarian, if I have access to the map cabinets myself. Often it is possible to thumb through a drawer and tell at a glance that the maps are of no use, or glimpse something of infinite academic value that I would never have thought of writing down on the application form. My most rewarding hours in libraries have almost always been when I have been let loose in this manner, hopefully to the benefit of others.

Of course, this is easy enough when the library has a modest collection of maps, perhaps in a vertical unit in the reading room, but less so if it is a large collection stored down below. A friendly librarian once remarked of me that my ideal library was one that offered me coffee. That is not (quite) true! My ideal library is, without shadow of doubt, one that allows me into the stack. What wondrous places they are! It seems to me that the space needed for the storage of maps means they are consigned to the remotest cellars, surrounded by pipes and girders and janitorial clutter, interspersed with unread magazines and council minutes, spiced with the distant echo of half-distinguished sounds, and the nearby scent of all-too-obvious smells. What treasures I have found here, and what dross; maps stacked five foot high on pallets (did the builders bring them here on forklift trucks?); plan chests that tear your fingernails to shreds; maps whose only reader these last 40 years has been a squashed spider; maps (horror of horrors) rolled so tight they spring shut the moment you unravel them, bashful to the light; maps covered with the dust of ages, or fading beyond recall; maps so grossly misfiled they must have been given up for lost a lifetime ago. Into such catacombs librarians have shut (even locked) me away, with a rueful comment of 'you know where to find me' – three stairwells, five corridors and a caretaker's broom cupboard away – and a pitying shake of the head. And here, so often, I have done my most rewarding work. No wonder librarians want to put their archives on to disk!

Conclusion

These rambling notes are, of course, subjective; yet it would, I think, be wrong to dismiss my 'user perspective' as unusual. Let us imagine just a handful of the uses to which paper maps are put. Transport historians, studying lengths of railways or canals far beyond the scope of any screen; industrial archaeologists, scouring a map for remains of old collieries and the cartographic 'moonscape' they leave behind; social historians, wishing to study urban deprivation in all its aspects. All of these will gain far more from the broad expanse of a map than from the tunnel vision of a computer screen.

Imagine too, the botanists and ornithologists, with their meticulously comprised atlases of habitat or breeding birds. Commonly with such projects grid squares, perhaps a kilometre square, are allocated to individual researchers across a region, yet how are these, working from home, ever to have access to identical computer systems? Planners too, and those opposing their plans on environmental grounds, need to see the broad effect played by new roads or building development; how many bad decisions are now being made because computer-bound bureaucrats cannot see the damage being done beyond the 100-metre radius of their computer screen? Perhaps the only researchers to whom scanned maps will bring unbridled joy are genealogists; yet I doubt whether even the most dedicated of academic map librarians is ready to play host to coachloads of family historians.

Of course, there are many exciting projects on computer, some local, some national. Within the UK many councils are scanning in the maps for their own area, which can be looked at in conjunction with nostalgic photographs, current planning applications, or the news that your house stands on contaminated land. In the cartographic field we look forward to the National Library of Scotland's work with its Timothy Pont maps (**http://www.nls.ac.uk/digitallibrary/map/pont.htm**), and relish the Library of Congress's many panorama maps (**http://lcweb.loc.gov/rr/geogmap/ gmpage.html**). The last is from one of my favourite websites; yet even here nothing can compare with the excitement of seeing these maps in (say) Denver Public Library before driving up into the mountains to visit Idaho Springs and Georgetown.

I have no doubt that I shall want to see maps on computer, to complement those I am looking at on paper, 'in the flesh'. I am equally certain that I and other professional users will want to see them at home, via the Internet, where we have control over the material. But for most of us, paper maps will continue to be our core cartographic resource, and for them we will still, of necessity, visit libraries. Map librarians who ignore this simple fact are in danger of consigning their profession to oblivion.

Reference

Metcalf, W and Florea, D (1999) Mapping in Romania, *The map report*, **17** (8), 14–16.

15

Perspectives on map use and map users in the digital era

David Fairbairn

This chapter presents a non-librarian's view of the impact of digital spatial data on the form of maps, their applications and use, and on users and curators. A number of trends in contemporary library use are noted, as are some likely expectations of map and spatial data users in particular. However, the major issue on the part of the curator is uncertainty about what each individual map user wants. Mechanisms for meeting possible needs, primarily those sourced in contemporary technology, are described. A number of case studies are examined to determine how usage patterns will develop, highlighting the British Digimap service, created to supply topographic map data to higher education institutions. From these, an impression is given of the way in which users and curators will interact in the future, the tasks for which spatial data will be used, and the impact of user needs and expectations on policy in the map library.

Introduction

As we cross the threshold into a new century, it is instructive to note that, in terms of map use, we are not starting a journey into uncharted territory. Whilst it is true that there is a widening scope to the definition of what can be termed a map, that there is a widening range of human activity to which mapping can be applied, and that there is increasing diversity in the map-using community, the development of map use can be seen as evolutionary, rather than revolutionary.

At the dawn of the last century, the person ultimately responsible for the Royal Geographical Society Map Room (at the time, the largest map collection in the world) claimed that the 'increased use that is made of our library and map-room proves that it is not only our numbers that are increasing, but also the intelligent interest that is taken in our science' (Markham, 1899, 4). Maps, map use and map users have clearly continued to change for at least a century as interest in all aspects spatial has increased. Map curators have not been slow to respond to the consequent demands placed on them. Indeed, as indicated elsewhere in this book, they have often been in the vanguard of developing and promoting such changes.

Perhaps the most radical of these changes, particularly in the last 20 years, has been the availability of spatial data in digital form, and this chapter is intended primarily to address the impact of such data on the form of maps, their applications and use, their users and, primarily, on the curator. In addition, some general comments on the nature of map library use, both actual and potential, are offered.

Using the 21st-century map library

The change in the nature of spatial data has been well documented throughout its developmental stages, but the subsequent changing nature of map use has been less well considered and it is thus difficult accurately to gauge the impact of the technological changes on types of map use in libraries and elsewhere. What is clear, however, is that these developing patterns parallel general observations regarding contemporary library and information use. Thus, trends such as

- improved information literacy in the library user community
- a move from teaching to learning as the prevalent mode of education
- an associated move to 'lifelong learning'
- the development of self-instruction programmes and distance learning as viable modes for study
- the use of computer facilities
- the use of networking

impact on the map library as they do on libraries in general (Riggs, 2000).

Unfortunately such an imprecise listing of factors does not specifically help the map librarian attempt to meet the particular needs of a community of users that increasingly varies in its definition and use of maps and its inherent abilities to address and handle the information presented in them.

The expectations of those approaching map libraries vary enormously (Parry and Fox, 1998). A significant proportion of map library users still have little knowledge of current technological changes. Ignorance of new methods of data archiving and delivery is widespread. However, there is also part of the user community that has unrealistically high expectations. Acquainted with the hardware, familiar with concepts of digital map data and, perhaps, with an application for that data that involves integration with other digital data sets, such users may expect the map curator to perform, on their behalf, complex data analysis and presentation.

The map librarian is faced, therefore, with uncertainty when approached by a user. To be prepared the contemporary librarian should be able to match the following user expectations in a number of different areas:

- Availability of *good quality information*: this can be obtained from in-house catalogues, from off-site indexing and bibliographic resources, and from the librarians themselves whose knowledge of their own stock should be of a high standard. This is to be expected as standard library practice.
- Accessibility to other *supporting material*, such as reference works, other records, almanacs, indexes of personalities.
- Assistance in locating and identifying information sources using index terms specifically for digital data, *metadata*, and other data description techniques such as *'quick-look' images* and web-based records.
- *No gaps* (temporal or spatial or thematic) in coverage: what is ideal (but, of course, unattainable) is complete access to a coherent set of map data. One of the perceived advantages of digital supply (either in-house or off-site) is that it should be able to overcome the physically restricted stock of the paper map library.
- *Good quality documents*: map librarianship involves curating physical stock and map users will expect this – clearly, there are ongoing conservation implications for as long as paper records are maintained.
- *Systematic organization*: as a major map use task, browsing, is aided by explicit or implicit linkage of documents and data, physical proximity may be expected, along with definitive 'route maps' for exploring digital data resources.
- *Ready access* to both hard copy and digital material is associated with this: the map user should not spend too long on forbidden or time-consuming searches and response times to off-sites should be short.
- Access to *multimedia*: even the most unsophisticated library user may potentially ask about use of material beyond paper – images, audio, video and digital data sets.
- *Software, hardware, and support staff*: such resources necessary to use digital data should also be available.
- *High quality technology*: electronic access to data, in particular, should be capable of being undertaken using, for example, high-resolution screens.
- *Provision of reproduction possibilities*: this may be necessary for hard-copy creation.
- Definitive advice on *copyright* and data dissemination: in all cases, users' responsibilities need to be categorically spelled out.

Meeting these needs requires a constant reassessment of a variety of factors, most covered elsewhere in this book. Issues of physical storage, physical access, nature of stock, technological facilities, personnel, hardware, Internet policy, costs and administration are all connected with the main purpose of the map library – to serve the users. The 21st-century map library may be in danger of failing its user community: to avoid this, it is essential that, in future, library organization is driven by a functional approach, predicated on user needs (Montanelli and Stenstrom, 1999).

Using 21st-century maps and the needs of users

Is the curator in a position, however, accurately to determine user needs? Just as predicting the nature of the next customer through the door is difficult, the actual task for which the map data are being sought may also be unpredictable. Map use can vary from very general browsing to a highly specific, focused enquiry.

Contemporary research into patterns of map use has been developed using a tripartite scaling of:

- levels of interaction with the map data
- levels of interaction with other players
- levels of knowledge acquired from the data.

These three scales form a visual cube (Figure 15.1) illustrating a space of map use (MacEachren, 1994). MacEachren further indicated the possibilities of placing typical map-use tasks at points 'within the cube'. Thus, use of a land registration map to determine public rights of way is an example of private map use (this is an individual inquiry), engaging in low interaction with the data (the viewer does not modify or 'add value' to the information) and accessing known information (in the sense that the user does not need to interpret the data beyond the method of presentation chosen by the cartographer). By contrast, use of data in a map library could follow a scenario of multiple access (by researchers in a video conference), to a web-based data set within which simulation exercises can be performed (such as plotting alternative land-use planning scenarios) and from which new conclusions and decisions can result.

A simpler distinction is made by Withers (1999) who suggests a difference between the utility-led map user and the curiosity-led map user: 'all map users lie somewhere along the continuum between these positions of the strictly utilitarian and the unremittingly curious'. The two extremes of this scale exemplify, on the one hand, specific problem-solving using maps and, on the other, general browsing.

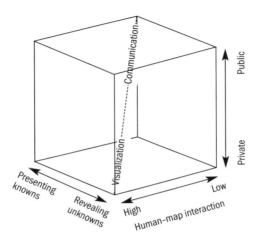

Fig. 15.1 *Map use 'cube' (after MacEachren, 1994)*
Reproduced from MacEachren, A M and Taylor, D R F (eds), 'Visualization in modern cartography', 1994, p6, with permission from Elsevier Science.

Both these models attempt to cover the vast range of potential map use, a range that, in reality, may be difficult to encompass. Attempts have been made to define *map use* in a narrower sense by equating it with *mapreading*, an activity that has been studied in depth by numerous psychologists and visual scientists. Some of this work has been followed through by cartographers (eg Board, 1984) examining typical map-use tasks such as region definition, point location and route planning. To these can be added further tasks familiar to map librarians such as determining the nature of transformation from one map reference system to another, accessing data sets of boundary information, noting the correct spelling of a geographical name and assessing the relationship between one thematic attribute of a location (eg the rainfall) and another (eg the dominant vegetation).

Clearly it is, in fact, impossible thoroughly to document every possible task: as map librarians are aware, map use often prompts further investigation and continued and extended access to other sources. The original map-use task may be considerably different from the range of procedures actually undertaken by the map user in their work within the map library.

A further issue that arises now is whether such tasks are approached differently dependent on media (ie paper or 'soft-copy' mapping). The use of digital multimedia, allowing for map data to be accessed and manipulated with considerable ease, could be regarded merely as the development of the paradigm of multiple information source access that libraries, incorporating map libraries, have afforded in the past. The information sought from spatial data is unlikely to be different whether the user in the past viewed paper maps or now accesses online sources.

To answer the question about how a map librarian can ascertain user needs, it is possible, from a practical viewpoint, to develop user surveys. These have, to date, been limited in scope. Gillispie (1990) indicated that much routine information on a variety of management issues – number of loans, waiting times, reader registrations, satisfaction surveys – is collected by large libraries. These are of little utility in a reference, specialist map library. Informal metrics, such as number of items needing to be re-shelved, visitor numbers and online transaction times, appear to have considerably more merit. McGlamery (1997) has used these, and further proactive surveys by e-mail, to build a profile of the user community to assist in collection building and enhancement.

Parry (1995) has questioned the overall benefit of such user surveys, indicating that concentration on the particular request, document or item is unrealistic: 'curators know that most map collection users seek information rather than a specific map, and, more often than not, it is the curator who defines the appropriate map source'. This makes planning and meeting targets difficult: if potential use is unpredictable and actual use is impossible to record, map librarians may face problems in justifying the existence of their specialist realm.

Demonstrating that curators are more proactive than reactive in their interaction with users is crucial, both in justifying their own future and meeting user needs. Personal knowledge on the part of the librarian is important, particularly when faced with an uncertain or novice user. Aspects of scale, resolution and differential compilation methods, knowledge of indexing, tiling and referencing, and understanding of geometrical aspects such as projection are all highly specialist spatial data-handling issues inherent in the management of both paper and digital records. Many users expect such expert guidance from the map librarian additional to their assumed knowledge about context and content.

Mechanisms for addressing user needs

It has been suggested that map use has changed in the last century only in the methods of inquiry and the possibilities afforded for subsequent data manipulation. Technological progress has changed *how* libraries do their work and not *why*. It is the resultant new patterns of map use that map libraries are now addressing. The roles of GIS, of Internet access and of electronic atlases are becoming increasingly important and these impact significantly on user needs and expectations (a number of which are *italicized* below and explored further). They also, however, bring to the map library mechanisms for meeting those needs.

An initial requirement may be to locate spatial data around a particular location or for a specific area. Traditionally met by catalogue resources, such an *inquiry* could now be assisted with online searching facilities using standard web search engines. The efficiency of such methods is debatable: they require exhaustive facilities for searching through vast resources and they rely on well documented metadata (Chapter 9). The development of expert systems, both for narrowing down location searches (Yu, 1999) and for 'mining' knowledge from vast and complex data sets is essential. Such systems can allow for incomplete or 'fuzzy' queries to be put to large bibliographic databases and to the web: a search string such as 'Pennine Hills' needs to be interpreted in definitive coordinates and as a match for the more common (and correct) name, 'The Pennines'.

The result of a search may be to note the existence of data sets not held directly by the library. Most notably, *digital data sets* can be seen as an increasingly important resource. Some spatial data are no longer routinely published in conventional printed form. Users may require digital data for their specific task (for example, precise coordination, data overlay or customized output). Digital data are ideal for integrating disparate data sets. All these potential user needs are met using data stored on CD-ROM and DVD. The implications for the map library are clearly immense. User needs are served by having regularly updated electronic media, viewable through contemporary hardware and capable of being 'sub-set', either as an image or as a data layer. Archiving possibilities using digital techniques are also of interest to the user (Chapter 10).

Increasingly, access to such data is through a remote site: it is this issue that is of most concern to map librarians, but offers great opportunities to map users. It is clearly most economic for regular, mass producers of spatial data (most notably national mapping agencies) to disseminate their data from a centralized site, probably using *access through the Internet*. Britain's Ordnance Survey have a web-based system, *Get-a-map* (available through the Ordnance Survey web site at **http://www.ordsvy.gov.uk**) from which anyone with Internet access can download current data. Dependent on the organizational policy for charging, a scenario becomes viable whereby the map library can be bypassed. Commercial suppliers of data are also able to make use of developing e-commerce possibilities (Chapter 16).

There are enormous opportunities to the map library, as well as threats, from open access through the Internet. Collaboration with other institutions, rather than competition, may be possible, allowing users to access pooled resources. *Remote access to map library resources* may result in fewer 'walk-in' visits to the physical site, but considerably more use of e-mail querying, remote access to digital resources mounted by library staff, and access to catalogues.

As has been seen, the use of data is widening and addresses a range of applications. The possibilities of data manipulation in GIS allow for map data to be integrated and added value to accrue. *GIS services* can be provided within the map library to satisfy user needs, but again there are significant implications. The creation of a fully functional GIS laboratory is only rarely an option for a resource-starved library institution (though compare Chapter 5). The issues of hardware acquisition, software choice, integration with existing institution facilities and personnel training are all likely to mitigate against GIS investment. Although initially some map libraries have tried to meet the possible GIS needs of users, it has become rapidly obvious that there are limits to what map libraries are able to offer in-house (Cobb and Olivero, 1997). Widespread contemporary policy is to rely on remote services (which are becoming increasingly sophisticated, with the introduction of static map and dynamic GIS resources served on the web) and on the user's own knowledge and resources. There is a perception that the library has a responsibility to acquire spatial data but that the user is expected to know how to use it (Deckelbaum, 1999).

In fact, there is a range of products and operations that expert and GIS-aware users are likely to demand. Browsing may result in the production of a user-defined (not user-designed or user-produced) map. Web sources capable of delivering such products include MapQuest.com (**http://www.mapquest. com**). More sophisticated operations may involve proactive data download, overlay, analysis and manipulation of spatial data, often in realtime. Added value can result from the generation of new material through such systems. Clearly, a user may need access to complex GIS, database and image-processing software packages to perform these tasks. Lamont and Bowles (1997) describe a system for users to operate a simple query, manipulation and map creation system to take county-based data and create and customize electronic thematic maps.

Such attempts to prepare 'municipal GIS' are typical of contemporary policy decisions which aim to bring information resources and their use to a wider public. They may well involve the opening up of the facilities offered by a map library to a potentially larger number of neophyte users. Without preconceptions of what the map library can offer, but aware of the fact that contemporary methods of map data handling are 'hi-tech' such users will require significant *training*. Offering courses is immensely time consuming, and of limited value to the 'one-off' or occasional user: there will still be demands, however, for advice and guidance on accessing and utilizing spatial data.

A final user need that must be met in a manner somewhat different from the past is the provision of *hard-copy mapping*. Copyright issues aside, mechanisms for creating a map that the user can physically take out of the library have developed from tracing through photography and photocopying to hard-copy plotting of digital data. There are implications for charging and technical support whenever a large-format plotter is installed in a map library.

The map library of the future will seamlessly integrate resources of paper mapping, electronic atlases (off-line repositories), software packages (for analysis), online access to data (spatial, image, (carto-)bibliographic), a combination of local software and online access to remote data and remote access to analysis/overlay/integration. In so doing, a wide range of uses and a wide range of users can be satisfied.

Resultant use patterns

There are few documented examples of the resultant patterns of map use by map library users. Much of the evidence of map-use patterns, purpose and methods is anecdotal, relayed by map librarians. Specific case studies have concentrated on particular constituencies of user (for example, university students) or on attempts to generalize the purpose of library use.

Milis-Proost (1990), for example, examined use made of map sources by historical researchers whose major aim was to examine contemporaneous mapping, looking for explicit historical indicators of human activity in the past (eg mills, roads, vegetation pattern). In addition, archaeologists and medieval historians were interested in the reconstruction of the landscape and the human settlement prior to the cartographic document itself, from the clues given on subsequent mapping. Further comparative use was made of maps of historical phenomena (eg demographic, medical, linguistic, etc). Finally, the study of the history of cartography itself was enabled by access to archival material.

Whether the historical community would benefit from access to material different from that already consulted, or in ways different from those already used, is not clear. There would clearly be benefit in integrating the study of map material and textual information.

A more generic view of map use is given in Parry (1995). In the context of a higher education map library the users are defined under the categories of reference, teaching, research and map production. It is suggested that some of these users (for example those engaged in research) engage in high-order map-use tasks, extracting added value from the map and associated data, whereas others (those using the map for reference and location purposes) are performing lower-order map-use tasks.

In both cases, however, electronic media can be used: for the former, access to sophisticated statistical software packages may be required whilst lower- order tasks can use straighforward electronic atlases. The distinction can be mapped to the map-use cube in Figure 15.1.

Berger and Hines (1994) have considered the needs of all library users, suggesting a number of functions of the library, again from the perspective of a university community: research, studying, assigned reading, browsing, socializing, non-academic research and casual reading. Such functions can also be translated to the specific case of the map library. Their resultant *desiderata* include accurate and speedy information retrieval, simplicity of use, computerized catalogues, computerized reading, full-text retrieval, wide availability of terminals, access to remote sites, 24-hour availability, expert staff and printed copies, all of which can be mapped to the wish-list defined above.

Contemporary map-use case study (the Digimap project)

A further example of the assessment of map use can be undertaken with respect to the Digimap project in the UK, a nation-wide scheme for supplying British Ordnance Survey topographic mapping to higher education organizations. An initial raison d'etre for this project was the perceived and actual difficulty of accessing large-scale digital mapping within the academic community (Steele, 1993). Rising prices, shrinking resources, the replacement of paper copies by digital data, the need for map curators to develop new technical skills, and the demands for the regular archiving of continuously updated spatial digital data all led to an acknowledgment that mechanisms for university access to and use of OS data needed to be completely redefined.

Under the auspices of the Joint Information Systems Committee (JISC), a body set up by university funding authorities in the UK to address issues of data provision and use in the higher education sector, a pilot project was undertaken, followed by a full implementation in 2000. This has resulted in a system that can replace access to limited stocks of Ordnance Survey mapping through separate institutional libraries by a web-based distribution system for map and data download. The development and administration of Digimap is documented elsewhere (**http://edina.ed.ac.uk**) and some assessment has been made of the impact of the system on its users and on the organizations that mediate access to the system (Millea, 1999). Currently, such use is permitted only through established institutional (but not necessarily library) facilities, primarily for the purposes of ensuring registration and access are only available to those entitled to exploit the Ordnance Survey data for educational purposes. There are strictly enforced procedures ensuring no data leakage, acknowledgment of the data source in subsequent use, and use for authorized purposes only. It is technically possible for any user, once registered, to access the data from any Internet-enabled terminal, thus bypassing the library facility completely and it is clear that many users follow this route.

The usage patterns for Digimap are recorded at source within the organization that runs the project (Edinburgh University Data Library). Again, the local libraries can only have a limited role in assessing users and usage from their site.

Initial use patterns from the pilot project (Digimap, 1999) revealed that under-graduate students have been the majority user community (49% of registrations), with disappointingly little use made by researchers. However, during the pilot project, researchers were in many cases unable to access Digimap as its use was restricted to research funded by the universities themselves or by UK research councils. Only a minority of research is actually funded through these channels, and this rule has been relaxed with the full implementation of the Digimap service. The primary usage of data was in teaching and demonstrating, both in formal classes and in the completion of set elements of practical coursework. Creating hard-copy maps from the system was the most common method of accessing data, followed by the downloading of raw data, presumably for inclusion in GIS. Down-loading plotfiles for subsequent plotting on in-house facilities, followed by viewing 'soft-copy' maps on-screen were the other usage patterns detected.

One aspect of note is the recorded disciplinary spread of Digimap users. Social sciences and economics, surprisingly, provide the largest number of individual registrations (25%), with engineering and physical sciences comprising 18% of the recorded users. Biosciences and natural environment are also significant sectors. Although the discipline of geography could be placed in any of these categories, an unusual result is the proportionately low number of geography students and staff registered for Digimap, compared with, for example, architecture and civil engineering users. To a certain extent this may reflect the nature of the data provided: primarily large-scale topographic mapping, ideal for creating and modifying site plans. In terms of spatial data usage, the creation of a map for recording purposes – delineating the nature of a small site or allowing for the manual plotting of field-collected data – appears to be a major function. Those downloading data or plotfiles are usually producing hard-copy maps for similar purposes.

The significance of the Digimap project goes beyond the presentation of statistics regarding map use and user profile. The model that Digimap presents is of longer-term importance. The technology of holding and supplying vast quantities of voluminous spatial data across the web is clearly of interest. The role of the map librarian is of interest: for many Digimap users their only link with the map librarian has been to register for the service. General librarians, not specialist map librarians, are perfectly capable of directing users to Digimap.

The project has employed skilled computer programmers, with expertise in Java and web programming, it has purchased considerable hardware to store and distribute the data, it has entered into ground-breaking agreements with a major data supplier, it has embarked on a massive education and training programme to ensure viable takeup of the service, it has altered the 'mind-set' of a significant number of library staff throughout the UK, it has set up a detailed registration system for individual users, and it has received and spent large sums of competitively awarded grant money. Is this the direction in which map libraries will inevitably go in the 21st century?

Future patterns of use

Information handling in the future will follow the paradigm exemplified by the Internet and other multimedia tools. Map-use tasks themselves rely on data integration: combining archival with contemporary sources, thematic overlay with topographic base, point locations with background aerial or satellite imagery. In addition, the map data can be stored, manipulated and queried with other data in a database management system or a GIS. Furthermore, there may be the need to bring map data alongside textual material, within the walls of a library or across the Internet.

Uses are clearly varied. Digimap is a very specific example, currently supplying topographic mapping to a limited community of expert or moderately skilled users. Future plans involve the potential supply of archival material and image-based data, possibly widening the constituency of users. The majority of users, however, are not familiar with the requirements and opportunities inherent in a system such as Digimap. Such users may be more interested in simple browsing than in amassing complete multi-scale coverage of an area. They may be context, rather than content driven: 'Can I use this map for my particular task?' rather than 'What tasks can this map be used for?'. They may be more concerned with the visual appearance of the map rather than its accuracy. There may be those for whom the message behind the map is more important than the data portrayed by the map itself. For all these groups of map users, and for those who have claimed, from childhood, that they 'can't read maps at all', there is an expanding role for the map librarian. To a great extent, they will be seen by such users as information brokers, skilled in handling spatial data of all types and aware of the possibilities afforded by their day-to-day immersion in map data. In some cases the patron may expect the map librarians themselves actually to perform the tasks of viewing, downloading, analysis and 'adding value'. In most cases such user needs can be addressed and the promotion of map librarian skills may be a valid advertising message.

For computer-literate, problem-specific users, needs may be met completely away from the physical resources of the map library, either from their own office through an Internet connection or through a system, such as that set up for Digimap, whereby the map librarian merely becomes an enabling conduit acting as an intermediary between service providers and end-users. For this group, map librarians may become superfluous, although it is clear that there are still significant hurdles to the idea of a virtual library. 'Libraries without walls are libraries with new walls – technologically bounded, legally restricted and administratively hamstrung' (Kuny and Cleveland, 1998, 113).

On the valid assumption that map libraries continue to exist and address the needs of, at least, those requiring information-brokering facilities, the question of their nature in the future arises. In the end, policy decisions based on resource availability and resource use are going to determine how capable map libraries will become in meeting user needs. The skills of map librarians may be directed by their paymasters towards answering questions such as how much *serious* use is made of your facility? What does cost–benefit analysis of your operation reveal? Can you quantify the use of your own in-house facilities compared with your patrons' access to other sources? What feedback mechanisms do you employ? How do you know that you are meeting user needs appropriately? The evolution of map libraries will continue to be driven by such inquiry.

References

Berger, K and Hines, R (1994) What does the user really want? The Library User Survey Project at Duke University, *Journal of Academic Librarianship*, **20** (5/6), 306–9.

Board, C (1984) Higher order map-using tasks: geographical lessons in danger of being forgotten, *Cartographica*, **21**, 85–97.

Cobb, D and Olivero, A (1997) Online GIS services, *Journal of Academic Librarianship*, **23** (6), 484–97.

Deckelbaum, D (1999) GIS in libraries: an overview of concepts and concerns, *Issues in Science and Technology Librarianship*, **21,** available online at **http://www.library.ucsb.edu/istl/99-winter/article3.html**.

Digimap (1999) *Digimap Project Annual Report 1998–99*, Data Library, University of Edinburgh.

Gillispie, J (1990) Exploiting cartographic resources. In Perkins, C and Parry, R (eds) *Information Sources in Cartography*, Bowker-Saur, 295–308.

Kuny, T and Cleveland, G (1998) The digital map library, myths and challenges, *IFLA Journal*, **24** (2), 107–13.

Lamont, M and Bowles, G (1997) Advancing the digital map library, *Information Technology and Libraries*, **16** (3), 121–4.

MacEachren, A (1994) Visualization in modern cartography. In MacEachren, A and Taylor, D (eds) *Visualization in modern cartography*, Elsevier Science.

McGlamery, P (1997) MAGIC transaction logs as a measure of access, use and community, *Journal of Academic Librarianship*, **23** (6), 505–10.

Markham, C R (1899) Address to the Royal Geographical Society, *Geographical Journal*, **14**, 1–14.

Milis-Proost, G (1990) *Map-use and user habits in the University Library of Gent, presented at the 1990 Groupe des Cartothécaires de LIBER conference, Paris,* available online at
http://www.kb.nl/infolev/liber/articles/pro-user.htm.

Millea, N (1999) Delivering digital data into the library: the Digimap project and its impact on the Map Room – the Bodleian Library Experience, *LIBER Quarterly*, **9** (2), 189–200.

Montanelli, D and Stenstrom P (eds) (1999) *People come first: user centred academic library service*, ACRL Publications in Librarianship 53.

Parry, R B (1995) The electronic map library: new maps, new uses, new users, *LIBER Quarterly*, **5** (3), 262–73, available online at
http://www.kb.nl/infolev/liber/articles/1parry.htm.

Parry, R B and Fox, J (1998) Digimap: hopes, expectations and realities. In Fairbairn, D (ed) *Proceedings, British Cartographic Society 35th Annual Symposium, Keele*, 3–8.

Riggs, D (2000) Editorial: A closer look at user services, *College & Research Libraries*, **61** (3), available online at
http://www.ala.org/acrl/crlmay2000.html.

Steele, G (1993) The acquisition of maps in digital form in an academic library, *The Cartographic Journal*, **30** (2), 57–61.

Withers, C (1999) Knowing one's needs. In Fairbairn, D (ed) *Proceedings of the British Cartographic Society 36th Annual Symposium, Glasgow*, 26–30.

Yu, L (1999) Knowledge discovery in spatial cartographic information retrieval, *Library Trends*, **48** (1), 249–63.

16
The map dealer

Russell Guy

> *Map librarians and map dealers could be said to enjoy a love–hate relationship. Since map libraries provide the major market for international map dealers, they also provide dealers with the bulk of their profits, a fact that may be detrimental to happy relations. Nevertheless, international map dealers have been able to offer an indispensable service to the map library community. Drawing on his experience as cofounder of a well known international map supply company, the author elaborates on the changing nature of map dealing, and explores the radical changes fuelled by the advent of the world wide web. The web has affected the type of map dealers who are in business, how a dealer advertises, their customer base, how they obtain maps and the kinds of maps they stock. The author has struggled with these changes for the past ten years and expects to struggle with them for the next decade as well.*

The changing context of map dealing

Any discussion of the changes in map supply in North America must be prefaced with a discussion of the effects of the world wide web, which has revolutionized the selling of maps like no other change in recent history. It has not only affected how dealers advertise, it has also affected their client base, who a dealer competes with, the product knowledge of a potential customer, the prices a dealer can charge, the size of their inventory and the items they stock, and the maps a dealer is likely to be successful selling.

Promoting the products

For many years the only effective way to publicize the maps a dealer stocked or sold was to publish catalogues, which is an expensive venture. Smaller, or more geographically specialized part-time dealers were not able to print large numbers of catalogues; they had to rely on simple flyers, word of mouth, or working the telephone, and this made it difficult to reach a large audience. Only the larger dealers could afford to publish extensive catalogues, such as GeoCenter's famous three-volume loose-leaf *GeoKatalog 2*.

Paper catalogues have many drawbacks: colour illustrations are expensive, tripling the cost of production, maps listed are expected to be available for the life of the catalogue, prices cannot be changed until the catalogue is revised, revision or production of a new catalogue is time consuming and expensive, and mailing costs are often expensive too, especially for shipping overseas. Paper catalogues and flyers also have advantages, the main one being that many people like to have a sheet of paper describing an item so that they can make notes, scribble questions, or put the paper into a 'do later' (or some other) pile.

The advent of the world wide web has changed how map dealers can advertise. Instead of having to publish monthly, quarterly or annual catalogues and flyers, and to ship by bulk mail and wait three to four weeks for delivery, a dealer can compose and send a simple e-mail advertisement to an unlimited number of people in literally minutes and at minimal cost. The ease with which a dealer can put a thumbnail image of a new product on their web page, let alone itemized lists of quadrangle maps, has meant that a dealer can advertise huge numbers of products, many more than they could afford to advertise in paper catalogues. For example, Omni Resources have listings of over 150,000 maps and 2200 colour images on their website; to produce a catalogue containing these images would be prohibitively expensive, well over US$50 per copy for a small print run.

For many map dealers, websites and monthly e-mail newsletters offer inexpensive, quick advertising and a way to keep in touch with customers. At Omni, we use these methods as our primary modes of advertising. We have a monthly *New Arrivals* web page where we list, often with index maps and illustrations, the items newly received in our warehouse. We also have monthly *Travelers* and *Librarians* mailing lists where we highlight maps and guides which are of particular interest to independent travellers or map librarians. It is our experience that part of our target audience will respond only to e-mail or web advertising, while another part of our audience will respond to paper advertising only, and a part will respond to both forms of advertising. This has forced us to continue to produce paper flyers and newsletters, typically for more expensive items such as national atlases or topographic map series, although we no longer produce a printed catalogue of all our products.

Dealer competition

The web has completely changed the nature of competition between map dealers. The larger dealers are the most adversely affected. In the past major dealers, such as GeoCenter in Germany and Edward Stanford in the UK were competing essentially against themselves. Now they find that they are not only competing with each other, but with every other map dealer and map retail store around the world and with nearly all of their suppliers. Using Yahoo for a search of the web for 'Nepal Map' will result in over 30,000 'hits'. Out of those results, only a handful of dealers actually stock a good quality paper map, many others offer only a simple online map; how does a reliable dealer stand out in this crowd? With the world wide web a local map retailer can now advertise worldwide and can present an image on the web that makes the store look like a major player in the market. For only a few thousand dollars a dealer can present a well-designed website with a shopping basket system. No longer do the smaller dealers have to find their own sources for new maps. Now they can check the websites of the major dealers to see what new maps they are offering, copy the information and any sample images, and have the same information on their own sites in a matter of hours. With the immediacy of e-mail and the ease of putting information on the web, a dealer who has sourced new maps and advertised them on the web stands to have the results of his hard work appear on his competitor's website within days. Often his price is undercut by someone else in a very public way: competing dealers have told me that they have sold topographic sets at a loss to cast a particular dealer as high-priced.

In addition to competing with other map retailers and book superstores, dealers must also compete with their own suppliers. In these times of 'cost recovery' for national map agencies, these agencies are finding that the web is a cost-effective way to advertise their products. A dealer now finds that a librarian knows exactly the retail price in Peru of a Peruvian IGN topographic map. Many government map agencies now accept credit cards, alleviating the university map library's difficulties of prepaying orders with foreign currency cheques. The dealer is often forced to price items based on a publisher's local retail price and a perceived acceptable margin, rather that passing on the total costs to the purchaser. In a discussion in 1999 on MAPS-L, the American map librarians' mailing list, one well known map librarian suggested that map dealers were nothing more than 'price-gouging middlemen' who were no longer necessary, and map librarians did not need to deal with them. In fact this same map librarian continues to deal extensively with map dealers because they have something to offer him that he cannot find elsewhere – new maps and a single source for maps from thousands of publishers around the world.

As it becomes easier for libraries to purchase maps directly from overseas government mapping agencies, many map dealers find that their sales are switching to maps that are harder to obtain. This switch in sales forces dealers to have a larger percentage of inventories in items that are difficult to obtain. These items may have lead times of 12 months or more, forcing a dealer to commit large sums of money on items that may or may not sell, or on items that may or may not arrive in time for that dealer's prime selling season. A map dealer needs to have those items with good margins that he sells on a daily basis – items that form a base sales level. Without those items a dealer is more vulnerable to increased competition and to cash-flow problems caused by overstocked inventory of poor-selling items and prepaid purchases that are months in coming.

Selecting, acquiring and maintaining map stock

When deciding which maps to stock, a map dealer such as Omni must balance current demand with anticipated demand, ease of obtaining maps, cash flow, delivery time, and political situations in foreign countries. We constantly strive to obtain mapping that has not been readily available. For many countries around the world this still requires travelling to the country and trying to obtain permission to purchase the maps or to develop in-country contacts that can obtain the maps for us. In choosing a country to target, we look at the anticipated availability of maps from that country, the cost of travel to the country, and the anticipated difficulty in obtaining permission to purchase and export the maps, all balanced by the anticipated demand for maps of that country. This means that we are unlikely to travel to certain countries, such as the small African countries that produce limited mapping, because we would be unable to justify the cost of the trip based on the anticipated financial remuneration. We also look at what countries are politically unstable, as maps from these countries tend to be in demand during the time of instability or political change. This is also the time when obtaining maps from these countries is the most difficult and most costly. While the image of an itinerant map buyer may be romantic, the reality is not Paris and Acapulco, but Bucharest and Managua. During our travels to purchase maps we have been robbed at gun point, shot at, arrested and strip-searched, among many other trials and tribulations.

Diversification in map dealerships

In the past few years, the web has changed how a map dealer controls his inventory. In the past, regional dealers were in control of what they stocked and sold. They would choose their next map-buying trip, usually in response to inquiries or demand, notify their main customers of the upcoming trip, and take orders for products from the countries. With the smaller, less developed market and typically a lack of financial resources, the smaller regional dealers relied on frequent trips rather than stocking inventory to satisfy their customers. Usually these regional travelling dealers had a second profession that was either their primary income or supplemented the income from the map business. For example, Bill Stewart, a US dealer who specialized in maps from the Andean countries, was a talented runner and running coach. In many cases a regional dealer, such as Steve Mullins, a Mexican map specialist in the USA, would not stock many maps, if any at all. Only a few of the largest dealers, such as GeoCenter and Stanford's, were able to stock any significant quantity of maps. Map librarians learned that they often had to purchase maps for a particular country when a buyer was going, not when it fitted the librarian's schedule.

With the advent of the world wide web, the customer has much more, albeit indirect, control over what a dealer stocks. As with a customer in any industry, map librarians have become just-in-time customers: they want the map they need to be available when they want it, at a reasonable price. For an international map dealer, meeting this expectation has become a never-ending challenge. It is essential for the dealer to understand the client base, to keep aware of changing political situations around the world, the changing popular travel destinations, and to be aware of new maps as they are published.

Because dealers now face many more competitors, as well as competing with their own suppliers, they have to find some way to distinguish their product lines or services. This has led to a diversification of the kinds of international map dealers. Some, such as Map Link in the USA and Nilssen & Lamm in the Netherlands, specialize in wholesale supply of international travel maps, others, such as Omni Resources in the USA and GeoCenter in Germany, specialize in international topographic and thematic maps. Some have emphasized their retail stores over mail order such as (hitherto) Stanford's in London and many smaller travel book and map stores in Europe and the USA. Several companies have adapted to the new digital technology and are supplying digital maps and services, such as BKS Surveys in Northern Ireland and Land Info in the USA.

Changes in map supply

Another factor in planning inventory is the huge increase in the number of maps that are now available on a world-wide basis. Prior to the change to democracy of the Soviet bloc nations, there were very few maps available from those countries. A dealer was able to concentrate on Latin American maps and the few Asian and African maps that were made available by other travelling dealers, as well as the typical 1:50,000-scale topographic maps for Western Europe. A map library with a large budget had the opportunity over time to build a relatively complete collection of the topographic maps that were then available. With the democratization of the former Soviet bloc nations, tens of thousands of additional maps were made available for countries for which few libraries had major holdings. For instance, when Omni Resources brought the Soviet military topographic maps to market, they made available nearly 100,000 topographic maps for the former USSR, Eastern Europe, Asia and Africa. In many cases these maps covered countries for which nothing else was available, for example China, Pakistan, Saudi Arabia, Egypt and northern Africa. Now map librarians have roughly double the number of maps to choose from when planning their budgets. As they concentrated on these newly available maps, sales of the Latin American and European topographic map series slumped. This has caused dealers to spread their financial resources over a much wider range of maps, forcing them to choose a deeper but more restricted inventory or a thinner but more inclusive inventory. This change in buying habits also affects buying trips by reducing the quantity of maps purchased on a trip to a given country. As sales of Latin American maps slumped, it became harder financially to justify trips to some of the smaller countries, such as Nicaragua. A dealer who stocks a true selection of international topographic and thematic maps is likely to have an inventory approaching US$1 million in value.

The demand for digital maps

This huge increase in the availability of maps has been accompanied by the development of digital maps, a revolution that is still underway, and that will affect map dealers significantly in the near future. Many topographic maps from around the world are now available in both paper and digital form. For many developed countries, the government map agencies produce and market the digital maps: for example, the British Ordnance Survey, the US Geological Survey (USGS), and the Australian Surveying and Land Information Group (AUSLIG). For the developing countries and those countries where mapping is controlled by the military authorities, digital maps are usually available only from one of the several companies specializing in custom digitization. Of the major map series only the Soviet military maps and the USGS maps are without copyright; essentially all other paper maps are copyrighted. The legality of producing a digital map from a copyrighted map without the permission of the copyright holder has not been fully resolved in the courts. Now the librarian must also decide between buying a paper map or a digital map and between a legal digital product and a digital product of questionable legality. At Omni Resources our experience has been that researchers and corporations will buy digital topographic mapping, while map librarians tend to buy paper topographic maps. Map libraries also purchase digital route planners or other digital products derived from the original source maps by the owner of the copyright. If digital maps are purchased, the librarian must be concerned with the format of the digital maps, controlling access to them if required by the licensing agreement, and training users in the use of digital maps and GIS systems. Map librarians are no longer simply map librarians, but are often forced to become GIS specialists as well. Some larger map libraries in the USA are adding a GIS specialist to their library staff, recognizing the separate needs of digital and traditional library patrons (Chapter 5). Computers and software are currently on an 18-month generation schedule. Older digital data are sometimes no longer usable with the latest software, or the latest digital products may not run on the older computers found in many smaller map or public libraries. This switch to digital data reduces the need for paper maps, again reducing the number of maps purchased on a buying trip, a problem only getting worse as the digital revolution broadens.

Supply and demand: matching the buying cycles of map libraries

The dealer must anticipate the demand for particular maps or atlases, especially those that are obtained through buying trips or that have long delivery times. This is complicated by the typical buying cycle of many university map libraries. Map libraries tend to do the bulk of their map buying in two short periods each year: at the beginning of the fiscal year when they first get their annual discretionary budget, and at the end of the fiscal year with leftover or end-of-year money. The new budget buying is easier for a dealer since most libraries accept back orders on items ordered at the beginning of the fiscal year. If the dealer underestimates demand, there is time to obtain maps and atlases from many countries within the library's time frame. The end-of-year buying presents more problems for the dealer. Maps purchased with end-of-year funds must be received, invoiced, and paid for within a very short time span, often just two or three weeks. End-of-year buying tends to be concentrated on expensive purchases, such as large topographic map sets or expensive national atlases. These are the types of item that a dealer is reluctant to stock in large quantities because of their cost, limited market, and the limited time period in which the dealer is likely to be able to sell the product. Since most libraries do not know how much end-of-year funds they will have available, it is difficult for them to plan ahead. Rarely do we get contacted by librarians before the end of their fiscal year with a list of maps and atlases that are high on their priority list, allowing us time to adjust our inventory accordingly. For Omni Resources, end-of-year buying can be a significant part of our annual business. We try, therefore, to anticipate the demand and to have appropriate items in stock. If we guess incorrectly, we are left with expensive inventory that probably will not sell until the next end-of-year buying season, if then, and we will also upset customers wondering why we did not have in stock the items they needed.

In the 1980s and early 1990s there were many countries where it was difficult or impossible to obtain government maps via mail. This was particularly true for Latin America and Africa. In the case of Latin America, the mapping agencies were usually controlled by the military and permission from the officer in charge was often needed to purchase maps or to arrange the best wholesale price. Sometimes this was straightforward, other times it could take several days to reach the correct person and to negotiate prices, and sometimes permission was unobtainable, making the trip an expensive failure. Quantity discounts often depended on which officer was in charge of the office at the time of the visit; a new officer could cost hundreds or thousands of dollars in additional fees. Carrying large amounts of currency to purchase large numbers of maps and obtaining local currency could be risky, leaving you at the mercy of the moneychangers, pickpockets and unscrupulous employees of the mapping agencies. Paying for the maps could take several hours, or even a full day of bureaucratic procedures, as for example on trips to Morocco and Italy. Once the buyer had obtained the maps, getting them packed for shipment and arranging shipment could also be difficult. Packing 2000–3000 maps for shipment was often difficult in many Latin American or African countries where normal packing materials were often not readily available.

With the advent of e-mail, the web and bank wire transfers, travelling to obtain maps has become the exception rather than the norm. Several countries still require the personal approach, such as Brazil, Paraguay, Indonesia and Taiwan. In the next decade, travelling to purchase maps will become rare. In Latin America the political evolution to democratic governments has meant the end of negotiated discounts, back-door purchases, and having your maps delivered to you at your hotel by a plain-clothed general and his staff. The main problem now is the lack of inventory in the central government warehouses. For instance, about half the available 1:250,000-scale topographic maps for Argentina are available only as colour copies, rather than as paper originals. About 25% of the topographic maps and 35% of the geological maps for Mexico have been unavailable for some time while Mexico has been converting from manual to digital cartography. Only recently has Mexico started to reprint these maps; however many of the 1:50,000-scale topographic maps are being published as two-colour rather than as full-colour maps. In some Latin American countries the price of maps is pegged to the US dollar to remove the effect of inflation. In these countries sales of maps to international map dealers can account for a significant percentage of annual sales. A few years ago officials in Bolivia told us that purchases by two North American map dealers accounted for over half of their annual sales. Our first purchase of Indonesian topographic maps was more than five times the total maps sales for the previous year. In cases like these a map agency often sees an opportunity to obtain additional cash without penalizing local customers.

Changes in North American map supply

For many decades North American map libraries had to rely on European suppliers such as GeoCenter in Stuttgart, or Stanford's in London for most of their international map needs as there were few, if any, international map dealers located in the USA or Canada. This changed about 25 years ago, with the rise of a few small geographically specialized buyers such as Bill Stewart and Steve Mullins mentioned above. These buyers all had primary jobs, with the map business being of secondary importance, for good reason. In the early years of map supply in the USA, the volume of business could not support full-time international map buyers.

By the late 1970s and early 1980s there was an increased awareness of geography in the schools and universities, air travel was becoming easier and less expensive, and the advertising efforts of such dealers as Stewart and Mullins were paying off. University libraries were looking for maps from locations that were not served by the speciality retailers and the cost of doing business with European dealers (exchange rates, shipping costs, long delays) continued to be a problem. By the mid-1980s the map market in the USA and Canada had grown large enough to support more than the few well-known geographically specialized dealers. In the early 1980s the founding of the companies Omni Resources and Map Link provided two full-time international map suppliers. From their beginning Map Link specialized in international maps, with owner Bill Hunt and other staff making frequent trips to Latin America. Omni Resources, on the other hand, spent their early years in the geological consulting and supply business with maps being of only secondary importance. In 1986 Omni's owners (including this author), started to make map-buying trips overseas, especially to Latin America and in 1988 their first of many trips behind the Iron Curtain. Omni Resources and Map Link, as full-time map dealers who maintained large inventories of international maps, were better able to meet libraries' needs than the part-time speciality buyer. They were also better positioned to attend conferences and advertise, and had better financial resources, which allowed for ever-larger inventories. As their inventories increased they were able to supply the needs of libraries from stock rather than have them wait, with long delays, for the next buying trip. These factors led to the decline and eventual demise of the part-time speciality buyer/dealer in North America. The rise of Omni Resources and Map Link also greatly affected the sales of Stanford's and GeoCenter in the USA, dramatically cutting into their US sales over a period of years. The ability to pay with cheques in US dollars instead of dealing with foreign currency, to know the final price in advance and not have to worry about exchange rate fluctuations, and the ease of checking stock with a 'local' company, led many libraries to switch some of their business from GeoCenter and Stanford's to US dealers.

Coupled with the development of both Omni Resources and Map Link was the development of a need on the part of US businesses for international maps and the realization by the various levels of government of the woeful state of geography education. This growing market was met with an expanded supply from both Omni Resources and Map Link, as both companies rapidly increased their international listings, while local map retailers were also able to supply local businesses and local and regional school districts.

The Gulf War in 1990 offered unprecedented publicity for maps and map dealers in the USA. The location of the war in a place few Americans knew anything about fuelled demand by the news media for maps of Kuwait, Saudi Arabia and Iraq. The use of the maps in the news media, and the demand for maps by parents of soldiers, put map suppliers and map stores into the spotlight. Many map dealers found themselves the subject of television and radio interviews, which had priceless advertising value – you knew when your 800 telephone number had been shown on CNN or the major networks!

In 1991 Omni Resources brought the Soviet military maps to market. These maps offered coverage of countries for which no other coverage was available. This included not only the former Soviet Union, but other countries such as North and South Korea; northern African countries such as Egypt, Algeria and Libya; Middle Eastern countries such as Iraq, Iran and Syria; and Asian countries such as China, Mongolia, Pakistan and India. With the removal of the Iron Curtain and the dissolution of the former Soviet Union, there was a new demand for maps of the former Eastern Bloc countries. The availability of Soviet military maps for the Eastern Bloc countries, Asian countries and Africa and the Middle East fuelled a purchasing frenzy not seen before nor likely to be seen again.

Initially these maps were available only from Omni Resources, and then additional sources began to market these maps, such as Eastview Cartographic. The availability of these maps from US sources and the initial lack of availability from the major European dealers allowed the US dealers to expand into the European markets, previously the almost exclusive domain of GeoCenter and Stanford's. The development of the web, which allowed a rapid communication and safe flow of information, the decrease in rates of courier services around the world, the increased safety and availability of bank wire transfers, and the rise in the use of credit cards helped reduce the reluctance of European librarians to buy maps from the USA.

According to statistical survey data from the International Map Trade Association, in the past few years the world wide web has led to increased sales to the general public and increased use of maps, both paper and digital. The increased competition among the retailers, publishers, and catalogue and Internet sales companies has led to consolidation and is part of the change from single-person companies run for the love of maps, to small multi-employee companies, to corporations run for the benefit of stockholders. Higher profits are made on selling large volumes of a limited number of maps, rather than on low volumes of large numbers of maps. The travel map business fits this criterion much better than the topographic and speciality map business. An illustration of this was the breakup of what had been the world's foremost map supply company, GeoCenter Internationales Landkartenhaus, in Stuttgart, Germany. Several years ago GeoCenter was sold to Bertelsmann Publishing, one of the largest publishing companies in the world. Very shortly after the purchase, Bertelsmann split the company, keeping the travel map publishing and distribution business and selling to an individual, Internationales Landkartenhaus (ILH), the topographic and thematic portion of the business that had made GeoCenter famous. ILH now has a reduced staff and reduced inventory, and is no longer the dominant global player it once was.

In the late 1980s and early 1990s the company Interarts became well known as a producer of popular world maps and world map apparel (the 'Wearin' the World' map jackets). A few years ago Interarts was purchased by Geosystems, a company that specialized in custom digital mapping. Geosystems developed a digital map base that they were able to convert to use on the web as a route planner. In early 1999 Geosystems changed their name to MapQuest and their stock became publicly traded. In early 2000 MapQuest was purchased by AOL for MapQuest's online map routing product. Whether or not AOL will continue the original line of Interarts world and US maps is unclear at this time.

The impact of the International Map Trade Association

The International Map Trade Association (IMTA) was founded in 1972 by a group of 12 retailers. It was originally established for the cooperative purchasing of laminating supplies. This quickly proved not to be feasible and the group focused its attention on matters affecting the retailer: training, importing maps, dealing with publishers and advertising. For the first 15–18 years the IMTA was a small North American association, with few members from Europe or elsewhere. About eight years ago, however, the IMTA made a concerted effort to expand its membership world-wide, culminating in 1995 in Dublin, Ireland, with its first convention off the North American continent. Currently the IMTA has more than a thousand members spread across five continents, divided into three divisions, each of which has its own annual convention.

The IMTA has had a significant impact on the ability of map dealers to offer a wide variety of products to map libraries. Prior to the expansion of the IMTA into a truly world-wide organization, the only major mapping convention open to retailers was the Frankfurt Book Fair held each year in October. This show is the largest wholesale publishing convention in the world. For many years it has had a 'Map Hall' dedicated to displays by both government and commercial map publishers, primarily from European countries. For small family-owned retail stores, taking time off in the important pre-holiday season to travel to Europe was expensive and difficult to do. Only a few, well-established dealers and importers made the annual trek, to reap the benefits of direct contact with the major European mapping agencies and publishers. With the expansion of the IMTA into Europe, Australasia and recently continental Asia and South America, the IMTA's North American annual convention (a de facto international convention) has expanded to have the largest exhibits of international map publishers in the world. Having these international publishers come to the North American convention has greatly expanded their visibility to dealers in the USA and Canada, allowing them not only to offer a wider selection of products, but to be more aware of what is available and where to obtain these items.

In its early years, the IMTA was an association of and for retailers. In time, in an effort to expand the membership, it allowed publishers to join as full members. Many publishers did so, seeing obvious benefits from close contact with their speciality retailers. Unfortunately these retailers, typically small husband–wife organizations, do not have the time and resources to devote to running a volunteer organization. With the advent of the 'book superstore' and the decline of the independent retailer, the publishers have come to dominate the IMTA. Publishers and retailers are often on opposite sides of an issue, for example incentives given to superstores but not to independent retailers, leading to further friction and alienation of the retailer. In 1997 this led a group of prominent US travel bookstores and map stores to form a new association, the Independent Travel Stores Association (ITSA). This association is currently open only to retailers who meet certain criteria of size, product selection and years in business. ITSA has been able to address retailers' issues that could not be addressed by the IMTA due to its broadened membership, such as issues of pricing, discounts, special sales and advertising. Currently ITSA is open only to US and Canadian stores, but it could serve as a model for similar associations elsewhere.

The coming decade

Map dealers face a very challenging future. In the coming years more and more maps will be available in digital form. With the increased bandwidth of high-speed data cable connections becoming more available, more affordable, and much faster, downloading 40 Mb digital map files will not be the daunting task that it is now. Large-format plotters are still generally not affordable for libraries, let alone the general map user. In the coming years the cost of these plotters will drop drastically to a point where every major public library will be able to produce large-format digital output. Patrons will be able to download and plot maps or other large documents for a minimal fee. As personal data assistants, GPS units, cell phones and other hand-held computing devices become more powerful and pervasive throughout society, digital maps will become easily downloaded directly from a map producer's website. Even now, sales of street maps are down sharply according to IMTA statistical data. The popular route-planning websites such as MapQuest.com, Maps.com and AOL have taken a significant portion of the domestic travel map business.

The most successful map dealers have always found a way to procure maps before they are generally available to the public. In the 1970s and early 1980s map dealers brought to market the main topographic map series from Latin America and maps from behind the Iron Curtain. In the past ten years, international map dealers have brought to market the Soviet and Chinese military maps, Taiwanese topographic maps, many smaller series such as the Quipos and Guzman Cordova maps for Bolivia, Tombazzi hiking maps for Africa, the Prannok maps for Thailand, and a host of individual maps and other small series. As more and more countries reduce restrictions on the sale of their government mapping, there will be fewer opportunities for map dealers to source out new map series, removing the main reason many map librarians choose to deal with them. Without the sales related to 'sole source' items, dealers will need to offer other benefits to entice map librarians to be their customers, such as better and faster service, a wider selection of products, and easy-to-use interfaces for downloading topographic maps.

Map libraries will have more access to information about new maps and will increasingly be able to purchase foreign topographic maps directly from government map agencies. As budget cuts affect both staff and discretionary budgets, map librarians are forced to make their budgets go further, and with the information available on the web they can be more aware of prices at source. Map librarians are more willing to endure the difficulties of obtaining large map sets from overseas if they can save a dollar on each sheet. They will therefore spend smaller percentages of their budgets with map dealers, and this will be concentrated on end-of-year buying. As librarians begin to buy directly, international map dealers find that they are losing a significant, steady base of sales, sales they cannot afford to lose. As dealers lose these sales, reduced cash flow and reduced sales volume hinder their ability to travel to obtain maps and to stock the same breadth and depth of inventory as in the past. Unfortunately map dealers will not be able to survive on end-of-year sales to libraries – they must have consistent sales throughout the year. Hopefully map librarians will recognize that map dealers do offer a service, such as convenience and specialized knowledge of what map resources are available, and that it is in their best interests to help map dealers survive and adapt.

For map dealers to survive in the long term they will have to find a way to provide a service to users, both map libraries and individuals, as a portal to download sites for digital maps. For the next ten to 20 years, while the older generations age out of map use, there will be map users who will prefer to use paper maps and there will continue to be many maps that are not available in digital format. These people will provide a shrinking sales base giving map dealers the time to organize and complete the change to a digital map provider. The dealers who remain in business in the coming decades will be those who best handle this change.

17
Is there a future for the map library?

Chris Perkins and Bob Parry

▶ *The concluding chapter of this book has been written in the form of a debate between the editors on the future of the map library in higher educational institutions. We have tried to argue from opposite standpoints, drawing freely on points made by other contributors. We wish to stress that we do not necessarily subscribe to the views we express and hope that our dialogue draws together some of the complex arguments appearing throughout this book. Perhaps a resolution of this debate lies in the readers' hands?*

CP The time has come to accept that the concept of the local map library serving its own user community may be ending.

Chapter after chapter in this collection has documented profound technological changes, affecting the medium of mapping and the administrative procedures used by map libraries. If all of these changes are compounded then the future of the map librarian as custodian of a fixed archive of mapping looks bleak indeed. But broader social, cultural and economic changes may mean that newer more interpretative roles will be taken up by other agencies, leaving the map librarian with no new role to adopt!

I suspect that the period from the 1950s to the 1990s will be seen as the heyday of the map library. The future is full of threats and our capacity to respond to these is limited.

BP I certainly agree that there have been profound technological changes whose effect has not been limited just to the medium of mapping but to many aspects of the management and distribution of spatial data. But your view seems to be premised on the notion that a map library necessarily has to be a fixed archive of mapping, by which I assume you mean primarily printed maps. In the first place, I do not accept that there is no future for such mapping, and interestingly nor does the recently appointed Director General of Ordnance Survey (GB), Vanessa Lawrence. In a press release (OS 46/00) she is quoted as saying, 'There's a long-term future for paper maps – and the great success of the new *Explorer* series demonstrates that there's a real demand for them. People who try to write them off are the same people who are convinced that books are going to disappear because information can be downloaded on to palm-top computers. I don't believe it.'

CP Let's start with the issue of the map library as a fixed archive. I accept that most map collections, in the sense that most people understand the term, are still fixed archives of paper mapping. I did not, however, mean to imply only the printed product, I meant fixed in the sense of items that could be recorded in library systems, such as electronic atlases, or even cartographic data on a physical CD-ROM. Nor did my view imply there is no future for such mapping. On the contrary I am quite prepared to accept that the paper map will continue to play important roles.

What I meant was that those funding collections of maps and spatial data are increasingly likely to favour the digital, and that publishers are increasingly likely to cease to publish the fixed format. Witness Ordnance Survey abandoning hard-copy publication of large-scale mapping, and general moves towards central maintenance of databases with mapped output from these data served over the web. The future lies with the networked digital data set, not with the mass-produced paper map.

BP Well, of course I acknowledge your wider definition of a fixed archive, but I wanted specifically to refer to the matter of paper maps because, as products of old technology, it is easy to say, as many do, that their day has come. Yet Russell Guy informs us that in terms of what they *buy*, map librarians still favour paper maps over digital data. There is also the question of preserving the old. As map librarians, we all know the importance not only of early (say pre-1850) maps, but also of maps superseded less than a decade ago. I anticipate your rejoinder that scanned images of many such maps can already be found on the web. The Library of Congress for example is putting a huge archive of mapping on the web, and in the UK, Landmark have created a nice website that enables the viewing of old OS six-inch-to-the-mile mapping. But do such offerings represent a satisfactory substitute for the maps themselves? In Chapter 10 Chris Baruth has pointed out the enormous cost and complications of building a satisfactory and internationally accessible digital archive.

In the UK, we recently learned that the Royal Geographical Society has had all its archive of pre-war 1:10,560-scale Ordnance Survey maps scanned and made available on CD-ROM. Developments like this mean that map collections and individuals *can* have easy access (though in this case not cheaply) to a storehouse of material usually only found in the most extensive of map libraries. Adding such CDs to the fixed archive of a map collection will extend not reduce its value to users. Meanwhile, will the RGS dispose of its paper originals? I think not.

However, let's move the argument on. There are clearly two questions here, and we should not get them confused. The first concerns the future of the 'fixed map archive', the second the future of map libraries (and implicitly the future of map librarianship) in the digital age. I accept that the dominance of paper maps may disappear and that the role of the map librarian has to change, but you seem to think that the new requirements imposed by changing technology and new models of distribution are out of reach for curators. Yet several contributions in this book (for example those by Carol Marley and Jenny Stone Muilenburg) show that the necessary adjustments *are* being made. Convince me otherwise!

CP   You are quite right that map librarians still prefer to acquire paper maps. They would wouldn't they! It's what libraries are good at, what the collection development policies encourage them to do and what some of their existing users want. I also accept that at present scanned images offer a less satisfactory alternative to the paper map. Just because map libraries are continuing to do what they have always done, and just because alternatives are at present perhaps less satisfactory, does not mean that we will continue to be able to use paper mapping. I can advance two important arguments here to illustrate my case.

Firstly the built-in obsolescence of the paper copy. Our archives are disintegrating around us; what percentage of published mapping in a collection is printed on archival paper? Very small I fear. How many collections have the resources to conserve printed items in a paper medium? Very few again. Like it or not the scanned paper map will predominate within 20 years in fixed archives. And if a mechanism exists to distribute these data, why do they need to be held locally?

My second argument concerns the costs of storage. Many institutions now recognize that the costs of storing material have to be set against the benefits that flow from the fixed archive – few collections can afford to grow and grow, without withdrawing items. Organizations must fund in order to reap the benefits of holding material. Few new collections have been established in the last decade, indeed the trend world-wide has been a decline in the number of map library posts, with a decline in the membership of professional map library organizations. Again the costs of establishing conventional map libraries are no longer justified.

Those holding the purse strings are more likely to favour a digital alternative, held centrally and distributed with no storage or maintenance overheads falling upon the local collection. What is best for the users is irrelevant: the real world responds more to economic and political factors than to quality.

However, as you say, let's move the debate on beyond the fixed archive to wider concerns about the nature of map librarianship and the future of map libraries. There *is* evidence that the new skills and knowledge imposed by changing technology and new models of communication are out of reach for most curators.

Evidence from practice and theory. First the theory. What new skills are required? Broadly, knowledge of data, software, hardware and how these impact upon potential visualizations. Compare the conventional map inquiry with a digital map inquiry, and the implications of shifting to a digital map library become rather clearer. As Carol Marley and David Fairbairn show in their chapters, there are significant learning curves to be climbed if support for users is to be offered. Do you have HTML experience? How about ArcView? Do you know how to convert an NTF file into MapInfo? Would you have the time to be able to construct a map for a non-GIS literate user? I fear most map librarians lack the time, flexibility and knowledge. The practice backs up this assertion. Jenny Stone Muilenburg's survey is based upon a worryingly low response rate. Even in the USA the majority of conventional map libraries have not adopted any GIS services and very few posts of Geographic Information specialists have yet been created in libraries. Yet GIS is central to federal and state information programmes and commercial vendors have invested heavily in training programmes aimed at the library market. How many map libraries in the UK offer GIS? How many map librarians can use MapInfo or ArcView, let alone Arc/INFO? Very few. The institutional structures discussed by Nick Millea militate against radical reskilling. Even the Digimap service in the UK shortcuts the map librarian, with users logging on themselves rather than through the map library. At best the map librarian offers a back-up.

So my argument is that GIS has devised its own support structures and courses, that the emphasis shifts to the user and away from the custodian, and that map libraries are tied to the fixed past. We may attempt to move with the technology, but it is very difficult and the majority will not make the move.

BP You seem to have considerable faith in the longevity of digitally stored data, but we have seen great change over the past two decades in the means of storing digital data. Major collections still manage to preserve paper maps that are several hundred years old. Admittedly there are considerable costs in storage as well as in conservation. But can we be sure of a trouble-free future for the conservation of digital data? So far the indications have not been good. Can you still access the data stored on your institution's main-frame 25 years ago? What of the costs incurred in producing the UK Domesday multimedia system, which relied on what is now long superseded hardware, and which is no longer supported and probably no longer functioning anywhere? Or what of the costs of re-engineering the Canadian Land Information System by the National Archives of Canada (Can$75,000) to render it readable using contemporary computer software and hardware? I tend to agree with Alan Godfrey, who states 'A paper map, with reasonable conservation, will still be of use in a hundred years; can we really be so certain of today's GIS systems?'

You mention the question of costs several times in your latest piece. I have to admit that in these times of accountability, funding is a powerful influence in determining what happens to map libraries in terms of staffing and structure as well as the nature, availability and distribution of spatial data. In many cases the problem of costs works in favour of your arguments, but I suggest not always. With the increasing commodification of spatial data discussed by Bob Barr in Chapter 12 and the need to limit and monitor their use to meet the licensing requirements of the owners of the data, isn't there a continuing role here for the map librarian? You mention that the Digimap service shortcuts the map librarian. But this is not the whole story: although the data are distributed centrally, and can be independently accessed, their use has to be closely monitored locally. What is more, many users need to be made aware of the potential uses of the data, and to be educated in aspects of cartographic representation using the diverse data sets. Who better to carry out these tasks than the map curator?

You mention new skills, and particularly those concerned with GIS. I acknowledge the need for the skills you list, and it is true that you can't always teach an old dog new tricks. But many map librarians *are* meeting the new challenges, and this is also apparent from some of the chapters by map librarians. In her chapter, Stone Muilenburg argues the case for libraries 'developing as a GIS resource'. I don't believe that the GIS industry can provide a satisfactory substitute for the kind of services required by the infrequent user of spatial data. You say that GIS is central to federal and state programmes, but these are specialized applications, not the diverse reference and research services we associate with map libraries in educational institutions. Cartwright and Peterson (1999, 1) describe the more sophisticated uses of GIS as 'cartography for the few'. Map librarians provide cartography for the many!

In a parallel profession, that of university cartographer, there has been wholesale reskilling. People who a little over a decade ago spent their working day at a drawing board, now sit in front of an Apple Mac and are fully proficient in a large range of new software and printing skills. In the case of map librarianship, there is a difference in that the old skills are not entirely replaced, but rather extended. We are in transition, and new recruits to the profession will have the necessary new skills. While GIS has indeed developed its own support structures, I suggest the emphasis has been on data manipulation, rather than understanding the provenance of those data, and on being able to match data sets to users' needs. That is the map librarian's domain.

CP   I accept the potential problems over the longevity of digital data. There is indeed no guarantee that we will be able to access all of today's data 25 years in the future. Economic and political factors may well make it impossible. However I fear you and Alan Godfrey underestimate the costs and difficulty of preserving the 20th-century paper archive in the paper medium. As Chris Baruth pointed out in his chapter, acid-free and archival paper do not predominate in map collections – most of our apparently permanent and convenient paper archives are rotting away and, like it or not, we will only be able to preserve the more important items in paper format.

Our impotence is also reflected in the ways in which map publishers have regarded the library community. The library market is tiny in relation to either mass production of paper mapping for recreation, or the digital production of spatial data for the GIS market. We have managed to exert very little influence on map publishers: when have they considered our views on pricing policy, or making metadata available to use in library systems, or on employing the most convenient format for data dissemination? The library role only becomes significant when statute forces producers to consider our needs.

I'd like to move the debate on to a more detailed consideration of the difference the web makes. It shifts responsibility on to the users and producers and away from libraries. Users can increasingly expect customized mapping delivered to their desktop, producers no longer have to worry about mass production and can maintain data quality.

Let's illustrate. McGlamery, Kraak, Peterson and Perkins in this book all agree that the number of maps served over the web will continue to grow. MapQuest.com has already produced more maps than any other publisher in the history of cartography. These maps are served to new users who are unlikely to have used maps in map libraries: their number already far outstrips map library user statistics. You might argue that such services at present only supplement more conventional mapping offered from libraries, but the nature of Internet-based mapping is also changing. Official mapping is increasingly being delivered via the web, census mapping agencies are following the US lead, data warehouses are being established to disseminate geoscientific mapping, and data servers such as Digimap are being established by a growing number of consortia organizations, to customize the delivery of mapping for particular markets. The commercialization of the web can only increase this trend. Oddens already estimates a third of map library inquiries can be met from the web and this figure grows at the same time as library acquisition budgets for fixed archives come under pressure.

You cite Digimap as an example of the potential new educative role for the map librarian – the gatekeeper evolving new skills. I'd like to make a number of comments here. A large majority of higher education institutions have not yet subscribed to the service and only 50 institutions were signed up late in 2000. Even well founded institutions have found the very reasonable costs involved in supporting Digimap too expensive. Also how many of the site representatives from subscribing universities are map librarians? Of the 50 sites subscribing to this service only 15 operate the Digimap agreement through their map libraries: just as many institutions provide the service from their central information and computing facilities, and many institutions offer no central support for the service at all! This suggests that whatever the potential, in practice others are taking on the map librarian's GIS support role. Also you fail to draw out the user statistics – how many of your Digimap users do you see? The service is deliberately set up to meet individual user needs, not to be served through the library. Extensive online help is available, and, like it or not, users do their own thing with the service.

I would like to suggest that the map librarian's domain is being 'shorted out'. Matching data to user needs will increasingly be an automated task, individual users will increasingly carry out their own map inquiries, and the range of online support materials helping in this process will grow. I don't think the public service map librarian will be able to do very much to change this trend, however much we might want to preserve a quality of service.

BP   Let me ask you a question about your own institution's map collection. Has it been busy lately? I can confidently say that ours is busier than it has ever been. You ask how many of our Digimap users we see. Quite a lot of them actually, because we make considerable use of our 'casual user account', using Digimap as a map library service to meet some of the unpredictable one-off requests that are the bread-and-butter of map library use. I don't contest that the map librarian's domain is being shorted out in the ways you suggest. But this is taking place against a growing interest in maps, stimulated in part, yes, by the Internet, and so also resulting in a burgeoning need for new users to turn to someone who *knows* about maps and digital data, what is possible and what is not possible, to satisfy user needs.

You talk about online help. Look again at Carol Marley's two interviews. Could the contributions made there to solve the user's problems have been as well served online?

I think we can justify the future of the map library and map librarian (some people might want to call them different names), but I have to concede that our perception of what is advantageous and necessary is often not the perception of our paymasters, who may well see the net as an opportunity for cutting investment in the traditional map library route to accessing spatial data. We have to argue the social and economic costs of ceasing to provide such local services.

CP   It seems that the root cause of our disagreement depends upon our interpretation of the changing economic, social and political context of the map library. Like you I am quite prepared to accept that map curators *can* offer qualitatively better services to their users, than an interface on a home page. However such a well-trained professional response depends on a library being well founded, and also assumes that the map curator is able to argue for the social and economic benefits of a high-quality local service. These are formidable assumptions to make and I fear that you are very over-optimistic in believing that most libraries can win these arguments.

I'd like to advance two new pieces of evidence to back up this pessimistic view, drawing upon legal and economic barriers to change, and with a wider global picture than is painted by most authors in our book.

We have tended to emphasize *technological change* in this book, and most authors have stressed the pace of the shifts impacting on our collections. The way these changes happen is, however, a function of the local context, as Nick Millea shows in Chapter 3 and as I demonstrate with reference to access and availability issues. Bob Barr shows, however, that there are also significant *legal changes* flowing from a move towards digital data, changes that may make it hard for libraries to offer the kinds of services that you describe. For example variations in data pricing that flow from legal variation, reflect significantly differing national state policies towards digital data. It may well only be the larger collections, in states with a freedom of information policy and a tradition of publicly funded libraries, that are able to resource a digital interpretation service. The brave new world described by Pip Forer, where geographically referenced data sets are accessed from spatial information centres, is very unlikely to extend to the developing world, or to poorer European nations, or even to the majority of collections in New Zealand, the UK or the USA! He may argue persuasively that most map librarians have to cut themselves away from a collective 'cartophilic past' – but he fails to suggest the practical mechanisms to help in the change, or to describe institutions that have successfully remade themselves for the new millennium.

The big expansion in the number of map libraries that took place after World War 2 and is described in our introduction reflects the spirit of that age. Our post-millennial, globalizing world differs significantly and the social and economic costs of maintaining local map library services are quite simply too out of kilter with our times for most paymasters to be able to support.

To summarize, I fear the barriers are greater than you recognize, and I fear that the lack of widespread global progress towards Pip Forer's model future supports my interpretation.

BP   Our argument has moved from the view that the alternative futures are limited to a simple choice between locally stored and curated data, and data that are warehoused remotely and distributed directly to the user. As you say, the issues are more about management and control of the data. There is a substantial need in the digital age to maintain levels of local control of data for just the legal reasons you have suggested, and why should the map curators, with their growing understanding of data management, not be among the ones to provide this control? You have acknowledged the value of this but rejected the notion that it is realistic to expect our paymasters to support us. You may be pessimistic about Forer's model future, and you may be right, but the needs and the opportunities are still there.

It is apparent in reading the chapters of this book that some contributors have found it hard to find future significant roles for the map library. The net has usurped many of its functions by providing superior ease and convenience of access to the public at large, and provision of much data at non-commercial costs. But the net is unmoderated and unfocused. As Forer says, maps have become 'transient representations', and the time-sensitive data from which they are constructed are often transient too. I agree with Forer that map libraries not only need to adapt to the transience of new mapping, but have to take an even greater role in capturing, organizing and archiving the spatial data that underpin these representations.

Whether our outlook on the future of the map library is optimistic or pessimistic, we have to agree that these are challenging and exciting times for the use of spatial data and their graphical representation as maps. There is work for map curators to do, and it is up to them to show the world that it needs them!

Reference

Cartwright, W and Peterson, M P (1999) Multimedia cartography. In Cartwright, W, Peterson, M P and Gartner, G (eds) *Multimedia cartography*, Springer, 1–10.

List of acronyms

AACR2	Anglo-American Cataloguing Rules 2nd edition
ADEPT	Alexandria Digital Earth Prototype
ADL	Alexandria Digital Library
AMS	Army Map Service
ANZLIC	Australia New Zealand Land Information Council
ARL	Association of Research Libraries
AUSLIG	Australian Surveying and Land Information Group
AVI	Audio Visual Interleave
BRICMICS	British and Irish Committee for Map Information and Cataloguing Systems
CCD	Couple Charged Device
CCQ	Cataloging & Classification Quarterly
CDi	Compact Disk interactive
CD-ROM	Compact Disk - Read Only Memory
CEN	Commission Européennes de Normalisation
CGI	Common Gateway Interface
CHEST	Combined Higher Education Software Team
CNN	Cable News Network
CORC	Cooperative Online Resource Catalog
CSDGM	Content Standard for Digital Geospatial Metadata
DCMI	Dublin Core Metadata Initiative
DBMS	Database Management System
DC	Dublin Core
DEM	Digital Elevation Model
DLI	Data Liberation Initiative
DLO	Document Like Object
DMA	Defense Mapping Agency
dpi	dots per inch

DRG	Digital Raster Graphic
DTD	Document Type Definition
DVD	Digital Video (or Versatile) Disk
EDINA	Edinburgh Data and Information Access
ESRI	Environmental Systems Research Institute
FGDC	Federal Geographic Data Committee
FMD	Fluorescent Multilayer Disk
FTP	File Transfer Protocol
GIF	Graphics Interchange Format
GILS	Government Information Locator Service
GIS	Geographic(al) Information System(s)
GPS	Global Positioning System
GSDI	Geospatial Data Infrastructure
HTML	HyperText Markup Language
IAFA	Internet Anonymous FTP Archive
ICA	International Cartographic Association
IFLA	International Federation of Library Associations and Institutions
IMTA	International Map Trade Association
IP	Internet Protocol
ISBD	International Standard Bibliographic Description
ISBD(CM)	International Standard Bibliographic Description for Cartographic Materials
ISBD(ER)	International Standard Bibliographic Description for Electronic Resources
ISO	International Standards Organization
ITSA	Independent Travel Stores Association
JISC	Joint Information Systems Committee
JPEG	Joint Photographic Experts Group
LAN	Local Area Network
LC	Library of Congress
LIBER	Ligue des Bibliothèques Européennes de Recherche
MAGIC	[University of Connecticut's] Map and Geographic Information Center
MARC	Machine Readable Catalog
MIF	MapInfo Format
MPEG	Moving Picture Experts Group
NBII	National Biological Information Infrastructure
NCP	Network Control Protocol

NCSA	National Center for Supercomputer Applications
NGDI	National Geospatial Data Infrastructure
NIMA	National Imagery and Mapping Agency
NIMSA	National Interest in Mapping Service Agreement
NOAA	National Oceanic and Atmospheric Administration
NSDI	National Spatial Data Infrastructure
NSF	National Science Foundation
NTF	National Transfer Format
OCLC	Online Computer Library Center
OPAC	Online Public Access Catalogue
OS	Ordnance Survey
PDA	Personal Digital Assistant
PDF	Portable Document Format
PICA	Project Integrated Catalogue Automation
RDBMS	Relational Database Management System
RDF	Resource Description Framework
RFC	Request For Comments
RLIN	Research Libraries Information Network
SGML	Standard Generalized Markup Language
SOIF	Summary of Object Interchange Formats
TCP/IP	Transmission Control Protocol/Internet Protocol
TIFF	Tagged Image File Format
TIGER	Topologically Integrated Geographical Encoding and Referencing
UMTS	Universal Mobile Telecommunications Systems
URL	Uniform Resource Locator
USGS	United States Geological Survey
VRML	Virtual Reality Modelling Language
W3C	World Wide Web Consortium
WAN	Wireless Area Network
WAP	Wireless Application Protocol
WML	Wireless Markup Language
WTLS	Wireless Transport Layer Security
XML	Extensible Markup Language

Index